WINSTANLEY AND THE DIGGERS, 1649–1999

BOOKS OF RELATED INTEREST

NEWS, NEWSPAPERS AND SOCIETY IN EARLY MODERN BRITAIN
Edited by Joad Raymond

THE EMERGENCE OF QUAKER WRITING
Dissenting Literature in Seventeenth-Century England
Edited by Thomas N. Corns and David Loewenstein

TELLING PEOPLE WHAT TO THINK
Early Eighteenth-Century Periodicals from *The Review* to *The Rambler*
Edited by J.A. Downie and Thomas N. Corns

PAMPHLET WARS
Prose in the English Revolution
Edited by James Holstun

AUTOBIOGRAPHY AND QUESTIONS OF GENDER
Edited by Shirley Neuman

EDWARD CARPENTER AND LATE VICTORIAN RADICALISM
Edited by Tony Brown

COLERIDGE AND THE ARMOURY OF THE HUMAN MIND
Essays on his Prose Writing
Edited by Peter J. Kitson and Thomas N. Corns

Winstanley and the Diggers, 1649–1999

edited by

ANDREW BRADSTOCK

FRANK CASS
LONDON • PORTLAND, OR

First published in 2000 in Great Britain by
FRANK CASS AND COMPANY LIMITED
Newbury House, 900 Eastern Avenue, London IG2 7HH, England

and in the United States of America by
FRANK CASS
c/o International Specialized Book Services, Inc.
5804 N.E. Hassalo Street, Portland, Oregon 97213-3644

British Library Cataloguing in Publication Data

Winstanley and the Diggers, 1649–1999
1. Winstanley, Gerrard, 1609–1676 – Political and social views 2. Winstanley, Gerrard, 1609–1676 – Influence 3. Levellers 4. Great Britain – Politics and government – 1625–1649 5. England – Social conditions – 17th century
I. Bradstock, Andrew
322.4′2′0942′09032

ISBN 0 7146 5105 2 (hb)
ISBN 0 7146 8157 1 (pb)

Library of Congress Cataloging-in-Publication Data
Winstanley and the Diggers, 1649–1999/editor Andrew Bradstock.
p. cm.
"This group of studies first appeared in a special issue of 'Prose Studies,' vol. 22, no. 2, August 1999" – verso t.p.
Includes index.
ISBN 0-7146-5105-2 – ISBN 0-7146-8157-1 (pbk.)
1. Winstanley, Gerrard, b. 1609. 2. Levellers. 3. Great Britain – History – Puritan Revolution, 1642–1660. 4. Radicalism – Great Britain – History – 17th century. I. Bradstock, Andrew. II. Prose studies.

DA429.W5 W56 2000
941–dc21 00-035875

This group of studies first appeared in a Special Issue of *Prose Studies* (ISSN 0144-0357), Vol.22, No.2 (August 1999), [Winstanley and the Diggers, 1649–1999].

Printed by Antony Rowe Ltd., Chippenham, Wiltshire

TO
CHRISTOPHER HILL

Contents

Preface

Seven of these papers – those by Aylmer, Alsop, Taylor, Smith, Hobby, Holstun and Rowland – were first given at the "Hearts and Spades" conference held on 9 and 10 April 1999 at Brooklands College, Weybridge and St Mary's Church, Walton (by kind permssion of the Vicar, Canon Timothy Sedgley). This conference was one of several events held in the vicinity of St George's Hill, Surrey, England, in 1999 to commemorate the Diggers' occupation of that site which began on 1 April 1649.

The editor would like to thank, for their help with the preparation of this volume, Tom Corns, Sonia Craig, John Gurney, Andrew Hadfield, Ann Hughes, Claire Jowitt, David Loewenstein and David McLellan. The advice and support of Ronald Corthell (editor of *Prose Studies*) and Joan Dale Lace (Frank Cass Ltd) was also very much appreciated.

After Winstanley himself the person most frequently cited in this collection is Christopher Hill, who, in an extraordinarily productive career spanning more than 60 years, has done more than any other scholar to stimulate research into the civil war radicals, in particular Winstanley and the Diggers, and bring them to a wider audience. Dr Hill was unable to take part in the events organized to remember the Diggers in 1999, but it was the wish of all at the "Hearts and Spades" conference that greetings be sent to him on their behalf. Perhaps the dedication of these essays to him will go someway towards conveying the affection, esteem and gratitude felt by all at that event towards him and his work, as well as reminding him – if any reminder were needed – that interest in the Diggers is still very much alive as we enter the new century.

Explanatory Note

When quoting from Winstanley's writings contributors have used either the Sabine or Hill editions, which are cited as follows throughout:

Works: George H. Sabine (ed.), *The Works of Gerrard Winstanley; with an appendix of documents relating to the Digger movement* (Ithaca: NY: Cornell University Press, 1941, and NY: Russell & Russell, 1965).

LFOW: Christopher Hill (ed.), *The Law of Freedom and other writings* (Harmondsworth: Penguin, 1973, and Cambridge: Cambridge University Press, 1983).

Introduction

ANDREW BRADSTOCK

One of the great ironies about the Diggers' attempt in 1649 to re-make the Earth as a "common treasury" is that the site they chose to begin this task is now as enclosed a piece of land as it is possible to conceive. The home of rock stars, TV presenters and other assorted millionaires, St George's Hill, Weybridge, is one of the most exclusive private estates in England, a sort of British counterpart to Los Angeles' Beverly Hills. Those who delighted in the Diggers' downfall, in their failure to stop the rich from "bagging and barning up the treasures of the Earth", could scarce have imagined how total that failure would ultimately turn out to be.

That the Hill bears no trace of its earlier communist settlers is therefore none too surprising: there is no plaque or memorial, no "Everard Avenue" or "Winstanley Way", no "Diggers' Fairway" on the beautifully manicured golf-course.[1] Yet if the Hill's present dwellers had been only vaguely aware of its historical significance before 1999, in the course of that year they were quickly projected up a steep learning curve as in April the nearby towns of Walton and Weybridge hosted a rally, conference, exhibition and march to honour the anniversary of the Diggers' occupation of the Hill, and in the same month a not entirely symbolic re-staging of that event took place on the Hill itself. The efforts of the latter-day Diggers to re-enact the past, which included turning the soil, planting crops and erecting temporary shelter, were not entirely appreciated by their involuntary hosts – this time not Francis Drake MP but the North Surrey Water Board – though the latter did go to some trouble themselves to ensure no historical detail would be missed by seeking the termination of their stay at the earliest opportunity. Within two weeks the new Diggers were off the Hill, though with the aid of some benign media coverage (the like of which Winstanley could only have dreamed) they had made public again the issue on which the original movement made its stand, the inequity of the practice of buying and selling for private gain that which "[i]n the beginning of time the great creator Reason made ... to be a common treasury", the Earth.

That this issue had been raised in this way, that the Diggers were not only being remembered but read, discussed and taken seriously at the end of the twentieth century, would have astonished their original opponents and detractors. So short-lived were their communities at George Hill[2] and later

Cobham, so total their defeat, and so quick to fade into obscurity their leader Gerrard Winstanley, that few who observed them at the time would have imagined their being talked about 350 *days* after their demise, let alone 350 *years*. If they were accorded a degree of fame (or notoriety) in their day, the Diggers seemed destined, after the brutal destruction of their venture, to be mere footnotes to the grander historical narrative being fashioned in the 1650s by the army, Parliament and Cromwell. Yet (to anticipate a point made by Nigel Smith in this volume), because Winstanley wrote, and did so with such clarity, passion, originality and courage, he continues to inspire his readers, and engage them with both his ideas and his digging, all these years after his heroic failure.

The legacy of those whose work has revived interest in him and his movement this century – Firth, Gooch, Bernstein, Berens, Petegorsky, Sabine, Hill[3] and some of the contributors to this volume – is that he and they are more written about, researched into and discussed today than at any other time in the last 350 years. In the last 60 years – to take the appearance of Petegorsky's study and the Sabine edition of Winstanley's works as a watershed – literally hundreds of articles, papers, books, theses, songs, films, plays and (more recently) web-sites inspired by the Diggers have appeared in every corner of the globe, such that any attempt at a comprehensive bibliography is almost certainly doomed to failure.[4] Considering so little is still known about them, that they flourished for barely a year, and that some of their writings lay undiscovered for more than 300 years, the influence and popularity of the Digger movement has been truly remarkable.

Indeed, this volume itself bears testimony to the Diggers' contemporary popularity, arising as it does from a conference held in Weybridge and Walton to commemorate the original George Hill occupation. This event, which took place against the background of the "second" occupation with which it enjoyed a symbiotic relationship, drew more than 200 participants from the UK, North America and the continent, who enjoyed, in addition to seven of the papers included here, a screening of the film "Winstanley" (with talkback led by Kevin Brownlow, the co-director, and Miles Halliwell, who played the eponymous hero); music from singer/songwriter Leon Rosselson, whose many compositions include the legendary "The World Turned Upside Down" about the events of 1649; readings from Winstanley's writings by members of the cast of the film; a work-in-progress report on the new edition of Winstanley from its three editors; and addresses by the veteran British Labour politician Michael Foot – who quoted from the Hamilton edition of Winstanley given to him by George Orwell – and environmental activist and journalist George Monbiot. The venue for the second day of the conference was St Mary's Church, Walton, which has strong connections with the Diggers: in 1649 some of their number were illegally imprisoned there, and on another occasion, as a contemporary newspaper report puts it, "[o]ne of their number getting up a great burden of thorns and bryers ... thrust them into the pulpit ... to stop out the Parson."[5] The re-enactment of this latter episode during the conference was, though dramatic, entirely symbolic, the present-day incumbent having proved an enthusiastic host of the event.

Given the occasion for these papers, it would be tempting to claim that they mark a watershed in Digger scholarship, but this scholarship is now so diverse that no one volume, certainly of this modest size, could ever claim to set down such a marker. Yet this is not to play down the value of these essays, representing as they do the latest thinking by scholars who have been in the forefront of research into Winstanley and his milieu in recent years. In so far as some of the main foci of this research have been Winstanley's life, background and influences; the identity of the other signatories to the Digger tracts; the significance of Biblical imagery and allegory in Winstanley's works; the role of the silent and unknown women in the Digger movement; and the influence of Digger writings in contemporary and subsequent political discourse and activism, these essays are clearly responding to current questions in the field. In addition, the broad range of disciplines informing the various contributions here – literary theory, biblical studies, historical analysis, women's studies, local history – reflects the remarkably eclectic nature of Digger studies at present, and the extraordinary fecundity, depth and originality of their writings. Things have clearly moved on from the days when it was thought necessary to apologise for studying the radicals of the mid-seventeenth century: now the attention paid to them by scholars, and the quality and quantity of their output, matches that long enjoyed by their more "illustrious" contemporaries.

These essays fall into two very general and non-discrete categories, historical analysis and textual criticism. In the first of the more broadly historical pieces, Gerald Aylmer sets out the context of the Digger project, and offers, *inter alia*, some reflections on why, despite operating in one of the last periods when a revolutionary situation of a traditional, rural, kind could have developed, the Diggers were ultimately unable to realize their vision. Then James Alsop, who over the last twenty years has done perhaps more than anyone to broaden our knowledge of Winstanley as a person, pulls together all of his research on this theme to offer a response to the question "Gerrard Winstanley: What Can We Know of His Life?" Picking up this question, and drawing upon his specialist and unrivalled local knowledge, David Taylor focuses on Winstanley's (and some of the other Diggers') connections with Cobham – the origins of which are brought into question in a postscript to this essay by John Gurney. By suggesting that Winstanley's father-in-law, William King, may not have been living in Cobham in 1643, Gurney raises the intriguing possibility that there were other factors drawing the Digger to the town following the closure of his business venture in London, possibly contacts already established with radicals in the region. Gurney's findings raise fresh questions about the origins and development of Winstanley's ideas.

Nigel Smith's concern is to demonstrate how vital was the pen as well as the spade to the Diggers' project. Though Winstanley appears to play down writing as no substitute for action, "the life of all", he did not give up writing until after he had stopped digging – though what he was effectively able to do, Smith suggests, was "dig" on the page as well as in the ground. If in this Winstanley proves himself a radical among radicals, in his views on gender roles he was decidedly more conservative, never seriously challenging, at least in print, the received wisdom of his day regarding the (inferior) status of women in society. As Elaine Hobby demonstrates, while there are occasional hints in the Diggers' pamphlets that their argument for equality might extend to women, this is never fully worked through – though many women contemporaries of the Diggers did themselves powerfully challenge traditional gender demarcations.

That Winstanley abandoned his project after barely a year was, of course, due largely to the attitude of his opponents, and John Gurney explores the dynamic between the Digger colonies and the local townspeople both at Walton and Cobham. Building on his earlier seminal work, and drawing both on contemporary sources and Winstanley's own writings, Gurney notes how, sensing a degree of local support for the Diggers at Cobham, the gentry there sought to characterize them as enemies of the state and provoke the government into taking action against them – a task made easier once Winstanley publicly claimed his right to dig on Crown land.

The significance of the religious imagery and biblical citations in Winstanley's writings has exercised scholars for many years, and his frequent metaphorical references to the Diggers as "Jews" appear particularly suggestive. In her chapter Claire Jowitt examines these references, and notes that, although writing against the background of improved relations between Englishpeople and Jews, Winstanley's interest in Jewishness is in the main historical. Though "Jewishness" was often considered the antithesis of "Englishness", the experience of the Jews as recorded in Scripture provides, for Winstanley, a powerful metaphor for the situation and aspirations of the Diggers. Another feature of Winstanley's writings is his tactic of appealing directly to those in power to recognize their common cause with "the people", and in exploring this theme Warren

Chernaik compares the Diggers with Milton and leading Levellers, with their stress on the right of "free born men" to "speak free" to those in positions of authority. If Winstanley and his contemporaries change tack somewhat in their later works, offering more of a lament for a loss of liberty than advice and counsel, this might, Chernaik suggests, be a consequence of their consciousness of defeat and recognition that the earlier convention of direct address had begun to break down.

Next Jim Holstun breathes fresh life into the debate about the supposed intellectual relationship between Winstanley and Marx, arguing that the point is not whether either or both men were in any sense "marxists" or "winstanleyans", but that both were *communists*. Marx famously rejected the label "marxist" for himself, and appeared to believe that the Russian *mir* might be the medium for an immediate transition to advanced communism without the "necessary" intervening stage of proletarian immiseration; and Winstanley, Holstun suggests, developed a materialist theory of history as class struggle, and envisaged the transition from oppressive enclosures to his communist utopia occurring through a dialectical process. Anticipating an objection that a comparison of Winstanley with Marx might lead to a "secularizing" of the former's ideas, Holstun argues a strong affinity between Winstanley, Marx and present-day liberation theology – a theme picked up and developed in the final essay by Chris Rowland. In his approach to the Scriptures, Rowland argues, Winstanley is close both to the later visionary William Blake and members of basic Christian communities in present-day Latin America, since all are concerned less to unlock the "meaning" of the Bible with the tools of scholarship and learning than to develop a new prophetic language to enable the text to speak to and interpret the reader's own context. In particular, radicals will want this language to provide a critique of hegemony and oppression, though as Rowland stresses, picking up a *leitmotif* of this whole volume, none will be satisfied with interpretation if it is not attended by action.

Research into Winstanley and the Digger communities seems certain to continue apace, not least since (as this collection clearly demonstrates) each new contribution to it, while appearing to respond to one question, will leave others in its wake. Despite the best efforts of Alsop, Taylor and others, our knowledge of Winstanley's life still consists of little more than tantalizing glimpses, and there is still a vast amount of work to be done on the men and women who joined him in digging the commons, both in Surrey and elsewhere.[6] The story behind his apparent drift back towards religious conformity against the background of at least some intermittent dialogue with the Quakers also needs to be teased out – not least in the light of what we are discovering about the practice of "occasional conformity" – as does the riddle now posed by Gurney about the basis of his connection with the part of Surrey which he began to dig. The fruitful results of reading Winstanley against other thinkers and activists – attempted in the last three chapters of this volume and in earlier work by Hill, Kenyon, Dawson and myself[7] – might also stimulate further such activity. A highpoint in Digger scholarship, and a major stimulus to further research, will be the publication within the next year or two of a new edition of the entire Winstanley corpus edited by Ann Hughes (Keele), Tom Corns (Bangor) and David Loewenstein (Wisconsin-Madison). Though we have been well served by the Sabine, Hamilton, Hill and, most recently, Hopton editions of the tracts,[8] the appearance of a comprehensive, scholarly edition, incorporating the early writings in full as well as those discovered since Sabine, is massively overdue. The editors, and Oxford University Press, are to be commended for their vision in conceiving, and hard work in executing, this project.

"[Y]et my mind was not at rest, because nothing was acted, and thoughts run in me, that words and writings were all nothing, and must die, for action is the life of all, and if thou dost not act thou dost nothing."[9] Winstanley's reflection on his literary endeavours, taken from the preface to his *Watch-Word to the City of London and the Armie* and emblazoned boldly on a banner hung high at all the anniversary events in 1999, was the most quoted of his statements at the commemorative conference – an irony not lost on speakers and participants alike. And here are yet more words – or words once spoken now presented in more permanent and accessible form – to add to the millions already produced in expounding, explaining and excoriating a man who saw only limited value in the written word. What he would make of them, or of our attempts to remember him and his movement, we cannot know, but perhaps his mind would still not be at rest if he thought our interest in him extended no further than merely *discussing* his vision of making the Earth once more a "common treasury". Might he want to ask our generation, as his contemporary John Bunyan asked theirs, "were you doers, or talkers only?"[10]

NOTES

1. Plans to rectify (in part) this omission are in hand, and it is likely that the striking memorial stone sculpted by Andrew Whittle for the 350th anniversary in 1999 will be sited on or near to the Hill sometime during 2000. It is also worth noting that Elmbridge Borough Council recently named two new streets in Cobham after Winstanley.
2. This was the name commonly used by the Diggers, who, like all good Puritans, ignored the saints of the established church.
3. C.H. Firth (ed.), *The Clarke Papers: vol II* (London: The Camden Society, 1894); G.P. Gooch, *History of Democratic Ideas in the Seventeenth Century* (Cambridge: Cambridge University Press, 1898); Eduard Bernstein, *Sozialismus und Demokratie in der grossen Englischen Revolution* (Stuttgart, 1908); ET, *Cromwell and Communism* (London: Allen & Unwin, 1930, and Nottingham: Spokesman, 1980); L.H. Berens, *The Digger Movement in*

the Days of the Commonwealth (London: Simpkin, Marshall, Hamilton, Kent, 1906); David W. Petegorsky, *Left-Wing Democracy in the English Civil War* (London: Gollancz, 1940, and Stroud: Alan Sutton, 1995); Sabine, *Works*; Christopher Hill, *The World Turned Upside Down: Radical Ideas During the English Revolution* (London: Temple Smith, 1972), which has perhaps done more than any other book to put Winstanley on the map in the last two or three decades (though Hill's numerous other writings on the seventeenth-century radicals all include substantial references to the Diggers and Winstanley). Hill has of course also edited *LFOW*.

4. Though riddled with typographical errors, one of the best recent attempts appears on pp.255–62 of the 1995 reprint of Petegorsky's *Left-Wing Democracy in the English Civil War* edited by Ivan Roots. This should be read in conjunction with Petegorsky's own (1940) bibliography. For another useful (though shorter) list of secondary sources see Andrew Hopton (ed.), *Gerrard Winstanley: Selected Writings* (London: Aporia Press, 1989) pp.116–17.
5. *The Kingdomes Faithfull and Impartiall Scout*, Numb. 13, 20–27 April 1649, in Joad Raymond (ed.), *Making the News: An Anthology of the Newsbooks of Revolutionary England* (Glos.: Windrush Press, 1993), p.394.
6. John Gurney is working on the Surrey Diggers. David Mulder included useful biographical notes of all the signatories to the Digger tracts in *The Alchemy of Revolution* (New York: Peter Lang, 1990, pp.299–331), and in an amusing piece based on Colonel Shapcot's assertion (at the trial of the Quaker James Nayler in 1656/7) that the Diggers came "out of the North country" where originate "the greatest pests of the Nation", Jim Paton argues that an analysis of known Diggers' surnames suggests the majority came from the south, particularly the south-west (privately published and circulated manuscript).
7. Hill compares Winstanley and Hobbes in *The World Turned Upside Down*, pp.387–94; Timothy Kenyon discusses More and Winstanley in *Utopian Communism and Political Thought in Early Modern England* (London: Pinter, 1989); David Dawson, "Allegorical Intratextuality in Bunyan and Winstanley", *The Journal of Religion* (1990), pp.189–201, explores the use of Scripture in both writers; and I attempt to identify common themes in Müntzer and Winstanley (and contemporary liberation theology) in *Faith in the Revolution* (London: SPCK, 1997). David Boulton is currently undertaking a close textual comparison of the writings of Fox and Winstanley, and has recently re-examined the relationship between the Digger leader and the Quakers in *Gerrard Winstanley and the Republic of Heaven* (Dent: Dales Historical Monographs, 1999) and "Winstanley and Friends", *The Friends Quarterly* (2000).
8. Sabine, *Works*, Leonard Hamilton (ed.), *Selections From the Works of Gerrard Winstanley* (London: Cressett, 1944); Hill, *LFOW*; Hopton, *Gerrard Winstanley: Selected Writings*.
9. *Works*, p.315.
10. Cited in Hill, *The World Turned Upside Down*, p.407.

The Diggers in Their Own Time

GERALD AYLMER

I have three themes, but will not divide my paper into three rigid divisions. The possible prerequisites for a successful revolution seem to me to include the existence of (i) a revolutionary class; (ii) a revolutionary idea; and (iii) a revolutionary situation. And I shall suggest that, while one of these existed in ample measure, the other two only did so in part, and that they did not come together in such a way as to make a popular revolution possible in mid-seventeenth-century England.

As to the revolutionary idea, by any standards we must surely agree that Gerrard Winstanley's critique of society as it existed in his own time qualifies under this heading. His demands, or if you prefer his programme, included common ownership of the land, the abolition of the buying and selling of land, the communal practice of agriculture and likewise – though this is rather more by implication from his writings – the communal operation of forestry, mining and manufactures, the abolition of the payment of rent and of wage labour. Almost the only thing that he did not want to abolish but actually to strengthen was the monogamous, some would say the patriarchal, family unit. Certainly what his contemporary, the republican theorist James Harrington, called "the superstructure" would have been entirely swept away if Winstanley's idea had been put into practice. He wanted to see a totally different legal system, with virtually the entire existing law and above all the system of professional lawyers being abolished. He wanted the existing church to be swept away, together with all its ministers. Not that he was anti-religious, or on his own terms anti-Christian; he was indeed a deeply religious man whose vision of a communist society had come to him in a mystical trance, so he tells us, before the digging experiment had begun. But he had no use at all for the church as it existed, or for the Puritan sects; not for the established church as it then was, a kind of Presbyterian-Congregationalist mixture – the Anglican Church having been overthrown a few years before. Nor had he any use for the existing system of higher education; the "higher" should be emphasized here because he would have been sympathetic to village schools where the basic skills of reading, writing and simple arithmetic were taught. He was by no means against education as such, and he was not anti-intellectual. If his works are read carefully, it can be seen that he had a concept of technological progress; the only honours which he allowed were for people who made important scientific discoveries, thereby almost anticipating a republican version of the later Royal Society. But he excoriated the existing system of higher education in grammar schools and above all in the universities.

By any standards, all this amounts to a revolutionary programme. It did not of course come from nowhere. It arose partly from the radical heritage of the Protestant Reformation in the sixteenth century; and in the shorter term from the ferment of ideas which came bubbling forth during the Civil Wars of the 1640s and in their immediate aftermath. Winstanley's ideas can be seen taking shape in his early pamphlets, but the most important ones for our purposes are those associated directly with the Digger experiment of 1649–50; and before that the one in which he announces that he has had a vision of the earth as a common treasury and will begin such an experiment when the time is ripe. *The New Law of Righteousnes,* in which he describes his mystical trance, was published just before the execution of the King, in January 1649. His last, longest and most comprehensive, though not in every respect his most effective work, *The Law of Freedom in a Platform,* he tells his readers was drafted during the Digger experiment, an extraordinary thought in itself when we reflect on the conditions under which he was living during the winter of 1649–50. He relates that he returned to it after the digging was over; he then added a Preface addressed to no less than Oliver Cromwell, not yet Protector but Lord General and the most powerful person in the country, appealing for the great man's support and his help in implementing the ideas set forth in it. This is dated November 1651, and *The Law of Freedom* was published in February 1652, well after the Digger experiment was at an end, but none the less quite clearly a product of that experience. So we have here a programme, adding up to a fully revolutionary idea, available in print by 1649–52.

We must now turn to consider the social and economic background, because it is essential to have at least a general picture of this in our minds in order to understand both how the Diggers came into existence at all, and why they did not achieve greater success. It is important to remember that, while the total population of England and Wales was probably only about one-ninth of what it is today, a far larger proportion of these people were living in rural areas; indeed many parts of the countryside would have been absolutely, as well as relatively, a lot more densely populated then than they are today. And far more people, of course, depended for their livelihood on agriculture in one form or another. So quite small changes affecting farming and people's way of life in the countryside could have an altogether disproportionate effect on the well-being of large numbers, indeed sometimes on their very existence. Bad weather leading to harvest failure was perhaps the most serious danger of all, except for plague and other epidemic diseases. There was a sequence of two, if not three, bad harvests in the late 1640s, producing exceptionally high grain prices, and thus pushing up the price of bread to an alarming level for many of the poor both in town and country. Therefore, in that sense a potentially revolutionary situation already existed. But man-made changes were also involved. These included enclosures of common lands, the reorganization of field systems, the drainage of fens and marshes, the clearance of woodland and closing of forests: all these were changes of land use which could make a big difference to the living standards of many people in rural areas.[1]

I would agree with those historians and economists who argue that, in the longer run, the development of capitalism and the extension of a national market probably did make most people better off than they had been in the Middle Ages. This is not to say that capitalism is the complete and ultimate answer to all of humanity's problems; I happen to believe that it is not. But in the context of the transition from medieval to early modern times the capitalist system was the way to greater prosperity. In the short run, on the other hand, because of these changes in the structure of the rural economy, it could mean that things got worse for numbers of people over relatively long stretches of time, and sometimes acutely so.

If we ask, why was there not a mass upheaval, a popular rising against these conditions, part of the answer lies in the existence of what we might call safety valves. First of all, the years before the Civil War, especially from 1630 to1640, had seen very considerable emigration to the New World – the West Indies and North America, as there had been earlier to Northern Ireland. Another form of emigration was internal, marked by the enormous growth of London, which together with Westminster, Southwark and the suburbs, was fast beginning to rival in size any other city in Christian Europe, if not in the world, by the end of the seventeenth century. In this way London had long overflowed the traditional boundaries of the City. And there were of course many other urban centres, lesser towns, all of them small compared to London, let alone by modern standards, but which also absorbed people from the countryside. Evidence advanced by historians of epidemic disease and of population movements strongly suggests that the death rate was much higher in London and in other towns than in rural areas, so the urban sector was recruiting people by attracting them from the surplus rural population, and in this way may fairly be seen as another safety valve, like emigration overseas.

Another, of a rather more cruel, brutal kind, arose from the casualties and general disruption caused by the civil wars of the 1640s. Although historians disagree about the number of those killed, let alone seriously injured, there can be no doubt that these are to be numbered in many tens of thousands. This is in spite of the fact that the Civil War was not as bloody in England as it was in Ireland, nor quite as much so as in Scotland; the English generally treated each other with slightly more restraint, in the way of killing prisoners and the wounded and savaging non-combatants, than they did the Irish or on occasion the Scots. None the less, the wars must have constituted a setback to the growth of population, with men being away from home for long stretches, many families losing husbands and fathers, and domestic life generally being disrupted by losses and damage to property, crops in the ground and farm animals.

Thus, for whatever combination of reasons, it does appear that from about the middle of the century the rate of population growth slowed down; it may indeed have begun to do so before the beginning of the Civil War in 1642, but certainly had done by the 1650s. And the total population may be thought of as bumping along on a kind of uneven plateau, with ups and downs but no large sustained increase, as there had been in the later sixteenth and early seventeenth centuries, until well into the eighteenth century. Moreover, associated with that – and it may be left to specialists in demographic and economic history to argue about what was cause and what was effect here – the price rise of Tudor and early Stuart times had also come to an end. Apart from the short-term fluctuations due to bad and good harvests, to which I have already referred, the overall trend of prices was no longer upward; indeed by the later seventeenth century agricultural prices and even rents were tending downwards. Real wages, the purchasing power of earnings, were no longer declining, and may even have risen by a modest amount after 1650. Therefore, in this sense the situation was becoming less potentially explosive. Perhaps the mid-seventeenth century was the last occasion when a revolutionary situation of a traditional, *rural* kind could have developed. Potentially revolutionary situations certainly existed again in the late eighteenth and earlier nineteenth centuries, at the time of the French Revolution and again in the age of the Chartists, but these were of a very different order.

Historians of rural society and of radical movements in the countryside do not altogether agree about the divisions among the different social groups involved. The American historian Buchanan Sharp, who wrote a very interesting book about the disturbances in the West Country, in and around the forests of Dorset, Gloucestershire and Wiltshire, especially in the years either side of 1630, concluded that those involved in taking direct action were not peasants or agriculture labourers but artisans, propertyless in terms of land but dependent on access to forest and woodland for raw materials, to gather what they could and to graze such animals as they possessed.[2] It is worth remembering that a successful anti-enclosure riot, the pulling down of fences, the levelling of hedges and ditches, even temporarily, did – in the phrase used at the time – "make things in common", because those involved gained or (as the case might be) recovered common access to woodland and waste for gathering and grazing; but that this was by no means the same as the practice of communal agriculture, based on collective ownership of arable and meadow or pasture. This is a fundamental distinction. And there is no evidence that those who promoted anti-enclosure riots wanted to practise collective farming, as we might think of it today; they wanted open access for families and individuals.

Another historian, Keith Lindley, who wrote an excellent book on the Fenland disturbances, particularly but not exclusively in the 1630s, argued that there were differences and even conflicts of interest between various groups who had or who sought access to property rights, or perhaps more strictly land use, in the fens. The fenmen were not without their own traditional rights; it was rather that these were being overridden by the promoters of large-scale drainage, but again they were individualists rather than collectivists.[3] So it is not altogether obvious or easy to say whether those who were most likely to join something like the Digger experiment in communal farming were landless agricultural labourers – who were literally being pushed beyond the limits of what they could endure, due to the low level of their earnings in relation to the high prices of food and basic necessities – or, alternatively, people who had, or had had some access to land and – even if they were not freehold owners or secure tenants – at least had a copyhold or customary tenancy, but had been disadvantaged by some or other of these various changes which have been briefly described here. Or else possibly, like Winstanley himself, they were people who had lost out as a result of the changes in the pattern of trade and the resulting setbacks in some sectors of the urban economy during and after the Civil War, and had come from London to rural Surrey in order to try to recover their fortunes by making a fresh start there. Although some excellent research has been done by local and other historians of the Diggers, I doubt if a large enough number of individuals can be identified for any reliable statistics to be possible. Certainly not all those who have made the closest studies of these rural movements and disturbances would see them as a simple conflict between the propertied and the propertyless.

Looking back a little in time, it might seem that people squatting on wastes, living in improvised cottages and cabins, who promoted some of the anti-enclosure riots, resemble the Diggers of 1649; and in some respects they surely do. The largest and most dramatic of these upheavals since the mid-sixteenth century had been the Midland Rising of 1607, centred in Northamptonshire but spilling over into neighbouring counties, which had ended in a pitched battle when forty or fifty of the so-called rioters had been killed. It was then that the very words "Leveller" and "Digger" were first used, to begin with (it seems) by the participants to describe themselves, and later by their enemies as terms of abuse.[4] Clearly the words remained in oral memory, but there is no evidence of their use in writing between the early 1620s and the late 1640s. More important, there is no evidence that the objectives of those involved in the Midland Rising were the same as those of the Diggers in 1649. The midlanders of 1607 wanted to restore open-field strip cultivation and to regain common rights, but not to practise common ownership or collective farming.

The best recent general account of the Diggers, putting them in a wider agrarian context, is by Brian Manning, an ex-pupil of Christopher Hill (with whose interpretations I have not always agreed) – in chapter 3 of his book *1649*.[5] For Winstanley's ideas we can go to the well-known writings of Hill himself,[6] besides those of his critics, but on the actual digging experiment and the participants I would recommend Manning in preference to Hill. In a recent article there is also a very interesting suggestion, from a more local perspective, that Winstanley and the others moved from St. George's Hill above Walton-on-Thames to Cobham Common because the inhabitants there, including the property holders, were less hostile towards them.[7] It has to be said that this is somewhat relative, for they seem to have been charged in the local court at Cobham as well as being physically attacked. None the less, this is a useful reminder that, even within one small region of the country, there could have been differences in the local rural economy and the social structure which might have affected the reception given to something like the digging experiment.

As to why there was not something more like what might be called (to offer alternative metaphors) a snowball or a brush-fire effect, we can find several reasons. First of all there were the actual counter-measures, both physical and legal, the sheer repression of the Diggers and the destruction of their habitat. Secondly, we have to remember in the days before the modern media, that although ordinary people could and did move about the country, they could only travel slowly, while news too moved uncertainly and communications were very uneven. Winstanley incidentally, in his last book, does call for a national postal system; he saw the importance of news and communications for ordinary people, and did not want these to be a monopoly of the Crown and the upper classes, as had largely been the case hitherto. Next is the point already touched upon in discussing the work of agrarian historians, what I would – if it is not too portentous a phrase – call the stratification of the peasantry and of the rural population as a whole. For many, indeed for most people in England at that time, life was not as bad as in most other countries in pre-modern times. This must be emphasized because otherwise one cannot understand the seventeenth century.

Compared to the inhabitants of France, for example, or of Spain, or many other parts of Europe, the living standards and conditions of a large proportion of the English population were not as terrible as some accounts might lead us to suppose, except for the periodic threats of epidemics and harvest failures. We may fairly conclude that many of them, very possibly an absolute majority, were better off, or perhaps we should say less badly off, as they were than they would have been as Diggers trying to scrape a living by cultivating waste and common land on St George's Hill or at Cobham.

Finally, there is the classic argument, which will take us into highly debatable territory intellectually speaking, that voluntary, unforced communism is incompatible with human nature. There had been another small communist experiment not long before this in the English-speaking world. The Plymouth Pilgrims, who had gone to New England as religious refugees in 1620, had subscribed a covenant before they landed, based on their financial obligations to their merchant backers in England, which involved common ownership and communal agriculture, which they practised for the first two or three years. It may have been partly due to the sadly premature death of their original, charismatic leader, John Carver, and the fact that his successor William Bradford, the second leader and historian of the infant colony of Plymouth Plantation, though a worthy and a resolute man, lacked these qualities. Certainly Bradford was persuaded, so he tells us, by some of the more energetic and hard working families to divide the land up in severalty, that is, to institute private ownership and individual family farming, which he says led to increased productivity (though the debt to the founding Company was never fully repaid). The more industrious men, he says, particularly objected to their wives having to help support the households of the more idle.[8] Actually this would not have happened if Winstanley's system had become more widely and firmly established, since he was keen to maintain family units in separate households. Be that as it may, I should perhaps have built in a fourth prerequisite for the success of any such undertaking: charismatic leadership and complete commitment among everyone involved. Winstanley clearly had some of these gifts, though not all; his associate in the early weeks of the digging, William Everard, also seems to have been a remarkable personality, even though he was regarded as mentally unbalanced by some of the army officers who had dealings with the Diggers.

This brings us to a serious mistake in Winstanley's tactics. He seems to have persuaded himself and the other Diggers that they could rely on, and expect the support of, the state. He had come to believe that the victory of Parliament in the Civil War, and the subsequent abolition of kingship, meant or should mean that the government would cease to uphold the authority of landlords, notably lords of manors, against their tenants and against those without any rights of property at all; also that the existing legal system and the burden of unequal taxation would be swept away, along with the rights of lords of manors. Why he should have believed this can only be worked out from a detailed analysis of parts of his writings, but for our purpose the important thing is the fact of his having held this belief, and thus having proceeded in a non-violent way, trying to persuade people to join the Diggers by the powers of argument and example. This helps to explain some extraordinary episodes. He and Everard had two interviews with Cromwell's immediate predecessor as Commander-in-Chief, Sir Thomas, by then Lord Fairfax. Once they went up to London to see him, and once he actually came down to Surrey and saw the Diggers at work. Although a fierce man on the field of battle and a strict military disciplinarian, Fairfax was in some ways a gentler, more equivocal character than Cromwell; and, if left to himself and not pushed to take action by the civilian authorities, he might not have ordered the suppression of the Diggers, since the evidence suggests that he regarded them as relatively harmless. The experiment could perhaps only have had a chance of being allowed to continue if they were indeed seen merely as harmless eccentrics; but in Surrey the lords of manors, clergy and other local property holders were not prepared to tolerate them; they twice got the Army called in, as well as taking direct action themselves against the Diggers, their dwellings, animals and crops.

Only in one of the other contemporary Digger experiments, at Wellingborough in Northamptonshire, is there a suggestion that any members of the existing landed classes, the property owners, were sympathetic. The evidence is slight, but according to those who have studied the sources in greatest depth Wellingborough had for various reasons grown very rapidly in population over the previous two or more generations; it formed a kind of congeries of industrial villages and hamlets concentrated in one district, with employment for many of the inhabitants being highly sensitive to trade fluctuations, and in the mid-seventeenth century with an exceptionally large number of people on poor relief. And the suggestion is that the local property owners who were sympathetic to the Wellingborough Diggers saw their undertaking as a way of getting poor people off the rates by setting them to work in communal agriculture, instead of having to support them by local taxation and private charity.[9] While this certainly seems plausible, unfortunately we do not have any comparable evidence about local reactions to the other experiment of 1650, at Iver in Buckinghamshire.[10] But we should note from the dates that these other Digger communities, if they lasted long enough to be so described, only seem to have begun after the original experiment in Surrey had collapsed, and its members had dispersed, having lasted almost exactly a year in the face of exceptional hardship and unremitting hostility. Again this underlines the lack of co-ordination and continuity which would have been essential for a truly revolutionary movement to have developed.

Lastly we come to the question of whether it is correct to see a fundamental shift in Winstanley's thinking, in Digger ideology. The case has been persuasively made, from having believed in what might be called revolutionary spontaneity, that sheer example would serve his purpose and that other people in society at large would simply be converted by peaceful persuasion, Winstanley moved to the notion of state power and coercion as a necessary means to achieve his communist objectives. This in essence is the argument put forward by J.C. Davis (now Professor of History at East Anglia, once paradoxically a pupil of Manning and myself at Manchester).[11] Even if one is only half persuaded by Davis's argument, it is a grave, some would say shocking, inconsistency in a revolutionary thinker that while Winstanley apparently believed that communism, his new vision of a just society, could be brought into existence by peaceful means, once achieved it could and should be upheld by coercive state power. It is worth remembering, however, that he was not alone in this. The Levellers, too, believed in non-violent means to achieve their ideal of a more democratic and fair society, with a very decentralized political system, something more like an English federation, and with a strict separation of powers between the different branches of government; but they also maintained that after their new constitution, or *Agreement of the People*, had been accepted and implemented, it would be right for the state to proceed criminally against anyone trying to reverse it and to bring about a return to the old order, thus treating counter-revolution as equivalent to treason. Not that this in itself would justify Winstanley's change of front. But the question is: how far did he change? If it is the case that he had actually drafted most of *The Law of Freedom* during the time of the Digger experiment, and that he only polished it up and added the preface to Cromwell afterwards, it is straining the facts to say that he moved – in a chronological sense – from a kind of anarcho-communism to state communism. Indeed, the Preface to that last book still envisages the coexistence of the two systems, old and new, with the new triumphing by example, not by force. To be fair to Professor Davis, he does not, I think, use the word "Stalinism" of Winstanley's mature ideas, but there is clearly some lurking implication that Winstanley had been converted to a belief in the use of coercive state power with the end justifying the means, as in Arthur Koestler's *Darkness at Noon* and George Orwell's *Animal Farm*.

The Diggers' belief in operating by persuasion and example can also be seen in the way they proceeded in practice. They did not attack, or attempt to occupy and take over private property as such; they were careful to limit their efforts to what they believed were commons and waste grounds. They got into legal difficulties both at Walton and at Cobham, because some of the local landowners (and possibly their tenants too) denied that these were wastes and commons; but that was their objective, and they did not intentionally invade privately owned farmland. It is worth speculating for a moment on how they would have fared if they had had a better opportunity; that is to say, if they had been operating on prime agricultural land with the best quality implements and animals of the time, rather than having had to scrape a bare living under the most miserable conditions on marginal scrub and woodland – which the film "Winstanley" brings out marvellously well. Simply to offer an opinion, the experiment might well have lasted longer and perhaps have gained more support; but unless some kind of cumulative process had taken place and the number of Digger settlements had grown so fast that they could exchange goods and services between them (as Winstanley envisages in his system of "storehouses" which were to replace shops where money passed), it is hard to see how things could have been so very different from what they were.

Yet it is worth emphasizing the grave disadvantages under which they operated; although they refer to ploughing, it is not clear that they even had proper ploughs, or draught animals as opposed to milking cows. Their agrarian technology was more like that of the pre-Roman Iron Age than that of Stuart or republican England. So, given better quality land, less local hostility, and the best farming methods of their day, it is not logically impossible to envisage the Diggers having been more successful and the experiment having lasted for a number of years. But all of these "might-have-beens" added together come near to saying, "if mid-seventeenth-century England had been other than it was …". If we look at experiments in common ownership and communal farming, even in the nineteenth and twentieth centuries, we see that it needs exceptional qualities of idealism and practical determination, besides a minimum measure of toleration on the part of the authorities, for these to survive, let alone to prosper. Nor is there any evidence to date of any country in which a completely communist system of land ownership and use has come into existence by spontaneous example. Peasants have seized the property of landowners, but not (either in Russia in 1917–18, or elsewhere in the twentieth century) in order to practise communal agriculture themselves; this has invariably been introduced, not to say forced upon them, as a result of state policy and by coercive action. So even applying anachronistic modern standards into our analysis, it is very hard to imagine how Winstanley's vision could have been translated into successful reality. Although it is theoretically possible that what I have called the snowball effect could have taken place, with more and more such communities springing up, first coexisting with, and then eventually superseding the whole previous social and economic system, given the historical reality of mid-seventeenth-century England in practice the experiment was bound to fail. The Diggers may have been heroic and admirable, but they were a failure all the same.

NOTES

1. For the general background, see Joan Thirsk (ed.), *The Agrarian history of England and Wales*, IV, *1500–1640* (Cambridge, 1967), and V, (Cambridge, 1984); C.G.A. Clay, *Economic Expansion and Social Change: England 1500–1700* (2 vols., Cambridge,1984); J. A. Sharpe, *Early Modern England: A Social History 1550–1760* (1987).
2. B. Sharp, *In Contempt of All Authority: Rural Artisans and Riot in the West of England 1586–1660* (Berkeley: University of California Press, 1980); see also A.R. Warmington, *Civil War, Interregnum and Restoration in Gloucestershire 1640–1672* (Woodbridge, Suffolk, for the Royal Historical Society, 1997), ch.5, esp. pp.140–42.
3. K. Lindley, *Fenland Riots and the English Revolution* (London: Heinemann, 1982); also C. Holmes, *Seventeenth-century Lincolnshire* (Lincoln: Society for Lincolnshire History and Archaeology, 1980).
4. John Burgess, "The Social Structure of Bedfordshire and Northamptonshire 1516–1700" (D.Phil. thesis, University of York, 1978), pp.273–80.
5. B. Manning, *1649: The Crisis of the English Revolution* (London: Bookmarks, 1992).
6. C. Hill, *The World Turned Upside Down* (1972); *LFOW*; *The Religion of Gerrard Winstanley* (Past & Present Supplement, 5, 1978).
7. J. Gurney, "Gerrard Winstanley and the Digger Movement in Walton and Cobham", *Historical Journal* 37 (1994), pp.775–802.
8. *Bradford's History of Plymouth Plantation* (ed. Boston, MA, 1928), pp.162–4; D.B. Rutman, *Husbandmen of Plymouth: Farms and Villages in the Old Colony 1620–1692* (Boston: Beacon Press, 1967), pp.5–7, 12–13, 82.
9. Burgess, "The Social Structure", pp.322–4.
10. The pamphlet of the Iver Diggers was only discovered relatively recently, by Keith Thomas; it is reprinted in the same volume, edited by the historian of science and of the British National Health Service, Charles Webster, as the piece by Winstanley himself which I was lucky enough to come upon in the Library of Worcester College, Oxford (C. Webster, *The Intellectual Revolution of the 17th century* (London: Routledge & Kegan Paul, 1974), chaps. ix, x and xi). The Wellingborough Declaration is in the Appendix to *Works*.
11. J.C. Davis, *Utopia and the Ideal Society. A Study of English Utopian Writing 1516–1700* (Cambridge: Cambridge University Press, 1981), chap. 7.

Gerrard Winstanley: What Do We Know of His Life?

JAMES D. ALSOP

The story of the life of Gerrard Winstanley is prefaced by the story of this research endeavour. Twenty years ago the February 1979 issue of *Past & Present* carried my "Gerrard Winstanley's Later Life". That was my first academic publication. As is frequently the case, the article was the result of serendipity: in the course of conducting research on one topic, I was diverted onto a path which proved to be far more fruitful and important. This would not have happened at all if not for the publication in 1973 of Christopher Hill's Penguin edition, *The Law of Freedom and Other Writings*. As is true for so many of my generation, that book brought Winstanley out of the university libraries and into the homes of many a budget-conscious undergraduate student, to be read, pondered and questioned. For that, and for so much besides, we all owe Christopher Hill a notable debt. What has been, what is and what will be accomplished for Winstanley and the Diggers rests upon his encouragement, his dedication and his wisdom. Although Winstanley has rarely been at the centre of my academic pursuits, he has remained in my thoughts and writing for two decades, and my appreciation for him has grown over time. This was a remarkable man, and the equally remarkable story of his long-time neglect and triumphal resurrection as an informal "yardstick" for measuring pre-modern radicalism deserves, at some point, to be told.

The task at hand is the life of Gerrard Winstanley: what do we know? What can we know? Biography possesses an immediate appeal, for it is here that we see – if only at a distance – real people living, laughing, loving, crying and thinking. In this pursuit, Winstanley poses particular problems. It is beyond question that one of the most impressive figures in early modern European history, the foremost radical of the English Revolution, has long remained remarkably obscure in his personal life and career. The root of this limitation lies in Winstanley himself.

Nothing can alter the fact that all Gerrard Winstanley's published writings and known correspondence fall into a brief four-year period of his middle age, 1648–51. We possess nothing from his hand, apart from a few signatures, for the first thirty-nine years of his life, and only several Chancery depositions for the last twenty-five. It is, of course, highly significant that he was profoundly stimulated and provoked by the momentous events of the later 1640s to participate in the radicalism of the era, both through his religious and socio-economic tracts and his involvement in Digger activism. That is why he is deemed to be worthy of study. However, all assessments of Winstanley recognize the severe limitations imposed by the wholesale lack of evidence for his intellectual development. Winstanley's silence in his writings on his background and earlier beliefs is almost total, never mentioning his parents, wife, children, friends, acquaintances, schooling, or even the books which he read. Winstanley had certainly studied the scriptures intensively, but only in the late 1970s was there detected a passing, certain, reference in his work to as basic a text as Foxe's "Book of Martyrs".[1] When it takes sustained scholarship to establish that Winstanley had read what virtually every other literate Englishman of his era is assumed to have known, we can appreciate how difficult, and contentious, studies of Winstanley's intellectual influences must be. Lacking a contemporary eulogist, bereft of sustained disciples, and largely forgotten by the public long before his own death, knowledge of Winstanley suffers from both unintentional, self-imposed obscurity and contemporary neglect.

Historians, like nature, abhor a vacuum. There exist a number of biographies of Winstanley which inform us what he must have thought at various times in his life, which authors he probably read, and what conclusions he drew from their writings. Some of this is sensible. We know that the past is remarkably pliable. With a figure such as Winstanley, of whom so little is known outside of a few intense years, scholars are under a particular obligation to state clearly that which is demonstrably in evidence, that which is thought to be probable (for clearly stated reasons), and that which is possible, plausible or partisan. What follows will be limited almost entirely to the aspects of his life and career which are either certain or probable. In this, the study builds upon the labours of several generations of scholars. In one area, however, I will venture directly into the realm of the possible. In 1940 David Petegorsky wrote: "It might be interesting to speculate as to the persons with whom he came into contact or the preachers to whose sermons he listened ...; but Winstanley has left us nothing on which to build."[2] This is, indeed, of very considerable interest. While it is true that Winstanley in his writings left us exceedingly little upon which to build, his biography, especially for the years of late adolescence and early manhood, provides intriguing possibilities.

Winstanley was baptised at Wigan, Lancashire, on 10 October 1609, the son of one Edward Winstanley, mercer.[3] The identities of his mother or of any possible siblings are unknown. Wigan was a large parish of 29,000 acres, taking in all of Up Holland, Orrell, Billinge, Pemberton, Winstanley,

Ince and other hamlets in addition to the borough of Wigan itself. In 1590 there were an estimated 3,000 communicants.[4] A very substantial number of Winstanleys were spread throughout the parish, and they do not appear to have been close knit. In excess of twenty adult male Winstanleys were heads of household in the parish during the period circa 1600–1620, including at least three named Edward. The status of these males ranged from gentleman, yeoman and husbandman, through mercer, glover, slater and pauper.[5] Most scholars have followed Petegorsky's lead in identifying Gerrard's father with the Edward Winstanley, town burgess of Wallgate, Wigan, who was buried on 27 December 1639.[6] Although not unlikely, this remains unsubstantiated. Even if the relationship is accepted, this was a town where there were 138 burgesses in – for example – 1628, most of distinctly humble circumstances. In a borough where the mayor in the same year was an artisan of limited estate and a total inventory of effects upon his death valued at £146, including uncollectible debts, Winstanley the burgess was never sufficiently prominent to serve as either alderman or mayor. All indications are that Gerrard Winstanley came from an artisanal family of distinctly modest means, not the urban pseudo-gentry of some recent biographies.[7]

Early Stuart Wigan, like most of Lancashire, was divided between papists, church papists and Anglicans. Nothing can be said about Winstanley's early religion other than that it was almost certainly protestant. But what form of protestantism? Devout Calvinism was present in the parish, the legacy in large measure of the labours of Edward Fleetwood, rector of Wigan from 1571 to 1604, whose influence could be felt as late as 1647. However, Fleetwood met sustained challenges from both religious conservatives and other protestants, and neither of his successors could be called Puritan.[8] Indeed, the dominant ecclesiastical figure in Wigan during Winstanley's youth was the king's chaplain Dr John Bridgeman, rector from 1616 and from 1619 concurrently bishop of Chester. The rector was also lord of the town and manor of Wigan, and Bridgeman engaged in drawn-out public confrontations and lawsuits with the parishioners over tithes, tenancies, markets and leet courts.[9] The Wigan of Winstanley's youth, therefore, was a contested space which emphasized the economic power and assertiveness of the established clergy. Bishop Bridgeman's endeavours highlighted the central role of the church in the local economy, administration and politics. When this was undertaken in an atmosphere of incriminations, lawsuits and petty vindictiveness it could not help but alienate many of his tenants and parishioners, including the members of Winstanley's family circle. In his own version of events, Bridgeman was not lacking in Christian charity, but his attention was focused directly upon the wealth, dignity and fabric of the church.

Of Winstanley himself, we learn nothing prior to the year 1630. Did he attend school? The Winstanleys were numerous but hardly distinguished; Humphrey Winstanley, who Bishop Bridgeman in 1620 referred to as 'chief of the name & family of Winstanleys in the Parish of Wigan', was, like others of this name, illiterate.[10] However, the Wigan grammar school received substantial endowments in 1613 and 1618, and attracted the bishop's personal attention in 1620, so opportunity existed for the younger generation. The reason scholars believe that Winstanley may have attended a grammar school for a time is his occasional use of Latin in his writings. But if he was enrolled at the Wigan school in the years 1620 to 1622 he would have come face-to-face with headmaster John Lewis, an individual later described by his own patron, Bishop Bridgeman, as a haunter of alehouses, an excessive gamester, a blasphemer, a night walker, a fighter and dueller, and one who had four young wives who all died soon after their portions were spent.[11]

It would be excessive to state that Winstanley's later contempt for the established church had its creation in Bishop Bridgeman's Wigan. After all, the experience did not radicalize the townsmen of the borough: their defence against the rector was based upon precedent and tradition; the borough several times returned Bridgeman's brother to Parliament in the 1620s; and Wigan was royalist in the civil war.[12] In different conditions the episode might have meant little to Winstanley in his later life. However, we know that Winstanley, in the period of spiritual crisis during 1647 which immediately preceded his first publications as a religious radical, engaged in contemplation of his past life.[13] When he then engaged in strident anti-clericalism, could he have failed to reflect upon Bishop Bridgeman's role in early Stuart Wigan?

On 25 March 1630, Winstanley, aged twenty, began an apprenticeship in London with one Sarah Gater (1605–56) of the Merchant Taylors' Company.[14] Twenty was well within the normal age range for apprentices who arrived in London from the provinces,[15] but in this instance Winstanley was placed in a small, intimate household with a female employer only four years older than himself. Who was Sarah Gater? She was one of the eight children of John Rogers (d. 1615), a clothworker free of the Grocer's Company, and widow of William Gater (d. 1624). Her deceased husband had entered the Merchant Taylors' Company only in the year preceding his early death; prior to this he had taken BA and MA degrees at Emmanuel College, Cambridge (1616, 1619), been ordained (1616), and served as lecturer at St Andrew Undershaft, London.[16] Sarah Gater herself was exceptionally devout, and exceptionally learned, possessing by her death in 1656 a sizeable library on theology and medicine, including her manuscript notes on physic and surgery.[17]

Winstanley and Gater were not thrown together by chance. This can be demonstrated through reference to the Lancashire Mason family. The three families of Winstanley, Gater and Mason were almost certainly connected by blood and/or marriage. With so much missing information for the female side of all three families it is impossible to be more definite. The Mason family of Wigan is important in demonstrating that close ties existed prior to the apprenticeship contract of 1630. Gilbert Mason, tanner, of Wigan, was related, in some way, to the Winstanley family. His younger son Henry immediately preceded Winstanley as Gater's apprentice, 1623–30. Henry had been taken on by Gater's husband; Winstanley, the second apprentice, was the first to be bound by Sarah Gater herself. Henry Mason remained in her employment as a journeyman servant up to 1656. She called him her nephew, although, as mentioned above, the precise relationship remains unclear. Meanwhile, Gilbert Mason's eldest son, Matthew, began his career in London before 1616 as a servant to the bishop of London's chaplain.[18] That chaplain was his uncle, another Henry Mason (1573?–1647), brother to Gilbert, born at Wigan as the son of a minor tradesman. This Henry Mason entered Brasenose College, Oxford, in 1592, graduated BA (1594) and MA (1603), and was rector of St Andrew Undershaft (1613–41) and concurrently prebendary of St Paul's Cathedral (1616–37).[19] William Gater had been his lecturer at St Andrew Undershaft, and the youthful William and Sarah Gater his parishioners. In her widowhood, Sarah Gater moved to the parish of St Michael, Cornhill, before 1630, but she remained close to Henry Mason. She eventually obtained a large portion of his library, and considered him to be her spiritual mentor.[20]

Remaining a widow up to her death in 1656, Gater carried on an independent minor retail trade with modest success. Winstanley served his apprenticeship under her in St Michael, Cornhill, from 25 March 1630 to 20 February 1638. The household was small, consisting of Gater, her infant son William, Henry Mason the journeyman, Winstanley and one or two female servants. In 1634 a second apprentice joined the establishment, George Dalton the son of a London tailor, and then in late 1637, as Winstanley prepared to depart, a new apprentice, Peter Smith of Middlesex, took his spot.[21] We know nothing of what passed within this household, of either a personal or a professional nature. Winstanley has left us just one minor clue: although he came to criticize so many institutional and customary features of seventeenth-century England in *The Law of Freedom* of 1652, he displayed unreserved admiration in his model society for the practice of apprenticeship.[22] For Gater we also possess one clue: her September 1654 last will and testament included favourable mention by name of all her previous apprentices then living, with the notable exception of Winstanley.[23] For the relationship of the 1630s this reveals nothing, but the omission might suggest alienation from Winstanley the True Leveller.

As a pious employer and relative, Gater can be presumed to have followed the advice of the prescriptive literature of her age to attend to the spiritual well-being of her apprentices. Perhaps it was in this household where Winstanley acquired a smattering of Latin, rather than at grammar school. Winstanley in his middle age demonstrated an interest in, and knowledge of, medicine;[24] here is a possible origin for that pursuit.

When Winstanley in his tracts of 1648–49 informs us that he had long been a conventional worshipper and a "strict goer to Church",[25] what exactly did he mean? Throughout his twenties, Winstanley almost certainly worshipped alongside Gater before rector William Brough, chaplain to Charles I and subsequently canon of Windsor (1639) and dean of Gloucester (1643). Resident in the parish up to 1641, Brough was a high church Anglican. The sequestration order of 1643 stated that he had corrupted his parishioners:

> wth the Leaven of popish and superstitious doctrines of bowing to or before the Alter, Worshipping toward the East, Wasing away of Originall Sinne by Baptisme ... and the error of Arminiasme of vniversall Grace, and ffree will in man fallen, and the Apostacy of the Saintes, and hath expressed great Malignity against the power & proceedings of the Parliament, That they ... should intermeddle wth Spirituall matters, Inveighing against such as Trayters to God and his Church ...[26]

How was this theology received within the Gater household? Apparently very well. Sarah Gater identified two spiritual influences upon her beliefs, her mentor and relation Henry Mason, MA, and her close friend and cousin, the poet and religious biographer Isaak Walton. Walton, best known as the author of *The Compleat Angler*, was a high church divine who had himself begun his career in the London cloth trade and who was resident in the city throughout the 1630s.[27] Mason was a noted anti-Calvinist. He had played a role in the controversies at Oxford in the opening years of the century, authored a series of controversial devotional tracts between 1624 and 1635, and in 1633 co-authored the unlicensed Arminian work, *God's Love to Mankind*.[28] Winstanley, thus, had direct personal knowledge of Arminianism. In particular, Mason's writings were present within the Gater household, and at least some circulated from an early date at Wigan;[29] could they have been among Winstanley's early reading? We, of course, do not know Winstanley's reaction, or even whether he had a reaction or a developed point of view. He informs us later that the religion of his life before 1647 had been ritualized, devoid of deep inner feeling: "I myself have known nothing but what I received by tradition from the mouths and pen of others: I worshipped a God, but I neither knew who he was nor where he was, so that I lived in the dark, being blinded by my flesh, and by the imagination of such as stand up to teach the people to know the Lord."[30] Had he been a conventional Arminian?

That question is unanswerable. However, four pieces of information from the years 1639 to 1643 shed light upon his development. First, we can answer a related question: once freed of his apprenticeship where did Winstanley turn? He established himself in another Arminian parish, where he speedily became an active parishioner. Winstanley secured his company freedom on 21 February 1638, and by 21 May 1639, at the latest, he was a householder and shopkeeper of Saint Olave, Old Jewry.[31] In September 1640, at the age of thirty, he married Susan King, three years his junior, second eldest child of William King, barber-surgeon of London, resident in the nearby parish of St Lawrence Jewry.[32] The circumstances which led to this marriage are obscure. In 1641 he began paying his parish's poor rate and at the same time began active participation in the open vestry, one of a small minority of ratepayers to engage in this activity.[33] The parish had speedily conformed to the high church innovations of the 1630s and its vicar, Thomas Tuke, was removed in 1643 by Parliament because he,

> is not only superstitious in practisinge and pressinge the late Innovations in the worshupp of God and the Prophanacon of the Lordes Day but hath refused to read the Declaracons of Parliamente. And when he had suddainly before he considered it, Read the Ordinance for listinge [enlisting] of Souldiers for the Service of the Parliamente, help vpp his hand and crydd in the Church, The divell confound All Traytors Rebells and Turbulent spiritts, and added that if he had considered itt before hand he would not haue reade it and often inveighes in the Pulpitt against them that bringe in plate and money in aide to the Parliament as men for sworne, and that haue broken their protestacon, and that they doe itt to maintaine a Warre against the Kinge, to the greate dishonor of God.[34]

Winstanley apparently settled in without difficulty, and remained an active parishioner under Tuke when sectarianism flourished in the early 1640s. That is, Winstanley throughout his residence in London never abandoned the established church.

We first secure glimpses of a political Winstanley in these years of escalating tensions. One incident involves the disputed elections for the London Common Council in December 1641, which occasioned city-wide disputes over electoral procedure. In theory, the common councilmen were elected in their respective wardmotes by all inhabitants who paid scot and lot; in practice in a number of wards the custom had developed whereby each precinct or vestry within the ward made the selections before formal, usually uncontested, election at the wardmote.[35] This latter procedure placed considerable influence in the hands of the more conservative aldermen and parish elites. The Saint Olave, Old Jewry vestry met on 4 January 1642 to determine its position on the selection issue. By majority vote, the vestry maintained a conservative position: the attempt to break with custom and choose councilmen at the general assembly of the wardmote was deemed to be a prejudicial innovation. For the only time during this period a dissenting opinion was recorded in the minutes. Fourteen signed in favour of the declaration; three – including Gerrard Winstanley – registered disagreement.[36] Here is Winstanley, for the first time, among the ranks of the "reformers".

The third piece of the puzzle in these years for the character of the newly independent Winstanley is something he failed to do: Winstanley did not appear for one of the best attended vestry meetings of the period, on 13 October 1642, when the presbyterian Ralph Robinson was appointed divinity lecturer for the parish.[37] Indeed, Winstanley was absent for all three divinity lecturer appointments of May 1641, December 1641 and October 1642.

Did he possess no religious convictions? That seems highly unlikely, for on Sunday 8 October 1643 he took the Solemn League and Covenant for the reformation and defence of the protestant religion. This was a notable development, which demonstrates his growing concern for religion and politics. It was not, though, within the parish a controversial, or perhaps even a partisan, action. A sizeable majority of the heads of household in St Olave, Old Jewry took the oath. Indeed, a number of married women quite unusually signed below their husbands' signatures, although Susan Winstanley was not among their number.[38] The Covenant came in time to be a rallying symbol for Presbyterianism, but in 1643 it appears to have been less controversial, and considerably less partisan, in parochial life. Winstanley was taking a stand, but what exactly was he standing for?

The developing political crisis of the early 1640s coincided with a financial crisis for Winstanley. When the youthful merchant tailor established his retail cloth trade in St Olave in 1638/39 he was among the poorer of the self-reliant householders, and his relative position never altered to any notable degree. From the outset his commercial enterprise was undercapitalized. From at least 1641, and probably earlier, he financed the trade on credit. By early 1642 that business was experiencing severe problems with cash-flow. Bad debts and undercapitalization were the causes.[39] Shipments of cloth to Ireland in 1641 produced uncollectible debts with the outbreak of the Irish rebellion. Following the initial period of the English Civil War, Winstanley was from early 1643 on the edge of bankruptcy. In May of that year he was reduced to repaying a portion of his debt due to one supplier in kind, with cloth. Later in the year he ceased trading altogether, and on 30 November divided up his remaining stock-in-trade amongst his creditors as far as it reached, in partial repayment. By 20 December 1643 Winstanley had settled his affairs as best he could, surrendered occupancy of his house and shop, and moved out of London to reside close to his wife's family at Cobham, Surrey.[40]

How might Winstanley's development by 1643 best be summarized? Out of the national polarization of politics and religion during the years 1641 to 1643 Winstanley emerged as a supporter of Parliament. His acceptance of the Solemn League and Covenant and his action in 1642 in regard to the Common Council election attest to this. Much later, in 1650, he was to write that "for my part I was alwayes against the Caveleers cause".[41] Precisely how enthusiastic Winstanley was remains uncertain. He subsequently blamed the "late unhappy wars" for driving him out of business, and in 1649 he credited "the burdens of and for the soldiery in the beginning of the war" as one of the reasons for his insolvency.[42] In looking forward to Winstanley's future beliefs and activities, we may note that while Winstanley can be considered a "parliamentarian", there is no reason to believe that up to his departure from London he had become an "activist" or had been "radicalized". He did not embark upon the writing and publication of tracts, nor did he engage in sectarianism. Indeed, he remained a member of his parish vestry up until at least October 1643, even though the royalist Tuke continued as vicar.[43] Perhaps he was preoccupied with his failing business; perhaps he, like so many, was genuinely perplexed and confused by national developments. Was he aware of the proliferation of ideas and viewpoints in his own London? Perhaps. Was he set on a course which would lead towards the Digger agitation of 1649? Almost certainly not. It would be surprising if Winstanley's residence in London during the 1630s and early 1640s did not affect his later thought and writing, but this period of his life – as far as we can observe – did not constitute for him a "high road to revolution".

Winstanley came to Cobham, presumably, because it provided a retreat from his financial collapse in London. His father-in-law, the barber-surgeon William King, was a property holder of Ham manor, possessing Stewards Mead in Church Cobham.[44] Although Winstanley later wrote that he went "to live a country life",[45] implying perhaps a time of solitude and seclusion, we know that he visited London occasionally over the next several years,[46] and Cobham's location, on the main London–Portsmouth road, was hardly isolated. Winstanley threw himself into the work of financial improvement. He became a grazier: renting land, buying cattle, fattening the stock, selling it at market.[47] In this he may well have been aided by his father-in-law, but he acquired an independent residence – in April 1646 he was a householder in Street Cobham – and was not an object of charity, or of derision.[48] He settled in and began in 1646, alongside other manorial tenants and officeholders, to assert disputed rights to dig peat and turf on the manorial waste.[49] The winter of 1647–48 in good measure ended Winstanley's aspirations for an economic revival. The 1647 harvest was poor, creating exceptionally high grain and hay prices and, with an exceptional drought, a dearth of livestock.[50] Almost simultaneously, Surrey experienced a dramatic increase in the charges of free-quarter for the parliamentary army.[51] Under this combination of afflictions Winstanley's economic position deteriorated.[52]

Precisely how critical Winstanley's finances became, however, is difficult to determine. Winstanley's writings leave the impression of total, abject failure and collapse: the loss of all friends and worldly estate.[53] This is an essential element in his spiritual message, and is indicative of his mental state in 1648. However, Winstanley never appears to have lost his friends, or to have been reduced to abject poverty. Consider, for example, the little which can be deduced about his position during the life of the Digger colony. Far from being the "wandering mechanic, preacher and cowherd" of legend,[54] Winstanley retained a settled residence away from the Digger colony at St George's Hill,[55] most likely the one he held in Street Cobham in 1646. All his statements point in one direction: Winstanley was a modest grazier, not a hired herdsman, immediately before *and during* the Digger episode. His property included grazing land upon which he kept his own cattle and pastured others for money.[56] He contracted with a local landlord to purchase, and reap himself, the harvest from several acres of land for winter fodder.[57] Of course, all the Diggers arrested for trespass on St George's Hill in Walton parish during July 1649, Winstanley included, were described as labourers of Walton.[58] This has been accepted uncritically to demonstrate his itinerant humble status in 1649. However, the description was a legal fiction.[59] Many of the Diggers are known to have originated in Cobham, and a number of those charged could not realistically be considered labourers.[60] The designations were not an accurate representation of the geographical origins or occupational status of this group as a whole, or of Winstanley in particular.

On the theme of religion, Winstanley's personal beliefs in the era 1643–48 are once again difficult to reconstruct in detail, although the broad outline is clear. Beyond doubt, this was the crucial period for his spiritual development, when he abandoned the Church of England, and moved through sectarian involvement to individual religious mysticism. How rapid was the transformation? The alterations most likely occurred after the vicar of Cobham, William King (a supporter of Parliament later ejected from Ashtead rectory in 1662 and possessing no known family connection to Winstanley's father-in-law), abandoned his cure in September 1644. Thereafter the parish was without a settled ministry until 1656.[61] At some point Winstanley became a Baptist, for he stated in 1648 that he had "gon through the ordinance of dipping".[62] There is, however, no justification for the belief that he was an itinerant Baptist lay preacher in these years.[63] Seeking spiritual solace, for the first time we learn that he read widely, although the particulars are elusive and Winstanley states that he found little comfort.[64] At some point prior to February 1649, he became closely associated with John Fielder, the Kingston-upon-Thames religious independent and future Quaker who was imprisoned in 1645 for establishing a conventicle. One of the leading members of Fielder's sect would later become a Digger on St George's Hill.[65] And, as is well known, Winstanley was in 1648 a close associate of the former army radical William Everard, his future Digger companion.[66] It is relatively easy to establish connections between Winstanley and other sectarians *from* 1648; it is extremely difficult to determine whether he may have been influenced by any prior to the end of 1647. This in itself is a significant point in respect to the timing of this individual's emergence as a radical thinker. Winstanley leaves the impression that his spiritual awakening during the winter of 1647–48 was sudden, complete (and unaided by mankind).[67] That is a vital component within his message of revelation and renewal. Beyond question, Winstanley himself considered the critical feature of his life to have been this spiritual enlightenment. That is the reason why he dwelt so little in his works on his prior life, family or thoughts. As W. Schenk stated: "When one believes oneself to have been favoured with a revelation one does not pause to consider much besides."[68]

I will not dwell at length on the features of Winstanley's life, writings and actions at Cobham and Walton during the late 1640s and early 1650s. Others deserve their say, not least Mr David Taylor, who over the years has been most generous in sharing his knowledge of Winstanley, Cobham and vicinity.[69] Winstanley arose virtually overnight in 1648 as a powerful, albeit at first hardly original, socio-religious thinker, whose intellectual development over the succeeding three years proceeded at an astonishing pace. With Everard's departure in 1649, Winstanley emerged as the unrivalled Digger leader and spokesperson. The story of the collapse of the Digger activism on St George's Hill in August 1649, the movement to Cobham Heath, and the subsequent dispersal of the Diggers in April 1650 is well known.[70] At some point before or after these events, Winstanley came into contact with the religious radical Lawrence Clarkson, and, possibly, Samuel Highland, a supporter of the Levellers who led an important separatist church in Southwark.[71] In the autumn of 1650 Winstanley found employment for himself and some of his "poor brethren" on the estate of the early Stuart mystic Lady Eleanor Douglas, or Davies, at Pirton, Hertfordshire, apparently serving as her estate steward. The relationship came to a speedy conclusion in December of the same year, amidst bitter, mutual accusations.[72] Thereafter, there is a protracted silence.

Winstanley was apparently back in Cobham, as a resident, by 15 June 1652 when he witnessed the will of the former Digger John Coulton.[73] He then re-emerged in the historical record in 1657. Around that time, his father-in-law transferred to Gerrard and Susan Winstanley the use of customary land within Ham manor.[74] We do not know precisely where Winstanley lived up to 1657, how he earned his livelihood or how he occupied himself. His last extant writing, *The Law of Freedom in a Platform*, was published in 1652 with a dedication dated 5 November 1651.[75] However, from at least 1657, as a landholder and son-in-law to William King, who held the status of yeoman and had been a subsidyman,[76] Winstanley had a presence at Cobham. He became a waywarden of Cobham parish in 1659, overseer of the poor in 1660, waywarden again in 1666, churchwarden in 1667 and 1668, and one of the two chief constables for Elmbridge hundred in 1671.[77] This succession of local offices reveals Winstanley's position and moderate stature within his parish. In 1660–62 he fought off an attempt by the executors of a deceased creditor to force him to repay monies due at the time of his insolvency in 1643.[78] The documents in this case reveal that Winstanley now bore, for the first time, the title of gentleman. An extant court roll for the manor of Ham of March 1662 shows him listed as a tenant, engaged in relationships with other customary tenants which originated with his wife's grandfather a half-century earlier.[79]

Susan Winstanley died prior to the date of her father's will of 6 June 1664, and the King property was later transferred to her sister, Sarah King.[80] We possess no knowledge whether Winstanley's first marriage ever produced any children. In July 1664, in the London parish of St Giles Cripplegate, Winstanley married Elizabeth Standley or Stanley.[81] She was the daughter of Joan and Gabriel Stanley and co-heiress, in 1665, of Hugh Turner of Middlesex, gentleman.[82] The couple had two sons, Gerrard, born about 1665, and Clement, baptised at Cobham on 7 October 1670, and a daughter Elizabeth, baptised in the parish on 3 January 1668.[83] The two sons died in 1683 and 1684, respectively; no further reference to the daughter has been located.[84] By 1675 Winstanley was resident in the parish of St Giles in the Fields, Middlesex, when involved in a complex lawsuit regarding the estate of his wife's deceased uncle.[85] In September 1676 the burial register of the Westminster Quaker monthly meeting recorded the burial of Gerrard Winstanley, aged approximately 62, corn-chandler of St Giles in the Fields; Quaker sources subsequently noted the remarriage of his widow Elizabeth and death of his sons Gerrard and Clement.[86] Winstanley appears to have died intestate.

Documentation is far too sparse to account fully for the series of changes in Winstanley's existence between 1652 and 1676. In material terms, his economic circumstances at first improved noticeably, although incautious decisions made by him between 1665 and 1669 as administrator of the estate of his wife's uncle produced a large personal liability and may help to explain his eventual removal from Cobham and return to trade as a corn-chandler.[87] The principal puzzles, as always for Winstanley, concern his beliefs and his value system. It is perhaps surprising that the millenarian who denounced trade in the 1640s as unjust and often dishonest eventually re-entered London commerce as a Quaker. It is directly contrary to the customary portrayal of Winstanley that the outspoken heretical critic of established religion became a churchwarden, and the Digger agitator who disrupted society held office as a chief constable – particularly when these activities took place at Cobham, the scene of his radicalism. However, the evidence is straightforward. John Gurney has demonstrated that the Digger agitation had received support from elements of the propertied residents of Cobham, and Winstanley was not the only former Digger subsequently to hold local office during the 1660s.[88] Cobham society was not as polarized as we once thought, and Winstanley, moreover, had again become respectable. Certainly, there can be no doubt that Winstanley the Digger was enjoying a moderately prosperous existence at Cobham in the early 1660s, largely as a result of the favour of his father-in-law. When William King placed him and Susan in possession of property in Ham manor around 1657, he laid the foundation for Winstanley's return to respectable life. Thus, Winstanley was socially acceptable as a parish waywarden in 1659. From there he progressed to be overseer of the poor and churchwarden, and crowned his moderate rise within his local community with selection as a chief constable. Winstanley was neither wealthy nor particularly successful in his later life, but, as has long been suspected,[89] he did enjoy comparative prosperity.

Much has been written upon Winstanley's "retreat" from radicalism during the later 1650s and 1660s. Space does not permit a complete reassessment of this theme, but several observations are relevant to the present investigation. First, we know that Winstanley was not the only Digger to return to respectability in Cobham. Hence, the answer may well lie in societal, not biographical, considerations. In view of Winstanley's silence in these years, we cannot know the extent to which his actions arose from personal intellectual choices, or as a consequence of the widespread reunification of society and community in the later 1650s. Second, Winstanley's retreat (if we wish to employ that value-laden concept) was the logical outcome of his own beliefs. He steadfastly refused to sanction violence, and he retained a respect for properly sanctioned authority. When, therefore, the inner light failed to grow within his fellow countrymen he had no recourse short of violating his belief system. As Winstanley stated in his dedication to Oliver Cromwell of *The Law of Freedom* in November 1651:

"[I] do quiet my own spirit. And now I have set the candle at your door, for you have power in your hand ... I have no power."[90]

It is particularly difficult to relate Winstanley's communion in the Anglican church during the 1660s with his death as a Quaker, especially if he was the "Wilstandley" noted by a London commentator, Edward Burrough, to be sympathetic to the Quakers in 1654.[91] It has been suggested that Winstanley was not a Quaker: at the time of his death his second wife, aware of his radical past, merely arranged for a Quaker funeral service to avoid burial within the established church.[92] This is improbable, but it may well have been Elizabeth Winstanley who was closer to the Quakers than her husband. Certainly she remarried and had both her children buried with the faith. Winstanley had little need of Quakerism as a religion of convenience; however, the paucity of evidence for him as a Quaker and his silence as a writer may indicate a lack of commitment. Nevertheless, this does not explain the apparent transition from millenarian radical heretic, to Anglican communicant and parish officer, to Quaker. Winstanley, in accepting parish office from 1659, acquiesced in the revival of the established church at Cobham after a long period of disruption, 1644–56. In 1659 this was, of course, not Anglicanism, and this fact may have assisted Winstanley's transition. But during the 1660s he was fully active at the parish level in the reconstructed church which he had criticised so strongly only a decade earlier.[93] For the early 1660s tantalizingly imprecise evidence suggests a link between Winstanley and the leading latitudinarian John Wilkins.[94] Could this aid us in comprehending Winstanley's about-face? Winstanley could not have foreseen the shift to a narrow orthodoxy which would take place in Anglicanism with the Clarendon Code. The subsequent persecuting Anglicanism, the tensions of the early 1670s, or the preference of his second wife could possibly have taken him towards the Quakers. This remains speculation, for we know so very little for this period of his existence. It is noteworthy, however, that Winstanley, up to the point of his acceptance of Quakerism, at an unknown date after 1670, had adhered to the established church consistently throughout his adult life. Only at Cobham, with no settled ministry between 1644 and 1656, did he depart from the practice. Perhaps this reveals more for his sense of community than of his personal beliefs. That would give added importance to the last alterations.

In attempting to understand Winstanley, I return to the only well-documented period of his life, 1648–51. Here we see a powerful, adaptable and rapidly evolving intellect. Are we doing Winstanley an injustice to expect consistency, or linear development, during a lifetime in which he and other Britons experienced disruption and revolution? Winstanley appears to me to have been impressionable in the best sense; that is, he was in touch with the temper of his times. He caught the radical tone of the late 1640s –

the fraught years when Parliament had successfully won the war but was struggling to win the peace – and made it his own. And at that point, and that one alone, he had a vocation and a public mission. This was not an individual born to be on the public stage: silent for the first thirty-nine years of his life; silent for the last twenty-five. The provocation – that is, the English Revolution – made him who he was, and its absence made him into something else.

Winstanley remains a challenging figure. He defies our desire to pigeonhole the personalities of the past. Outside the years 1648–51 we will never be able to answer the burning question: what did he think? We can, however, picture a life. This was a life in which there was no high road to revolution prior to 1642, and no one blueprint for change thereafter. It was a life which was as complex, and as interesting, as the seventeenth century itself.

NOTES

1. Thomas Wilson Hayes, *Winstanley the Digger. A Literary Analysis of Radical Ideas in the English Revolution* (Cambridge, MA: Harvard University Press, 1979), p.42.
2. David Petegorsky, *Left-Wing Democracy in the English Civil War: A Study of the Social Philosophy of Gerrard Winstanley* (London: Gollancz, 1940; republished Stroud: Alan Sutton, 1995), p.122.
3. Gerrard Winstanley, *The Mysterie of God Concerning the Whole Creation, Mankinde* (London, 1649 edn.), sig. A.2; Joseph Arrowsmith and F. Wrigley (eds.), *The Registers of the Parish Church of Wigan in the County of Lancaster. Christenings, Burials, and Weddings 1580–1625* (Wigan: Lancashire Parish Register Society, 1899), p.74; Wigan Record Office (W.R.O.), P/W1 (unfoliated); Guildhall Library, London (G.L.), microfilm 316/20 (Merchant Taylor Company apprenticeship binding register), vol. 10, p.91.
4. Public Record Office (P.R.O.), SP 12/235, fo. 7.
5. Arrowsmith, *Registers, passim*; J.P. Earwaker (ed.), *Lancashire and Cheshire Wills and Inventories at Chester* (Chetham Society vol. 3; Manchester, 1884), III, pp.116–20; Lancashire Record Office (L.R.O.), WCW (Consistory Court of Chester wills), *passim*; W.R.O., Borough Court Leet roll 3, fo. 32.
6. Petegorsky, *Left-Wing Democracy*, pp.121–2; *LFOW*, p.11; Olivier Lutaud, *Winstanley: Socialisme et Christianisme sous Cromwell* (Paris: Didier, 1976), p.40; Hayes, *Winstanley the Digger*, pp.3–4; G.E. Aylmer, "The Religion of Gerrard Winstanley", in J.F. McGregor and B. Reay (eds.), *Radical Religion in the English Revolution* (Oxford: Oxford University Press, 1984), p.93; W.R.O., P/W1, 27 Dec. 1639.
7. J.D. Alsop, "A High Road to Radicalism? Gerrard Winstanley's Youth", *The Seventeenth Century* 9 (1994), pp.12, 19–20.
8. Christopher Haigh, *Reformation and Resistance in Tudor Lancashire* (Cambridge: Cambridge University Press, 1975), pp.305–7; R.C. Richardson, *Puritanism in North-West England: A Regional Study of the Diocese of Chester to 1642* (Manchester: Manchester University Press, 1972), pp.34–5, 40, 188, 172–3; J.S. Leatherbarrow, *The Lancashire Elizabeth Recusants* (Chetham Society, vol. 110; Manchester, 1947), *passim*; Charles Jackson (ed.), *The Autobiography of Mrs. Alice Thornton* (Surtees Society, vol. 62; London, 1875), p.37.
9. Alsop. "High Road to Radicalism?", pp.13–18.
10. L.R.O., WCW, Edward Winstanley, 1603, Anne Winstanley, 1642; P.R.O., SP 14/107, fo. 100; W.R.O., D/DZ A13/1, pp.86, 91, 187.

11. Alsop, "High Road to Radicalism?", pp.17–18.
12. David Sinclair, *The History of Wigan*, 2 vols. (Wigan and London, 1882), I, pp.196–9, 226; B.G. Blackwood, *The Lancashire Gentry and the Great Rebellion, 1640–60* (Chetham Society, 3rd ser., 25; Manchester: Manchester University Press, 1978), p.8.
13. Brief observations are contained throughout the 1648 works. Some are examined in J.D. Alsop, "Ethics in the Marketplace: Gerrard Winstanley's London Bankruptcy, 1643", *Journal of British Studies* 28 (1989), pp.97–119.
14. Petegorsky (followed by later writers) states that Winstanley was apprenticed on 10 April 1630, citing unspecified Merchant Taylor Company records: Petegorsky, *Left-Wing Democracy*, p.122. The entry in the Company binding book is undated; it comes after one for 9 April 1630, but is followed by consecutive entries dated 30 March and 31 May: G.L., microfilm 316/20, vol.10, p.91. The binding therefore probably took place in April; it was to run for eight years from 25 March.
15. Steve Rappaport, "Social Structure and Mobility in Sixteenth-Century London: Part I", *London Journal* 9 (1983), pp.115–16; Steven R. Smith, "The London Apprentices as Seventeenth-Century Adolescents", *Past and Present* 61 (1973), p.157n.
16. J.D. Alsop, "Sarah Gater", *The New Dictionary of National Biography* (forthcoming).
17. P.R.O., Prob. 11/254, fos. 150–52v.
18. Alsop, "High Road to Radicalism?", pp.14–16.
19. J.D. Alsop, "Henry Mason", *The New Dictionary of National Biography* (forthcoming).
20. Alsop, "Gater".
21. G.L., microfilm 316/20, vol. 10, pp.91, 434, vol. 11, p.99; P.R.O., E179/147/568, m. 1v, E179/147/577, fos. 24–8.
22. Alsop, "Ethics in the Marketplace", p.113.
23. P.R.O., Prob. 11/254, fos. 150–52v.
24. Christopher Hill, *The World Turned Upside Down* (London: Temple Smith, 1972), p.299.
25. Gerrard Winstanley, *The Saints Paradice: or, the Fathers Teaching the Only Satisfaction to Waiting Souls* (London, 1658), sig. A2; Winstanley, *Mysterie of God*, p.11; *Works*, p.243.
26. *Dictionary of National Biography*, sub. William Brough; John Venn and J.A. Venn, *Alumni Cantabrigienses* (Cambridge, 1922), I, i, p.230; Chester, *Registers*, pp.128, 234–5; G.L., Ms. 4072/1, pt. 1 (Saint Michael Cornhill, vestry minute book, 1563–1647), fos. 168v, 169v.
27. P.R.O., Prob. 11/254, fo. 152; Margaret Bottrall, *Izaak Walton* (London, 1955), pp.9–11; John R. Cooper, *The Art of the Compleat Angler* (Durham, NC, 1968), pp.14–28.
28. Nicholas Tyacke, *Anti-Calvinists: The Rise of English Arminianism. c. 1590–1640* (Oxford: Oxford University Press, 1987), pp.67, 99, 134; Nicholas Tyacke (ed.), *The History of the University of Oxford. Vol. IV. Seventeenth-Century Oxford* (Oxford: Oxford University Press, 1997), pp.574, 598; Alsop, "Mason".
29. P.R.O., Prob 11/254, fos. 150-2v; Henry Mason, *The Cure of Cares* (London, 1627), STC 17605, endpage.
30. Winstanley, *Saints Paradice*, sig. A2.
31. G.L., Ms. 4415/1 (Saint Olave, Old Jewry, vestry minute book, 1574–1680), fo. 90v; G.L. microfilm 351/56 (Merchant Taylor presentment book, vol. 2), unfoliated.
32. Reginald M. Glencross, *A Calendar of the Marriage Licence Allegations in the Registry of the Bishop of London, 1597 to 1648* (London, 1937), p.210; P.R.O., E 179/251/22 (1641 poll tax assessments for London companies), Barber Surgeons' Company, fo. 7; A.W.H. Clarke (ed.), *The Register of St. Lawrence Jewry, London, 1538–1673* (London, 1940), pp.32–5, 38, 40; P.R.O., PROB 11/320, fos. 103–4; T.C. Dale (ed.), *The Inhabitants of London in 1638*, 2 vols. (London, 1935), I, p.84; *Surrey Wills, Part I* (Surrey Record Society, vol. 3; London, 1915), p.145.
33. G.L., Ms 4415/1. fos. 90v–118.
34. Ibid., fo. 113v; J.D. Alsop, "Revolutionary Puritanism in the Parishes? The Case of St. Olave, Old Jewry", *The London Journal* 15 (1990), pp.30–31.
35. Alsop, "Revolutionary Puritanism", pp.33–4.
36. G.L., Ms. 4415/1, fos. 98, 101v, 103v, 107v.
37. Ibid., fo. 118.
38. Alsop, "Revolutionary Puritanism", pp.34–5.

39. Alsop, "Ethics in the Marketplace", pp.97–119; J.D. Alsop, "Gerrard Winstanley: A Reply", *Historical Journal* 38 (1995), pp.1013–15.
40. Alsop, "Ethics in the Marketplace", p.104; John Gurney, "Gerrard Winstanley and the Digger Movement in Walton and Cobham", *Historical Journal* 37 (1994), p.790.
41. *Works*, p.389.
42. P.R.O., C9/412/269; *LFOW*, p.127.
43. G.L., Ms. 4415/1, fos.109v, 110, 118.
44. H.E. Malden (ed.), *The Victoria History of the County of Surrey, III* (London, 1911), pp.442–7; T.E.C. Walker, "Cobham: Manorial History", *Surrey Archaeological Collections* 58 (1961), pp.47–78; J.D. Alsop, "Gerrard Winstanley: Religion and Respectability", *Historical Journal* 28 (1985), pp.707; cf. John Gurney, "William King, Gerrard Winstanley and Cobham" in this volume.
45. *Works*, pp.6, 315.
46. P.R.O., C9/412/269, C5/415/123.
47. J.D. Alsop, "Gerrard Winstanley: The Origin of a Radical" (forthcoming).
48. Information from the steward's papers for the manor of Ham, provided to the author by Mr D.C. Taylor; Gurney, "Digger Movement", p.790.
49. Draft court baron and draft view of frankpledge for Ham manor, 10 April 1646 (formerly in the possession of D.C. Taylor).
50. Peter Bowden, "Statistical Appendix", in Joan Thirsk (ed.), *The Agrarian History of England and Wales, 1500–1640* (Cambridge: Cambridge University Press, 1967), pp.821, 828. Contemporary observers noted the extreme dearth of cattle caused by the exceptional drought, for example: *Mercurius Rusticus* (dated 12 November 1647 in Thomason Tract E 414.5), p.2.
51. John Rushworth (ed.), *Historical Collections: The Fourth and Last Part, Containing the Principal Matters Which Happened From the Beginning of the Year 1645, to the Death of King Charles the First 1648*, 2 vols. (London, 1721), II, p.936.
52. Alsop, "Origin of a Radical".
53. Winstanley, *Saints Paradice*, pp.33–4, 60.
54. Quoted from Roger Manning, review of Hayes, *Winstanley the Digger*, *Albion* 9 (1979), p.277.
55. *LFOW*, pp.139, 141.
56. Ibid., pp.139–45.
57. Ibid., pp.146.
58. Petegorsky, *Left-Wing Democracy*, pp.171–2.
59. Of all the information included in early modern criminal indictments, the exact occupation and residence of the defendant were among those categories most frequently inaccurate: J.S. Cockburn, "Early Modern Assize Records as Historical Evidence", *Journal of the Society of Archivists*, 5 (1974–77), pp.222–5; and idem, "Trial By the Book? Fact and Theory in the Criminal Process, 1558–1625", in J.H. Baker (ed.), *Legal Records and the Historian* (London: Royal Historical Society, 1978), pp.62–3.
60. For the Cobham origins of the first Diggers, see Charles H. Firth (ed.), *The Clarke Papers*, 4 vols. (London, 1891–1901), II, p.210; Surrey Record Office (S.R.O.), PSH/COB/1/1, *passim*. For the social status of individual Diggers: Gurney, "Digger Movement", pp.782–5, 790–93.
61. T.E.C. Walker, "Cobham Incumbents and Curates", *Surrey Archaeological Collections* 71 (1977), pp.208–9.
62. *Works*, p.141.
63. Withrop S. Hudson, "Gerrard Winstanley and the Early Quakers", *Church History* 12 (1943), pp.191–2; Richard L. Greaves, "Gerrard Winstanley and Educational Reform in Puritan England", *British Journal of Educational Studies* 17 (1969), p.167; Robert W. Kenny (ed.), Gerrard Winstanley, *The Law of Freedom in a Platform* (New York, 1973), p.11. Note also, Christopher Hill, *The Religion of Gerrard Winstanley* (*Past and Present* Supplement 5, 1978), p.9.
64. Gerrard Winstanley, *The Breaking of the Day of God. Wherein, Four Things are Manifested* (London, 1648), pp.7, 16; idem., *Saints Paradice*, sig, A2, p. 90; *LFOW* pp.155–7.

65. Leo F. Solt, "Winstanley, Lilburne, and the Case of John Fielder", *Huntington Library Quarterly* 45 (1982), pp.119–36; Huntington Library, San Marino, Ms. HA 13814; *The Humble Petition and Appeal of John Fielder of Kingston Miller, to the Parliament of the Common-Wealth of England* (London, 1651), pp.3–4; *LFOW*, p.108.
66. *Works*, pp.99–146; Richard L. Greaves and Robert Zaller (eds.), *Biographical Dictionary of British Radicals in the Seventeenth Century*, 3 vols. (Brighton: Harvester, 1984), I, p.260; Oliver Lutaud, *Winstanley: Socialisme et Christianisme sous Cromwell*, p.133.
67. Winstanley, *Mysterie of God*, sig. A2; *idem.*, *Breaking of Day*, sig. A5v. (Cf. below, p.44.)
68. W. Schenk, *The Concern for Social Justice in the Puritan Revolution* (London: Longmans, Green, 1948), p.97.
69. See below, Taylor, "Winstanley in Cobham".
70. *LFOW*, pp.26–31; Gurney, "Digger Movement", pp.775–802.
71. Alsop, "Origin of a Radical".
72. Paul Hardacre, "Gerrard Winstanley in 1650", *Huntington Library Quarterly* 22 (1958–59), pp.345–9.
73. Gurney, "Digger Movement", p.791.
74. J.D. Alsop, "Gerrard Winstanley's Later Life", *Past and Present* 82 (1979), pp.74–5.
75. *LFOW*, p.290.
76. P.R.O., Prob. 11/320, fos. 103–4, E 179/186/437.
77. David C. Taylor, *Gerrard Winstanley in Elmbridge* (Elmbridge, 1982), p.4; Alsop, "Religion and Respectability", p.706.
78. Alsop, "Ethics in the Marketplace", pp.97–119.
79. St. George's Chapel, Ms. XI. M. 3, fos. 111, 112, 113v, 116.
80. Alsop, "Winstanley's Later Life", p.76.
81. G.L., Ms, 6419/7, St. Giles Cripplegate, parish register, 1663–67 (unfoliated). I am grateful to John Gurney for this reference.
82. Alsop, "Winstanley's Later Life", p.77.
83. S.R.O., PSH/COB/1/1. This document, the surviving eighteenth-century copy of the parish registers, includes three relevant entries: "Jeremiah, the son of Winstanley, bap. Nov. 15 [1665]"; "Elizabeth daughter of Mr. Gerad Winstandley bap. Jan. 3rd [1667/8]"; "Clement Win [*sic*] son of Gerad Winstandley bapt. Oct. 7th [1670]". There is no subsequent notice of Jeremiah. Winstanley's eldest son, identified as Gerrard, subsequently died in 1685, aged 8 (note 84, below). It is likely that this was the child born at Cobham in 1665, and that one of the documents incorresctly reproduces his name.
84. Richard T. Vann, "The Later Life of Gerrard Winstanley", *Journal of the History of Ideas* 26 (1965), pp.133–6.
85. Alsop, "Winstanley's Later Life", pp.77–9.
86. Vann, "Later Life of Winstanley", pp.133–6.
87. P.R.O., C5/581/55; Alsop, "Winstanley's Later Life", pp.78–9.
88. Gurney, pp.785, 790–93.
89. Petegorsky, *Left-Wing Democracy*, pp.229–30.
90. *LFOW*, p.285.
91. Friends' House Library, London, William Caton Ms. 3, p.147. I am grateful to Barry Reay for this reference.
92. Hayes, *Winstanley the Digger*, p.246.
93. Alsop, "Religion and Respectability", p.709.
94. J.D. Alsop, "John Wilkins and Winstanley", *Notes and Queries* New Series 36 (1989), pp.46–8.

Gerrard Winstanley at Cobham

DAVID TAYLOR

As with most of Winstanley's life, his time in Cobham poses more questions than answers. He is usually cited as having come to the Cobham area in the early 1640s, and he himself refers to being in Kingston, just eight miles from Cobham, in 1643. It seems likely that it was a family connection which brought him to the area, as his first wife, Susan, was the daughter of William King of Cobham.[1] His business in London having collapsed, he became a grazier of cows, which was something more than a simple cowherd and would have involved renting land and taking charge of other people's cattle. In April 1646 Winstanley is listed as a householder in Street Cobham, a part of Cobham which straddles the old Portsmouth Road and which is nearest to Walton on Thames. Until this century Church Cobham and Street Cobham were two separate communities. Street Cobham owed its existence to the Portsmouth Road, and many of the people living there were of "the middling sort": rather than being tied to the land, their trades and occupations were related to the passing traffic, and for this reason Street Cobham was marked by a sense of independence. It was here that the Quakers built their Meeting House in 1679, and, two centuries later, the Congregationalists built a chapel after having met for several years in a room above one of the many inns in the area. It is interesting that Winstanley appears to have lived at Street Cobham, which was also the part of Cobham nearest to St George's Hill.

Exactly where the Diggers were on St George's Hill is uncertain. Contemporary reports speak of them being "on that side of the hill next to Campe Close".[2] The late George Greenwood, historian of Walton and Hersham, thought that this was "somewhere near Silvermere Farm on the Byfleet Road rather than on the unprofitable slopes of St George's Hill itself". Greenwood also considered that "the Diggers were not poor men in the modern sense, but rather younger sons taken by the sheer logic of Winstanley's ideas: indeed, early Fabians".[3]

The story of the Diggers' attempt to set up their commune on St George's Hill between April and August 1649 is well enough known, though perhaps less attention has been paid to the second episode in their history, which was acted out wholly in the parish of Cobham. After the Diggers were forced to leave St George's Hill they moved to Little Heath in

Cobham where they remained for at least eight months, a period twice as long as the one spent on St George's Hill. Cobham's Great Heath is now represented by the Fairmile Common between Esher and Cobham; the Little Heath is still to be found about two miles to the east where the parishes of Cobham and Stoke D'Abernon meet. Like St George's Hill, this was also common land: the Diggers did not attack private property as such.

It was this second phase of the digging that incurred the wrath of Parson Platt of Cobham; he does not seem to have been unduly worried about St George's Hill as it was outside both his parish and manor. Winstanley himself writes a dramatic account of the ending of this settlement in the spring of 1650:

> Thereupon at the Command of Parson Plat, [the attackers] set fire to six houses, and burned them down, and burned likewise some of their householdstuffe, and wearing Clothes, throwing their beds, stooles, and householdstuffe, up and down the Common, not pittying the cries of many little Children, and their frighted Mothers, which are Parishoners borne in the Parish.[4]

In the autumn of that year it is known that Winstanley and some of his "poor brethren" hired themselves to Lady Eleanor Davies of Hertfordshire, a remarkable self-styled prophetess. However, Winstanley's connections with Cobham did not cease with his eviction from Little Heath, and in 1652 he was witness to the will of John Coulton of Cobham.[5] Five years later, in 1657, William King of Cobham made over property in the manor of Ham to Gerrard and his wife Susan, and perhaps it was this change in Winstanley's circumstances that led to his acceptance and respectability in the parish. Ham manor consisted of islands of property within the manor of Cobham: it was in Chertsey parish and became part of the foundation grant of St George's Chapel, Windsor. Steward's Mead, which was part of the land held by Winstanley's father-in-law, was by the River Mole, opposite the present Cobham Mill.[6] The whereabouts of Winstanley's home is not known, though an early seventeenth-century house, still standing in Church Street, appears to have been the home of *a* William King in the 1640s. This William King was, like Winstanley's father, a mercer.

The White Lion Inn, where, in August 1649, a boycott of the Diggers was organized, still stands, but is now known as The Cobham Exchange and serves hamburgers and cocktails instead of the "sack and tobacco" which the Diggers' opponents consumed.[7] The only house still standing in Cobham which can be linked to the Diggers with any certainty is a medieval warrener's cottage on Cobham Fairmile. This was at one time the home of Anthony Wrenn, who I think we can safely assume was the same person as the Digger of that name.[8]

Beginning in 1659 Winstanley's name starts to appear in surviving parish records: in that year he was appointed waywarden for Church Cobham, and, in 1660, Overseer of the Poor.[9] By 1664 Susan Winstanley was dead and Gerrard had married Elizabeth Stanley. In 1665 a "Jeremiah Winstanley" was baptised in Cobham parish church. In 1666 Gerrard was reappointed waywarden and in 1667/68 a daughter Elizabeth was baptised at Cobham. In 1668 Gerrard became one of the two churchwardens and in 1669 another son, Clement, was baptised at Cobham. One final documented fact about Winstanley at Cobham was his appointment as one of the two chief constables for the Elmbridge hundred in 1671; after this date Winstanley is heard of no more in Cobham.

Yet even this documented evidence of Winstanley at Cobham raises questions: why and how did the radical Digger Winstanley become Winstanley the man of property and respected member of the community? Where was Winstanley living between his return from Hertfordshire in 1650 and his appointment as a chief constable of Elmbridge hundred twenty or so years later? Regrettably no documentary evidence has come to light to answer this and other questions, and, since manorial and parish records for this period are patchy, it is perhaps unlikely that any more will. Having said that, however, I have to mention a chance discovery of some manorial papers dating from 1646 which I found used as packing at the bottom of an old tea chest containing part of the archives of a local landowner just a few years ago. After some conservation work and research these scraps of paper were found to be the secretary's original minutes of manorial court proceedings, the fair copies of which are missing. One page carries the following note: "They present also that Richard Genman, Widow Whiterow, Gerrald Winstanley, Gewen[10] Mills, Edward Mills and Elizabeth Perrier have dug up and carried away peat on the waste of this manor without licence of the lord." For this they were each fined the hefty sum of ten shillings (50p). This is the earliest written evidence for Winstanley being in Cobham that has appeared to date, with one possible exception which I shall mention later. Among these papers was also the list of tenants for the tithing of Cobham Street for default of suit at the Court Leet held on 10 April 1646. This list includes a "Gerrald Winstanley". The previous list, dated 1642, does not include Winstanley, and he was probably never a tenant of the manor as he seems not to be included in any list of tenants at the Court Baron.

In a scholarly and detailed paper on Winstanley and the Digger movement in Walton and Cobham, John Gurney has researched many of the local aspects of the movement and helped flesh out some of the previously scant detail about both their supporters and antagonists. Gurney writes that:

> The middling sorts of Cobham were much more divided in their response to the Diggers than Walton's inhabitants had been, and there

> is no evidence here of a community united in its determination to resist an external threat. Most importantly, several locals joined the digging and would appear to have been among Winstanley's most active supporters.[11]

This is an interesting point, and does seem to confirm the presence of a strong underlying current of nonconformity and dissent in its broadest sense that can be traced in Cobham over a period of many centuries and which may well have assisted Winstanley in his local activities. Dr Gurney also refers to "Cobham's long tradition of landlord/tenant conflict".[12] The following examples, though not mentioned in Gurney's article, also point to the existence in Cobham of religious tensions over a long period. In the sixteenth century the vicar of Cobham, George Lyster, was indicted for "failing to wear the surplice", and a few years later his sister Joan was also indicted for using "scandalous words" in that she publicly said that "the Bishop of Canterbury and the Counsayle make fool of the Queens Majestie, and because she is but a woman she ought not to be governer of a Realme. And that the bishop of Canterbury was but a preest, and that the world would change err yt were longe".[13] In the eighteenth century the independents or congregationalists were very active in Cobham, and in the nineteenth century the village became the centre of a strong Wesleyan Methodist movement that spread throughout Surrey – much to the annoyance of the local vicar who was a man of high church tendencies.

No less important was the establishment of a Quaker meeting in Cobham in the seventeenth century. The Cobham area had been identified with Quakerism from its early days, and in 1665 Ephraim Carter of Cobham was committed to prison for holding a meeting in his house. In 1679 a purpose-built meeting house was erected on land at Street Cobham which had been purchased from the Vincent family, who had earlier been so opposed to the Diggers. However, here is yet another mystery. James Alsop has written of Gerrard Winstanley, the London corn chandler who was buried as a Quaker in London in 1676.[14] If this is our Gerrard Winstanley why did he not choose to identify himself with the movement in Cobham? Winstanley had been identified with Quakerism as early as 1647, when he acted as one of the arbitrators in an action for false imprisonment brought by the future Kingston Quaker leader, John Fielder. Fielder's other arbitrator was Henry Bickerstaffe, who must surely be the same person as the Digger of that name. In 1654 Edward Burrough the Quaker had written about a "Wilstandley" who was assisting him in London.[15] In 1678 Thomas Comber in his *Christianity No Enthusiasm* made numerous references to Winstanley and not George Fox as the father of Quakerism.[16] So why did Gerrard not choose to throw in his lot with the Cobham Friends instead of taking his place in the established church? This brings in the question of Winstanley's religious faith, and the fact that he claimed divine inspiration is sometimes overlooked or dismissed, some having argued that he simply used religious language to convey a political message. I share Winstanley's belief that God speaks to ordinary men and women in their time. Whatever his formal religious affiliations were, Winstanley believed that God spoke to him, and I believe that this is pivotal to understanding the man and his message.

I would like to close with one final mystery. Seventeenth-century parish records for Cobham contain a list of all villagers who were to be assessed for a levy to maintain the churchyard palings. As we run our eye down that list our attention will be caught by two references to Thomas Smyth who was charged for one "pain". Against each entry appears the name Winstanley and "Mr" prefixes one of these entries. This appears to indicate either that Smyth's property was then, or had been, occupied by someone named Winstanley. The title "Mr" implies a certain status. However, if we look again at the top of the page we will find that this assessment was made on 30 May 1631 – some *15 years* before Gerrard Winstanley is accused of wrongly digging peat from the common and *18 years* before the Digger episode. What does this mean? Was the name added later? Was it just coincidental? Were there other Winstanleys living in Cobham? Was it this that brought him here? More work is required on this matter.[17]

I once had the opportunity to discuss this with Christopher Hill some years ago. It was Hill who suggested that perhaps there were two Gerrard Winstanleys, and then, after a pause, added with a chuckle, "but that way madness lies"!

NOTES

1. Though see now John Gurney, "William King, Gerrard Winstanley and Cobham" below.
2. C.H. Firth (ed.), *The Clarke Papers* (London: Camden Society, 1894), p.210.
3. In private correspondence held by the author.
4. *Works*, p.434.
5. See John Gurney, "Gerrard Winstanley and the Digger Movement in Walton and Cobham", *The Historical Journal* 37/4 (1994), pp.791, 794.
6. John Gurney inclines to the view that the William King who held Steward's Mead was not Winstanley's father-in-law but someone else bearing the same name: see Gurney, below. King's Will is also discussed in James D. Alsop, "Gerrard Winstanley's Later Life", *Past and Present* 82 (1979), p.75.
7. *LFOW*, p.143.
8. See D.C. Taylor, "Old Mistral, Cobham: A Sixteenth-Century Warrener's House Identified", *Surrey Archaeological Collections* 79 (1989), pp.117–24; and idem. *Cobham Houses and their Occupants* (Cobham: Appleton, 1999), p.110.
9. In this respect I feel a strong affinity with Winstanley, as part of his job was to manage the accounts of charitable giving by the parish. Today the trustees of Cobham Combined Charities administer this task and I like Winstanley am the Clerk!
10. This name is unclear in the document: it could be "Gowen" or even "Gordon".
11. Gurney, "Gerrard Winstanley and the Digger Movement", p.790.
12. Ibid., p.775.

13. Surrey Quarter Sessions Records held at the Surrey History Centre, Woking.
14. Alsop, "Gerrard Winstanley's Later Life", p.74.
15. This reference was originally uncovered by Barry Reay.
16. See Christopher Hill, *The World Turned Upside Down* (Harmondsworth: Penguin, 1975), p.241.
17. The most likely explanation does seem to be that Winstanley's name was added later, and indeed the book appears to have been amended at various times to take account of subsequent changes in the occupation of particular dwellings. It has been suggested (by, for example, John Gurney, below, and in personal correspondence), that Winstanley's name was added to the 1631 list some years later, and if this is in fact the case, then we need not worry unduly about the presence of a Gerrard Winstanley in Cobham in 1631.

POSTSCRIPT

William King, Gerrard Winstanley and Cobham

JOHN GURNEY

It has long been known that Gerrard Winstanley moved from London to the parish of Cobham in 1643.[1] It is possible to date his move to between 8 October, when he took the Solemn League and Covenant in the London parish of St Olave Jewry, and 20 December, when Surrey's county committee ordered rates to be set in Elmbridge hundred for the two months' weekly assessment.[2] Winstanley was included in this assessment as a Cobham resident.[3]

Winstanley was later to write that when he left London he was "beaten out both of estate and trade, and forced to accept of the good will of friends crediting of me, to live a Country-life".[4] Since the important discovery by James Alsop of the will of Winstanley's father-in-law, the London surgeon William King, historians have assumed that Winstanley moved to Cobham because of his family connections.[5] Alsop demonstrated that King held property in Cobham as a customary tenant of Ham manor, and that in about 1657 he turned this over to Gerrard and Susan Winstanley.[6] In view of this clearly established connection between King and Cobham, scholars have felt no need to look beyond King to identify the friends who may have provided Winstanley with a retreat following the collapse of his cloth business.

Until now it has generally been accepted that King's links with the parish of Cobham were longstanding, and that he must have held property in the parish *before* Winstanley arrived in the autumn of 1643. He has usually been identified with the William King, son of William King senior, who acquired the customary property of Stewards Mead in Ham manor in 1615–16, following the death of his mother Judith King.[7] Recent research suggests, however, that the William King who held Stewards Mead was not Winstanley's father-in-law, but a Cobham yeoman of the same name. The confusion between the two is understandable, given that several individuals of this name had connections with Cobham during the seventeenth century, including a minister, a yeoman and a labourer, as well as Winstanley's father-in-law. Several other Cobham householders bore the surname King.[8] Every historian who has written about the Diggers in recent years has accepted that there was some sort of link between William King the London surgeon and William King the Cobham yeoman.[9] Even Robert Dalton, who in an important article on Winstanley's bankruptcy correctly identified King's parentage, accepted that King the surgeon had become a Cobham yeoman by 1621 at the latest and was therefore responsible for Winstanley's decision to settle in the parish.[10]

William King of Cobham was born around 1589.[11] He acquired not only Stewards Mead in Ham manor but also a substantial copyhold estate held of the manor of Cobham.[12] This had previously been held by his father William King senior, and before him by William Wrenne.[13] At the time of the 1598 Cobham manorial survey William King senior was the largest copyhold tenant of Cobham manor, with just over 132 acres of land.[14] King himself became one of Cobham's largest tenants in 1614, and was a regular member of the manorial homage.[15] His name is, however, absent from lists of jurors after 1631, when he sold his Cobham lands and moved to the home of his sister Katherine Wicks in the nearby parish of Chertsey.

His copyhold estate was sold for £800 to Bigley Carleton, a London merchant with Cobham connections, who bought it on behalf of his son Samuel.[16] King appears to have retained no property in Cobham after this date. He made his will as a Chertsey resident in March 1650, and he died in 1655, soon after having commenced legal action against Samuel Carleton, John Platt and other Cobham residents to recover £200 which, he claimed, remained unpaid on the sale of his former lands in Cobham.[17]

There is no evidence to connect this William King to Winstanley's father-in-law. The latter was baptised in the parish of St Lawrence Jewry on 18 June 1587, the second surviving son of Edward King, a citizen and barber surgeon of London.[18] Edward King died in November 1589, and Richard, his eldest surviving son, in 1597.[19] On 13 June 1609 William King was admitted by patrimony to the Barber Surgeons' Company.[20] He appears to have remained a resident of St Lawrence Jewry for most, if not all, the rest of his life.[21] The name of his wife is not known, but the registers for the parish contain details of the baptisms of six of his children including Susan, who was baptised on 13 December 1612.[22] She was to marry Winstanley in 1640.[23]

Winstanley's father-in-law can with some certainty be identified as the London surgeon who had become a liveryman of the Barber Surgeons' Company by 1636, and who became senior warden in 1646 and master in 1650.[24] He was elected an examiner in August 1645, which may have occasioned his gift to the company that year of a great tortoiseshell painted with the company's arms.[25] It was during his time as master that the company acquired a large banner decorated with the arms of the Commonwealth.[26] His will was drawn up in June 1664 and was proved in April 1666.[27]

King's will shows that he had acquired copyhold land in Cobham by 1657, and that by 1664 this property was in the possession of Winstanley.[28] Neither King's will nor any surviving manorial documents give an indication of when he first acquired the property, which was described in his will as a tenement or ten acres of land "lately Smythes".[29] The tenement is almost certainly the one occupied in 1631 by Thomas Smyth, who was charged for one pain in a parish assessment for churchyard palings in May of that year. The Cobham "Church Book", in which details of this assessment were entered, fell into disuse after 1631, and no further entries were made before 1657. The 1631 list is, however, heavily annotated with the names of later occupants of the properties included in the assessment, the names almost certainly being added in 1657 and later; the name "Mr Winstanly" was later added against that of Thomas Smyth.[30] Another property occupied by Winstanley was one that in 1631 had been in the possession of Thomas Emmett, a Cobham tanner; against Emmett's name were later added the names of "Mr King" and, in a different hand, Winstanley.[31] This was presumably therefore another property which passed through King's hands to Winstanley.

While it remains possible that Winstanley's father-in-law held property in Cobham before 1643, and was therefore responsible for his move to the parish, there is no evidence to show that this was the case. Other possibilities are that he acquired the property in or after 1643, in order to help his daughter and son-in-law settle in the parish of their choice, or that he acquired it after 1650, in order to assist their return to Cobham after the collapse of the Digger experiment. It is also conceivable, if he was the surgeon at St Bartholomew's Hospital who resigned in February 1655 owing to blindness,[32] that he acquired property in Cobham at around this time to be near his daughter, and that he later turned this over to her and her husband.

If King was not in fact responsible for the decision to move to Cobham, who might the friends have been who persuaded Winstanley to settle there? We cannot be at all certain, but two possible candidates are John Coulton and Henry Bickerstaffe, both of whom were Diggers or Digger sympathizers who had connections with Winstanley independent of the digging episode. It is not known when Coulton, a Cobham yeoman, first met Winstanley, but it is clear that the two became friends. Coulton described Winstanley as his friend in his will, and named him as an overseer of the will.[33] Coulton's son-in-law William Forder, a citizen and carpenter of London, was to join Winstanley in 1652 in appraising the goods of William King's deceased son-in-law, Giles Hicks.[34] He had married Mary Coulton in 1633, when he was a resident of the London parish of St Bartholomew the Less and she a resident of Whitefriars.[35]

Henry Bickerstaffe, who knew Winstanley by February 1649 at the latest, seems, like the Digger leader, to have been a failed merchant.[36] He had become a freeman of the Skinners' Company in April 1633, having been apprenticed to his elder brother Anthony, a linen merchant living in Newgate Market.[37] In 1636 and 1637 he was resident in the London parish of St Gregory by St Paul, but by January 1640 he had moved to Painshill on the borders of Walton and Cobham, where, after the death in September 1640 of his father, he was to manage the estates inherited by his brother Anthony.[38] In February 1649 he was to join Winstanley at the Surrey Assizes in defending the Kingston separatist and future Quaker John Fielder.[39] Bickerstaffe's background is an interesting one: one of his aunts was married to Archbishop Whitgift's secretary Michael Murgatroyd, while another was daughter of Philip Moyse of Banstead, who has recently been identified as a member of the Family of Love.[40] His brother Anthony was to become a leading supporter of the high Presbyterian movement in the City of London.[41]

In the present state of research it is impossible to say for certain why Winstanley moved to Cobham in 1643. Responsibility may lie with his father-in-law, but it may also lie with friends who in 1649 were to join him in digging on St George's Hill. If it is the latter, then it raises intriguing questions about Winstanley's first contacts with radical circles, and about the date of his emergence as a radical. It must remain possible that the ideas which lay behind the digging episode had a much longer gestation than is usually assumed to be the case, and that Winstanley did not develop them in isolation.

NOTES

1. D.W. Petegorsky, *Left Wing Democracy in the English Civil War* (London: Gollancz, 1940), p.124.
2. The date of the move is discussed in John Gurney, "Gerrard Winstanley and the Digger Movement in Walton and Cobham", *Historical Journal* 37/4 (1994), p.790.
3. Public Record Office (P.R.O.), SP28/245 (unfoliated), accounts of Augustine Phillips.

4. *Works*, p.315.
5. James Alsop, "Gerrard Winstanley's Later Life", *Past and Present* 82 (1979), pp.73–81. For the will see P.R.O. Prob. 11/320 ff. 103–4.
6. Alsop, "Later Life", p.75.
7. J.D. Alsop, "Gerrard Winstanley: Religion and Respectability", *Historical Journal* 28/3 (1985), p.707.
8. Surrey History Centre (S.H.C.) PSH/COB/1/1; London Metropolitan Archives (L.M.A.) DW/PA/7/13 f. 160 (will of Richard King of Cobham, yeoman, 21 September 1641); DW/PA/7/13 f. 225 (will of Mary King of Cobham, spinster, [1 November] 1642); P.R.O. Prob. 11/329 ff. 327v-8 (will of Thomas King of Cobham, mercer, 17 March 1669); Prob. 11/373 f. 344 (will of Elizabeth King of Cobham, widow, 16 July 1683); Prob. 4/3055, 15639; T.E.C. Walker, "Cobham Incumbants and Curates", *Surrey Archaeological Collections* 71 (1977), pp.208–10.
9. For instance Gurney, "Digger Movement", p.797.
10. R.J. Dalton, "Gerrard Winstanley: The Experience of Fraud 1641", *Historical Journal* 34/4 (1991), pp.975–6.
11. He described himself as being around thirty-two years old in May 1621: P.R.O. E134/19 Jas I/T2: deposition of William King of Cobham, yeoman. Cobham's registers of baptisms between 3 June 1565 and 10 May 1610 have been lost.
12. P.R.O. SC2/204/43.
13. P.R.O. SC2/204/43; LR2/190 f. 267v.; REQ 2/34/23; REQ 2/157/503; REQ 2/159/13, 192.
14. S.H.C. 2610/29/3.
15. P.R.O. SC12/22/34; S.H.C. K44/1/8; 2610/11/8/33, pp.2, 6, 7, 11, 15, 19, 25, 32.
16. P.R.O. C10/22/86; S.H.C. 2610/11/8/33, pp.47–9, 53–7.
17. P.R.O. Prob. 11/245 f. 13; C10/22/86.
18. A.W. Hughes Clarke (ed.), *The Register of St Lawrence Jewry London 1538–1676* (London: Harleian Society, 1940), I, p.21. He was not, as has been suggested, his eldest son, and he could not later have worked in partnership with him: Dalton, "Experience of Fraud", p.978.
19. Register of St Lawrence Jewry, pp.125, 129. For Edward King's will, see P.R.O. Prob. 11/75 f. 16.
20. Guildhall Library (G.L.) Ms 5265/1 f. 48v; Dalton, "Experience of Fraud", p.979.
21. See, for instance, G.L. Ms 10,091/21 f. 73; T.C. Dale (ed.), *The Inhabitants of London in 1638* (London: Society of Genealogists, 1931), p.84.
22. *Register of St Lawrence Jewry*, pp.32, 33, 34, 35, 38, 40.
23. G.L. Ms 10,091/22 f. 184v.
24. G.L. Ms 5255/1, accounts for 1635–36, 1646–47, 1650–51; Norman Moore, *The History of St Bartholomew's Hospital* (London: Pearson, 1918), vol. 2, pp.623–5; T.C. Dale (ed.), *The Members of the City Companies in 1641* (London, Society of Genealogists typescript, 1935), p.103; Dalton, "Experience of Fraud", pp.978–9.
25. G.L. Ms 5257/5, p.341; Moore, *St Bartholomew's*, pp.623–5.
26. G.L. Ms 5255/1, accounts for 1650–51.
27. P.R.O. Prob. 11/320 ff. 103–4.
28. P.R.O. Prob. 11/320 ff. 103–4; Alsop, "Later Life", p.75.
29. P.R.O. Prob. 11/320 ff. 103–4. Ham manorial records from 1623 until March 1662 are missing: Alsop, "Religion and Respectability", p.707. By November 1656 William King was also a tenant of Sir Anthony Vincent for Mill Field in Cobham: S.H.C. G3/4/17.
30. S.H.C. PSH/COB/5/1 (unfol.), church palings assessment 30 May 1631; David Taylor (above).
31. S.H.C. PSH/COB/5/1, church palings assessment. Both Smyth and Emmett's properties were in the tithing of Church Cobham: PSH/COB/5/1: receipts on accounts for 1631–32. Winstanley was a resident of Street Cobham in 1646, but had moved to Church Cobham by 1647: S.H.C. K44/1/9; 4398/1/10.
32. Moore, *St Bartholomew's*, pp.623–5; Dalton, "Experience of Fraud", pp.978–9.
33. Gurney, "Digger Movement", p.791. For the will see P.R.O. Prob. 11/224 f. 307v.
34. Corporation of London Records Office MC1/83/232. (For the case relating to Hicks, see Dalton, "Experience of Fraud", p.978.)

35. G.L. Ms 10,091/15 f. 22. He was the son of Richard Forder of Wokingham in Berkshire: G. L. Ms 21742/1. Coulton's grandson Elias or Eliah Forder, to whom he left £5 in his will, was admitted to the Carpenters' Company in 1664: P.R.O. Prob. 11/224 f. 307v.; G.L. Ms 21742/1.
36. Gurney, "Digger Movement", p.782.
37. Ibid., pp.782–3.
38. G.L. Ms 10,232 ff. 10v., 11; Gurney, "Digger Movement", pp.783–4.
39. Ibid., p.782.
40. Croydon Archives Service, Croydon parish registers 1538–1679 ff. 29v., 32v., 64v.; F.A. Crisp, "Surrey Wills", *Surrey Archaeological Collections* 13 (1897), p.178; W. Bruce Bannerman (ed.), *The Visitations of the County of Surrey ... 1530, 1572, and 1623* (London: Harleian Society, 1899), pp.149–50; Christopher W. Marsh, *The Family of Love in English Society 1550–1630* (Cambridge: Cambridge University Press, 1994), pp.163–4, 281.
41. Gurney, "Digger Movement", p.783.

Gerrard Winstanley and the Literature of Revolution

NIGEL SMITH

> Rich men receive all they have from the labourer's hand, and what they give, they give away other men's labours, not their own. Therefore they are not righteous actors in the earth.
>
> *The Law of Freedom* in *LFOW*, p.287.

In Winstanley's account of the genesis of Digger ideas, writing is abandoned in favour of working the land: "thoughts run in me that words and writing were all nothing and must die, for action is the life of all, and if thou dost not act, thou dost nothing."[1] Writing is not action; words are a useless distraction, or even a harmful illusion, that prevent man from meeting his true purpose: the return to Eden by union with the Godhead in the collective cultivation of the land. One recent commentator claims that digging was "not a text but a project".[2] We think of writing as the result of the fruitful deployment of the creative imagination, a meeting of pleasure and usefulness. For Winstanley, imagination was a facet of original sin.

And yet the spoken, written and printed word was essential for the elaboration of Digger ideology, especially if it is seen as the end result of a series of moves occurring in radical Puritan thought during the 1640s. The commune at St George's Hill would have lasted for less time, since Winstanley would have been unable to appeal to both Fairfax and the City of London. The plan for an extended series of communes across the nation could not have existed outside written form: hence *The Law of Freedom in a Platform* (1652). Winstanley knew well the opportunities for written expression and printed circulation in the political community of the early 1650s, and, as we shall see, he exploited them with notable expertise.

Without the writings, the Digger colonies would be to posterity a lot less than they are: scattered mentions in state papers and newsbooks, and traces left in local archives. In these circumstances, the Diggers would have become far more difficult to resurrect as a subject of inquiry and a cause worth remembering. Perhaps they might have figured as evidence in the social historian's account of the progress of land enclosure, rather than the important response to the political and religious crises of the period that they are now seen to be.

The injunction to action is not merely an abandonment, but, in the moment of picking up the spade, a rejection of writing. This is in part because Winstanley's earlier writings (certainly the first three) are so concerned with themselves as acts of writing, and because writing and publishing in print were so highly valued by the radicals of the 1640s. Winstanley's tracts that predate the digging of St George's Hill are classic pieces of radical Puritan declaration.[3] Their very end is their printed form, and the fact that these early tracts are absent from the Thomason collection suggests that they were designed for local distribution, as the proper accompaniment to the presence of the declaring prophet.[4] In fact, Winstanley never lost his drive to write. Even during the commune, this burden, so prevalent in the radical literature of the day, is evident:

> I was so filled with that love and delight in the life within that I have sat writing whole winter days from morning till night and the cold never offended me, though when I have risen I was so stark with cold that I was forced to rise by degrees and hold by the table, till strength and heat came into my legs, and I have been secretly sorry when night came, which forced me to rise.[5]

There is also another factor worth bearing in mind. The commune at St George's Hill was a short-lived experiment, the most prominent of several that grew up as a response to popular dissatisfaction with the new free state. Winstanley's early writing predates the commune (just), while *The Law of Freedom* postdates it, and gives further evidence of the circulation of Winstanley's works as time went by. The writing enables us to place Winstanley in a broader context, both before and after the time of the commune. In this way, we can come to a more informed view of his entire activity, as well as being able to see how parts of his vision were developed by like-minded contemporaries and successors.

To begin a consideration of Winstanley's works in the chronological middle of the sequence is to appreciate his powers as a writer of reportage. The pamphlets that sought to defend the attacks by local landowners on the Digger commune give the lie to those who have cast doubt upon Winstanley's expressive powers. These works, such as *A Watch-word to the City of London and the Armie* (26 August 1649) and *A New-Yeer's Gift for the Parliament and Armie* (1 January 1650), contain narratives of dispossession. They are attentive to the requirement of immediacy that characterizes civil war battle accounts. They present the resort of the local landowners to law, and the Diggers' response thereunto, as a kind of narrative in which the victimized Diggers are situated at the heart of the drama that dispossesses them. Documents presented to courts are included within this narrative arrangement. To this extent, Winstanley follows

Leveller strategy for dealing with the use of the law against them.[6] Several tracts are petitions, or imitate petitions, in their multiple signatures. We are not listening to Gerrard Winstanley so much as to the voice of England's poor spade operatives. But Winstanley is a good deal clearer than the Levellers in this respect, although, admittedly, the difference may be no more than an indication of a simpler set of issues than those faced by the London Levellers, rather than an example of Winstanley's superior polemical clarity.

Dispossession even becomes a *leitmotif* in these works. Brutalization of the powerless occurs in a version of property-concerned narrative known at least since the coney-catching pamphlets of the late sixteenth century:

> Then they came privately by day to Gerrard Winstanley's house, and drove away four cows, I not knowing of it; and some of the lord's tenants rode to the next town shouting the diggers were conquered, the diggers were conquered. Truly it is an easy thing to beat a man and cry conquest over him, after his hands are tied as they tied ours. But if their cause be so good, why will they not suffer us to speak.?[7]

As the narrative develops, what belongs to whom becomes confused (the cows do not belong to Winstanley), and other agents confuse matters ("strangers" free the cattle from the bailiffs), as the concept of private property is comically mocked. In this instance, the narrative is also intensely internalized (Winstanley presents us with himself walking along, mulling over what has happened), and apart from the presence of his theology, this inwardness – "the power of self at such over-flowing times"[8] – affords allegorization: "I feel myself now like a man in a storm, standing under shelter upon a hill in peace, waiting till the storm be over to see the end of it."[9] The allegory, with similes (the law is a "dragon's den or hornet's nest") affords access to a universal vision of exploitation. As is so often the case in Winstanley's writing, the abstract, the imagistic and the visionary turn out to be the sources for the revelation of the real, and they return to immediate practicalities. After all, for Winstanley, the imagination does not exist as a category outside of sinfulness. In Winstanley's terms, vision lives side by side with the fundamentals of existence, the birthrights of breathing and eating.

By extension, the narrative explains abstract concepts, such as law and property rights, in terms of the material signifiers of social division. The "Norman" powers of landlords are described as lordly horsemanship, which, after property and dress, was the most obvious sign of social ascendancy: "now if they get the foot fast in the stirrup, they will lift themselves again into the Norman saddle."[10] There is no sense of any difference between the two categories, because there is no assumption of rhetorical practice to force Winstanley or his readers to think about words as a performance, or indeed how words should be organized by decorum. Neither can we readily tell how successful these polemical works were, since, as with most controversial works, reprints were rare. Reference to them is equally uncommon (it is Winstanley's earlier theological writings and his utopia that are more frequently mentioned), but, again, this is no proof of lack of impact. Suffice it to say that Winstanley was writing in a calculated way that took careful notice of the opportunity to address superiors (hence prefatory epistles, and whole works constructed as letters to institutions (Parliament, the City of London) and influential individuals (Fairfax)). He was also manipulating extant genres (the Leveller manipulation of law and Leveller forms of self-presentation), civil war narrative, and visionary prophecy. What is most startling is the sheer originality of the result. The digging of the common land was remarkable, but the writing was possibly more so. This makes Winstanley's writings, in all their apparent simplicity, almost beyond analysis as works of literature: their clarity as a vehicle for the digging ideal is perfectly achieved, and there is nothing left to say. There are many different ways in which English civil war and revolutionary literature, or the early histories of the civil war, have this kind of impervious quality, and also a kind of "flatness" or lack of perspective due to its closeness to events. But Winstanley alone puts this kind of writing firmly into the controversial arena. George Fox divided up his discursive range, so that his tracts deal in prophecy, and the observation with narrative perspective comes later in his *Journal*. Winstanley stands out in fusing the two categories. He does more than this.

The apparently polished openness is sufficiently developed to let questions, and hence alternative narratives, or alternative economies, grow in the reader's mind. Who are the "snapsack boys" and "ammunition drabs" that so bedevil the Diggers?[11] If I have my etymologies correct, they were ex-soldiers and camp followers, the women camp prostitutes, who were bribed with food to help victimize the Diggers. The dislocation effects of the war produced many landless people, who were no less destitute and exploited than the Diggers. Except that most of the Diggers, Winstanley included, had some kind of local association. The picture we are given is of military vagabonds passing through Surrey.

Winstanley does things with figures too, however. "Snapsacks" (that is, "knapsacks") were worn by soldiers to carry supplies. After battle, they became the ready retainer for plunder, and were frequently mentioned as an essential part of military garb.[12] In Winstanley's text, they become embodiments of pure, primitive accretion, as opposed to the subtle and mystical Edenic communion with the land that Winstanley presents. Later on, in both Defoe's fiction and non-fiction, the bag features as the most potent image of accretion and its psychic drives. The awareness of consumption and of the need for proper regulation is made in sexual terms: soldiers, torn out of their homes, need sexual "ammunition". In the case of both usages, Winstanley's writing leads back to a profoundly conservative, or should I say, conservationist, vision: communes are founded through the coming together of local people in their own localities, as seems to have been the case with many of the personnel at St George's Hill.[13] All else is as harmful as the enclosure that is the church, and the church that is an enclosure.

The "snapsack boys" and the drabs are also described as "sutlers", that is, those who provision armies, or simply camp followers.[14] They are part of the "Norman" army that is placing a new slavery over the people.[15] By "Norman camp", Winstanley means the propertied establishment of the new republic, whose "line of communication" (that is, the means by which an army is supplied) is imagined as an enclosure, and which are the Rump ordinances maintaining the old property laws. Whether, then, there were around Cobham really "snapsack boys" and prostitutes falls into doubt: we have to accept the status of Winstanley's military figures. That status is visionary, and his text demands that we regard his army as if it were a biblical symbol: the "Norman camp" in "mystery". The mystery is greater in import than the mere history, and the presence of Winstanley's early works begins to creep back in. The text functions like a three-dimensional picture or a film where changes of perspective suddenly reveal the truth of oppression, just as you have to change your perspective to grasp Winstanley's heretical theology.

Behind this eminently practical symbology is the most starkly fragile economy where subsistence is barely attained, and where cows are the currency that guarantee life (the draper's shop has been left far behind). He makes us see the world from a cow-like point of view: elsewhere in *A Letter to the Lord Fairfax* (9 June 1650), the hostile locals of Cobham are likened to beasts, pushing with their "horns".[16] There is undoubtedly an economy of moderation here. The cows are there to provide milk and cheese, but not flesh (since they do not belong to Winstanley, he is not about to eat them, or sell them to be slaughtered), whereas they are readily imagined as the fleshy dinner for the growing Norman army. Carnivorous over-consumption, the ravenous maw of an army, a frightening demand for food beyond all capacity of the land to sustain (in which Winstanley includes the fees of lawyers), emphasizes the tyrannical property relationships that prevail, pointing back to the necessity for refounded Edenic community.[17] Winstanley reminds us that to dig the land is also to dig up the ideological infrastructure of social and state tyrannies.

Yet much of the force of Winstanley's writing remains in its association with the radical theology developed largely in the London Puritan circles of the early 1640s. We know that Winstanley was living in the parish of St

Olave's in Old Jewry in the early 1640s, before his business failed, and that he was apprenticed to Sarah Gater in the parish of St Michael Cornhill for most of the 1630s. It is here that he may have met the people or read the works that were having a profound impact upon the understanding of church, community, the self, the universe and political life. To regard, as he did, animals as rational beings, strongly suggests a debt to the future Leveller Richard Overton's *Man's Mortality* (1643).[18] The "brotherly one-nesse" of his second tract looks like the "spiritual I-hood" of the translated German mysticism circulating among the followers of John Everard and Giles Randall.[19] The resurrection of Christ being defined as a "vision" to the Apostles, the real resurrection being a spreading of Christ's spirit, through the Apostles, through creation, looks Paracelsan.[20] But Winstanley also confesses the strong influence of his parents' teaching. Was Winstanley's early religious experience, as Professor Alsop has argued, rooted in a parish with a Laudian incumbent?[21] Or was the young Winstanley in touch with the Puritans that had been influential in his parish, or even those further afield in the county who were immersed in lay scriptural interpretation, and who would eventually form the backbone of the early Friends.[22] And if Sarah Gater too had Laudian interests, at what point did Laudian ceremony and Arminian anti-predestination views modulate into universalism and anti-clerical, anti-university separatism?[23] Winstanley addressed the "children of light" in 1648: did he mean a Lancashire, London or Cobham group, or parts of all three? While these questions of biography require further research, it remains the case that, quite unconventionally for a Puritan, the writings of the commune period represent not a conversion from the wicked ways of the world (as in Bunyan and so many others) but a second conversion, or a deconversion, or better still, a recombination, in which grace finds nature, and, along the way, a new kind of narrative facility.

However we regard Winstanley's roots, the first five pamphlets, published between 1648 and early 1649,[24] before the commune began, are markedly different from the commune and post-commune writings. They are complicated, heretical scriptural commentaries, and they are not clear. Or rather, they would have been clearer to their immediate Puritan readership, perhaps more comprehensible than the later pamphlets. All five works are statements of "experimental" Christianity, and one in particular, *The Saints Paradice* (?1648), is a spiritual autobiography. *The New Law of Righteousnes* (26 January 1649) is written from the point of view of someone who was in, or who had been in, a gathered church.[25] The presentation of the self as a prophetically inspired agent would have made Winstanley immediately recognizable to other radicals like the Ranters Laurence Clarkson or Abiezer Coppe. They all had a sense that something of huge importance – the final arrival of liberty – was about to happen, as the public events of late 1648 and early 1649 took shape. The pamphlet literature of this period is full of various configurations and interpretations of biblical apocalyptic: it could be read in fact as a collective allegory of the trial and execution of Charles I. Mankind is about to endure a holy incineration for the sake of purification, which in turn causes a final restitution of all creatures. You can see the commune vision coming, but the steps that need to be taken in the universe of writing have not quite taken place:

> When man-kinde shall be restored, and delivered from the curse, and all spirited with this one power, then other creatures shall be restored likewise, and freed from their burdens: as the Earth, from thorns, and briars, and barrennesse; the Air and winds from unseasonable storms and distempers; the Cattle from bitternesse and rage one against another. And the law of righteousnesse and love shall be seated in the whole Creation, from the lowest to the highest creature. And this is the work of Restoration.[26]

It is, however, in this tract that the earth is declared unfulfilled until it is a common treasury, and that is a long way from the starting point of Winstanley's discussion, deriving from Colossians chapter 2, that men "wholly taken up into God, are called Angels".[27]

The vision here is based on a fusion of biblical reference with a sensitive awareness of natural processes. That the writing down of this vision involved some expressive peculiarities has been noticed before. There are explanations of the relationship between God/reason, nature and man that are logically inconsistent, or internally incoherent.[28] Elsewhere, there are webs of articulating images or metaphors that confuse or confound the reader. The most important word in a sentence may be not the noun or the verb, but an adverb, like "out", Winstanley's word for describing the Fall.[29] The order of language has to be challenged if a heresy is to be articulated: hence the difficulty Milton had expressing his monist world view using the inherited linguistic tools of dualist explanation in his divorce tracts of the early 1640s. Winstanley's dilemma was no different.

Winstanley returned to this ground in *Fire in the Bush* (19 March 1650), published just before the final dissolution of the Cobham colony. Significantly, it addresses the old enemies of the extreme sects, the Presbyterians, as well as the Independents, and any other religious grouping. The Independents and the Presbyterians, as well as the Baptists, were the major religious beneficiaries of the republic's religious policies. Winstanley centres his work in a definition of Eden as the "spirit of man", rather than a place, and proceeds to attack the visible churches for their selfish "inward covetousness". Being in an Edenic state of personal and/or communal regeneration finds echoes throughout radical literature, not only in the mid-century decades but down to the end of the century and beyond, as we shall see. Winstanley's preface to *Fire in the Bush* adopts in close tonal imitation the attack on the formalism of the Presbyterians and the gathered churches that characterized the Ranter pamphlets of the previous months and weeks. Indeed, here and elsewhere, several passages use scriptural texts beloved of the Ranters, and interpret them within the Digger system, since Winstanley was at pains to keep the purveyors of the community of flesh at bay, as much as he opposed the tyrannical formalism of the Presbyterians. Spiritual Eden requires an apocalyptic de-enclosuring that both frees the self and unlocks the treasure of the earth:

> When you know the son within, as you can talk much of him without, then the son will set you free; and truly he is coming on amain, to break down all your pinfolds[30] and to lay all open to the common; the rough ways he will make smooth, and crooked ways straight; and level mountains and valleys.[31]

Then follow some of the most powerful passages of Winstanley's pantheism. In the winter of 1649–50 Winstanley was busy reploughing his commune writings with the gleanings of his earlier mysticism.

Fire in the Bush is also a study in applied radical Puritan views of human psychology, as if Winstanley was trying to identify the problems in individuals and in groups that were besetting the commune. It is true that the tract contains a call for the abolition of property (whereas the earlier commune writings insist rather on the return of common land to their proper owners, the people). Yet it seems in this work as if Winstanley was already reaching out to another kind of readership, one that was interested in the relationship between divine universal love and its relationship with community, but one that did not necessarily see the solution in the digging of common land. Indeed, the text begins to produce a vision of unselfish people, together with a state rid of structures of domination (universities and the clergy), that would have appealed to many of those disaffected radicals who found common cause in the early Friends. Yet regeneration is still described as a purgation of bodies and a fusion of man with creation:

> Now this spirit of freedom, being rising up in some already in part, assures the creation and gives those bodies as pledges that he will rise up in the whole, and restore all mankind to himself. ... the pure creation of the living soul, the single life of the five senses, which is called the earth.[32]

In other words, I think Winstanley was exploiting a readership strategically, although at the same time *Fire in the Bush* represents an actual extension of his communist vision. *The Law of Freedom* is even more strategic, engaging in the battle that took place for the support of the New Model soldiers, once the safety of the republic had been established at the Battle of Worcester in September 1651.[33] Marchamont Nedham published editorials in *Mercurius Politicus* urging that the "free state" offered better protection for the rights of free men than the reforms that had been proposed by the Levellers. *The Law of Freedom* is a remarkably cogent as well as extensive attempt to apply and develop the Digger principles on a national scale.

In this respect, the critical perception that the Rump government had left the legal, clerical and economic structure of the old regime intact is expressed with an unsurpassed starkness. To this extent, *The Law of Freedom* is a contribution to the debate on the economic nature of the commonwealth. This debate was a broad-ranging exchange of views that took place within the "public sphere" of the free state. It was very much a post-civil war event, made in the context of an opportunity to redraw the map. At its heart was the definition of what a community was. In fact, economy, spirituality and communication all partook of the same space in this debate: these categories genuinely faded into each other. The Hartlibian reformers of science admired the Quakers for their emphasis upon communication. The Friends' interest in local means of economic amelioration remains relatively unexplored, but Winstanley's interest in inward, personal reformation associated with a free and just use of the land, and without the abuses of "buying and selling", belongs with it. It therefore becomes easier to understand how Winstanley may have become a Quaker. On the other hand, the vision in *The Law of Freedom* of a community made up of individual households, governed locally by magistrates, but with no private property, and with the intense accountability of political representatives, looks decidedly similar to the popular republic proposed by John Streater in 1653–54. Winstanley drew his model from ancient Israel, Streater from a series of classically rooted polities.[34]

These associations do not prevent Winstanley from presenting his utopia as cultivated land. The annual renewal of officers is thus likened to weeding and removing moss, while the roots of common preservation and self-preservation produce respectively the trees of magistracy and tyranny. But like Streater's disciplinary vision of intense production on the land, Winstanley imagines a highly diligent, rationally applied labour force making an abundance of foodstuffs from the land, which are then held for collection by anyone in communal warehouses. Supply outweighs demand, whereas in the commune writings, demand outweighed supply.

All of Winstanley's commune and post-commune writings do significantly more textual work than the other writings associated with the cultivation of the common land in 1649–50. Both the *Light Shining in Buckinghamshire* pamphlets, for instance, detail the unfairness of surviving feudal tenancy relationships, and they contain highly effective satire of political and religious institutions, but they do not do the work of digging in common in their texts, which is what I am claiming makes Winstanley's writings so exceptional.

The Law of Freedom does not look unremarkable among the works of reform that appeared in 1652, and thereafter down to the beginning of the Protectorate; nor indeed in the flurry of publications that followed the recall of the Rump Parliament in 1659–60. But what of the Commonwealth's aftermath, and the time thereafter, before Winstanley's works were openly resurrected from the late eighteenth century onwards? There seem to me to be two directions in writing and in practice by which Winstanley's beliefs and some of his practices, or his insights, were continued after the early and mid-1650s. Both are to do with diet.

The first is the tradition of vegetarianism that had its origins in some of the dietary practices of the interregnum years. I think that Winstanley was no strict vegetarian, and when he appears to have been one, it was through the forced sale of animals. And yet his use of animals as a living source for dairy produce rather than meat makes him begin to look like the moderate African carnivore of the Restoration vegetarian writer Thomas Tryon. Tryon's mystical cosmology looks very much like Winstanley's:

> And these secret and wonderful Operations cannot be performed any other way, but only by the five great Princes or compleat governors, called Senses; the Creator hath appointed each of them its province and government, who are always ready and on their guard to defend the Tree of Life, that is, that nothing should be communicated to the Central parts of Nature that could be injurious or hurtful.[35]

This is extremely close to the passage on the five senses or rivers in *The True Levellers Standard Advanced* (1649):[36] it is hard to see how Tryon could not have read Winstanley's tract (he certainly moved in the right circles in the 1650s and 1660s). Tryon's temperance recommendations do not disturb property relations as such, except that if everyone obeyed them, a kind of vegetarian (if not Digger) utopia would be achieved by the personal application of so many individuals. And this of course was far less threatening to the propertied than the Diggers. But the degree of accommodation in Tryon's writing is not so great, and could rather be seen as an intensification of Winstanley's vision, as applied to the context of colonial plantations. After trips to Barbados, Tryon attacked the slavery system, and voiced a black slave who attacks the quest for luxury among the west European propertied classes. A family-based system of agrarian labour and wool production is recommended as a solution: not quite Digger but very sheepy, and involving the whole household in optimal productiveness.[37]

Tryon was far more successful in exploiting the press than Winstanley, as his many practical books, some of them in several editions, testify. Less successful in print, but crucially revealing, were the obscure publications of my example of the second direction, Richard Franck, the New Model Army officer and culinary writer. Like Winstanley and Tryon, Franck had an interest in occult and hermetic philosophy. His account of his time as a soldier stationed in Scotland in the 1650s, his praise for the military prowess of Oliver Cromwell, and his ferocious attack on the fishing knowledge of Isaak Walton, in the name of his own piscatorial practice, and gastronomy, are documented elsewhere. His very last writings, like his earlier works, are also concerned with the achievement of an Edenic state of being, which was possible through contemplation and through the proper relationship with nature: a position reached by other civil radicals such as the General Baptist and Putney Debater, Robert Everard. Franck spent at least one long period in exile in colonial America, and his account of this period represents the inner world of a figure not encountered directly in Winstanley, although enough Diggers were like Franck – godly soldiers dislocated from their homes, and without all means of support.[38] The narrative mode here is pilgrimage (the debt to Bunyan's *The Pilgrim's Progress* is strong), but it expresses the sense of radical political loneliness or "Naked Space" of many a pike-trailor, effectively a consciousness of being reduced to frail basic birthrights when a person is removed from their habitual social context.[39] Franck uses Ovid's figure of Proserpina, who was taken to the underworld while gathering flowers in the fields of Enna.[40] For Franck, such innocent environments are the living Edens still available to us:

> In like manner the Ocean super-abounded with Fish, which by reason of their unctuosity become profitable to the Merchant; whiles some others not so unctuous are by renewed acts, fitted and accomodated for bodily Health; besides Shell-fish innumerable that are not so edible, which in another Case become useful and ornamental. So that what to say of the Treasures in the Ocean, since so vastly enrich'd by the Bounty of Heaven, my Pen wants Rhetorick to put an Estimate upon them.[41]

True recreation involves a prudent use of nature: catching and cooking a trout.[42] In *The Law of Freedom*, cattle are similarly abundant and available for eating from the communal stores. Franck's Protestant exile avoids the strictures of Winstanley's utopia, and relies instead upon boundless uninhabited space within which the pilgrimage takes place.

Had the commune lasted longer, had Winstanley engaged with dietary radicals of the 1650s, he might have had pause to reflect further on the relationship between production and consumption. One such contemporary who did, and who also controverted Winstanley, was William Rabisha, New Model soldier, cook and eventual author of cookery books.[43] There is for Rabisha no immanent presence of God in nature, and therefore no need to worry about the harm done to nature. His cookery book is accordingly a celebration of the festive dismemberment of dead animals, which he doubted were in Eden in the first place. Winstanley's moderation points in another direction.

My main point is simple: beginning in the later early writings, through to the commune writings, Winstanley did something quite remarkable, something achieved by no other contemporary. In developing an interpretation of the Bible as his did, he dug on the page, as well as in the ground. By reading him carefully, you the reader dig too. Or you begin to dig, and to see what digging meant. That we have ended up with eating is no coincidence. For all early modern people, eating echoed the eating in the service of holy communion. Eating a miracle, or the sign of a miracle, to remember that there might be redemption and restitution. For Winstanley, consuming to remember is replaced with giving to produce, whereby each man realizes the restitution within him and the world, as oneness is realized. You are bound to trip up in words if you try to express this, especially in 1649; trip up in the woods. Winstanley's reader is his garden, his allotment of the common land, and his cow-pen; he the Digger dug. Dig don't write? He did not stop writing until after he stopped digging.

NOTES

1. Gerrard Winstanley, "To the City of London, Freedom and Peace desired", in *A Watch-word to the City of London and the Armie* (26 Aug. 1649), in *LFOW*, pp.127–8.
2. Christopher Kendrick, "Agons of the Manor: 'Upon Appleton House' and Agrarian Capitalism", in David Lee Miller *et al.* (eds.), *The Production of English Renaissance Culture* (Ithaca, NY Cornell University Press, 1994), p.13.
3. *The Mystery of God concerning the Whole Creation Mankind* (1648), W3047; *The Breaking of the Day of God* (1648; dedication dated 20 May), W3041; *The Saints Paradice* (?1648), W3051; *Truth Lifting up its Head above Scandals* (1648; dedication 16 October), W3054; *The New Law of Righteousnes* (1649; dedication dated 26 January), W3049.
4. As was the case with several Seeker, Ranter and Quaker works; the publisher Giles Calvert published several works that were distributed in this way. Winstanley makes the connection between public speaking, especially in disputes with parish ministers, and print publication, in his defence of William Everard, "To the Gentle Reader", *Truth Lifting up its Head* (1648), in *Works*, pp.103–4.
5. Preface to *Several Pieces Gathered into One Volume* (20 Dec. 1649), in *LFOW*, pp.155–6.
6. For Leveller pamphlet strategy, see Nigel Smith, *Literature and Revolution in England 1640–1660* (New Haven: Yale University Press, 1994), chap. 4.
7. *A Watch-word to the City of London*, p.139.
8. Preface to *Several Pieces*, p.155.
9. *A Watch-word to the City of London,* p.141. But note that the visionary allegory is foreclosed: " ... many other things that my eye is fixed upon. But I will let this pass", *A Watch-word*, p.141.

10. Ibid.
11. Ibid., p.142 *Oxford English Dictionary* (OED): "Drab" n[1]2. Thomas N. Corns, *Uncloistered Virtue: English Political Literature 1640–1660* (Oxford: Oxford University Press, 1992), p.167, sees a Miltonic comparison here, but this is, I think, only apparent.
12. See *OED*; see also J.P., *A Spirituall Snapsacke for the Parliament Souldiers, containing cordiall encouragements* (1643).
13. John Gurney, 'Gerrard Winstanley and the Digger Movement in Walton and Cobham', *Historical Journal* 37/4 (1994), pp.775–802.
14. *OED*.
15. In *LFOW*, p.142.
16. In *Works*, p.282.
17. And in *The Law of Freedom*, *LFOW*, p.281, freeholders and gentry are blamed for overstocking common land with sheep and cattle, so that the animals of the poor are undernourished.
18. For Overton's views on animals, see now Susan Wiseman, Erica Fudge and Ruth Gilbert, *At the Borders of the Human: Beasts, Bodies and Natural Philosophy in the Early Modern Period* (Basingstoke: Macmillan, 1999); Erica Fudge, *Perceiving Animals: Humans and Beasts in Early Modern English Culture* (Basingstoke: MacMillan, 2000).
19. See Nigel Smith, *Perfection Proclaimed: Language and Literature in English Radical Religion, 1640–1660* (Oxford: Oxford University Press, 1989), Pt. 1; David Como, "Puritans and Heretics: The Emergence of an Antinomian Underground in Early Stuart England" (unpublished Ph.D. thesis, Princeton University, 1999)
20. See also Corns, *Uncloistered Virtue*, pp.156–7.
21. See above pp.19–36.
22. I disagree with Professor Alsop's description of early Stuart Lancashire religion as either papist, church papist or Anglican (see above) if he means this in an exclusive sense. The evidence of the Furness district, for instance, or the borderland with the Yorkshire district of Craven points to the existence of autochthonous or Familist-inspired heresy.
23. For another passage from a Laudian childhood into a Puritan adulthood, albeit a very predestinarian one, see the example of the Independent and Fifth Monarchist, John Rogers (*DNB*).
24. See above, n.3.
25. See, e.g., The *New Law of Righteousnes,* pp.114–15
26. Ibid., p.21.
27. *The Saints Paradice* (?1648), p.43.
28. See Smith, *Perfection Proclaimed*, pp.258–62, 264–7.
29. *The New Law of Righteousnes*, p.3.
30. Pounds for stray cattle (*OED* n.1b).
31. *Fire in the Bush,* in *LFOW*, p.216.
32. *LFOW*, p.261.
33. The preface is dated 5 Nov. 1651, but Winstanley states that he wrote the work two years earlier.
34. But Steve Pincus characterizes Streater as an economic liberal rather than a republican: 'Neither Machiavellian Moment nor Possessive Individualism: Commercial Society and the Defenders of the English Commonwealth', *AHR* 103 (1998), pp.705–36 at 723.
35. *Tryon's Letters, Domestick and Foreign* (1700), p.119.
36. In *LFOW*, p.77
37. See Tryon, *Friendly Advice to the Gentlemen-Planters* (1684); see also Nigel Smith, "Enthusiasm and Enlightenment: Of Food, Filth and Slavery", in D. Landry and G. McLean (eds.), *The Country and the City Revisited* (Cambridge: Cambridge University Press, 1999), pp.106–18.
38. Richard Franck, *Northern Memoirs* (1694); for Franck and Everard, see *DNB* references; for the former, see also Smith, *Literature and Revolution*, pp.330–36.
39. Nigel Smith, "'Naked Space': Cultural Boundaries in the Leveller Republic", in Peter Lake and Steven Pincus (eds.), *The Public Sphere in Early Modern England* (Manchester: Manchester University Press, forthcoming).

40. See Ovid, *Metamorphoses*, 5.376–571.
41. [Richard Franck], *The Admirable and Indefatigable Adventures of the Nine Pious Pilgrims* (1707), p.106.
42. Ibid., pp.163–4.
43. William Rabisha, *Adam Unvailed* (1649), R111; idem, *A Paralel between Mr. Love's Treason* (1651), R112; idem, *The Whole Body of Cookery* (1661), R113; see Smith, *Perfection Proclaimed*, pp.261–2; *Literature and Revolution*, pp.334–5; John Considine has prepared the life of Rabisha for the new *DNB*; William Poole of Linacre College, Oxford, is researching Winstanley and Rabisha and their disagreements in the context of the contemporary debate on the Fall.

Winstanley, Women and the Family

ELAINE HOBBY

When the Diggers mounted their challenge to the law of property by sowing and building houses on George Hill, the economic and social positions of the women and men were radically different. A woman's destiny was supposedly marriage, her salvation ensured by her obedience to her husband and her bearing of children ("she shall be saved in childbearing", 1 Tim. 2.15), her subservience symbolized in her silence in church (1 Cor. 14.34–5). In the words of a legal commentator of the time:

> In this consolidation which we call wedlock is a locking together. It is true, that man and wife are one person; but understand in what manner. When a small brook or little rivulet incorporateth with Rhodanus [the Rhone], Humber, or Thames, the poor rivulet loseth her name; it is carried and recarried with the new associate; it beareth no sway; it possesseth nothing coverture. A woman as soon as she is married is called covert; in Latin *nupta*, that is, 'veiled'; as it were clouded and overshadowed; she hath lost her stream. I may more truly, far away, say to a married woman, her new self is her superior, her companion, her master ... The common law here shaketh hands with divinity.[1]

If this defines the way that things were supposed to be, Amy Erickson's extensive research into the actual economic position of seventeenth-century women shows how, during a marriage, a woman usually was indeed overshadowed or eclipsed.[2] A "feme covert" or wife could not make a contract or a will, nor could she sue or be sued independently of her husband. The dowry a woman brought with her to a marriage would fall under her husband's direct control, and her chattels – movable goods such as money or debt, clothing, household furniture – became his outright. If her dowry included any leasehold or freehold property that was rented out to tenants, this would revert to her on her husband's death if she survived him; but in the meantime, any income from it would belong to him, not to her. In return for her dowry a woman who outlived her husband was entitled to jointure for her lifetime: that is, she would receive the income from one-third of the estate left at his death. If he survived her, by contrast, he was entitled to all of her property, as long as a child had been born to the marriage.

It was possible to prevent this complete male domination if a specific marriage settlement had been negotiated with the husband by the woman's family before the marriage: in such circumstances, for instance, property could be held in trust for a wife throughout her marriage, or she could be ensured of a small separate income ("pin money"). But most married women were not protected in this way. The more usual escape from conjugal subordination came from the fact that women did not marry until well established in adult life (24 was the usual age for first marriage for a woman), and the likelihood that the union would be ended by the early death of one of the parties. As a result, as Erickson explains, although in law and ideology "all women are understood either married, or to be married", in practice less than half the adult female population in the seventeenth century was married at any one time. Women were more likely to be either young adult virgins or widows than they were to be wives.

This reality is not, however, represented in the ideological writings of the day. Just as the power of the monarch had been justified, prior to the execution of Charles I, through the assertion that the king's domination of the country was as natural and necessary as the head's control over the body, a man's power over his wife and family was naturalized with a similar metaphor. Both hierarchies were claimed to be the direct result of God's will. In his speech to Parliament on 21 March 1610, for instance, James I had likened his own prerogatives to those of the corporal head: "the head hath the power of directing all the members of the body to that use which the judgement of the head thinks most convenient. It may apply sharp cures or cut off corrupt members, let blood in what proportion it thinks fit and as the body may spare, but yet is all this power ordained by God."[3] For the conduct-book writer Thomas Gataker, the comparison had another application: "the man is as the head, and the woman as the body ... And as it is against the order of Nature that the body should rule the head: so it is no less against the course of all good order that the woman should usurp authority to herself over her husband, her head."[4] The connection to Christian doctrine would have been clear in the day: women's subordination to men was the result of Eve's rebellion in the Garden of Eden. Eve could not be trusted to govern herself, so God had placed her under Adam's command (Gen. 3.16). As St Paul puts it in 1 Corinthians 11.3, "the head of every man is Christ; and the head of every woman is the man", and in Ephesians 5.23, "For the husband is the head of the wife, even as Christ is the head of the church". This godly and natural state of affairs also had the backing of science in the form of the emergent new anatomy.

In the words of the anatomist Helkiah Crooke (1576–1635): "That Females are more wanton and petulant than Males, we think happeneth because of the impotency of their minds; for the imaginations of lustfull women are like the imaginations of brute beasts which have no repugnancy or contradiction of reason to restrain them."[5] The necessary conclusion, Crooke assumed, was that men must rule these creatures who could not restrain themselves.

A fundamental element in the church's role in furthering this state of affairs was its promotion of St Paul's command: "Let your women keep silence in the churches, for it is not permitted unto them to speak; but they are commanded to be under obedience, as also saith the law. And if they will learn any thing, let them ask their husbands at home: for it is a shame for women to speak in the church" (1 Cor. 14.34–5). In the great overturning of the revolutionary years these beliefs came under direct pressure, as women as well as men formed and joined radical congregations, and argued that their divinely ordained role was one of action and intervention, not wifely obedience, or silence. A particularly striking example of the thinking that inspired this kind of activism, and of the terms in which the state responded, are the experiences of Dorothy Waugh. She was a Westmorland servant who travelled widely spreading her Quaker message, being gaoled in Norwich in 1654, Truro in 1655, Carlisle in 1655, New Amsterdam (now called New York) and then Boston in 1657. This is her account of the treatment she received in Carlisle:

> Upon a 7th day [i.e., Saturday] about the time called Michaelmas in the yeare of the worlds account 1655 I was moved of the Lord to goe into the market of Carlile, to speake against all deceit & ungodly practices, and the Mayors Officer came and violently haled me off the Crosse, and put me in prison, not having any thing to lay to my Charge, and presently the Mayor came up where I was, and asked me from whence I came; and I said out of Egypt where thou lodgest; But after these words, he was so violent & full of passion he scarce asked me any more Questions, but called to one of his followers to bring the bridle as he called it to put upon me, and was to be on three houres, and that which they called so was like a steele cap and my hatt being violently pluckt off which was pinned to my head whereby they tare my Clothes to put on their bridle as they called it, which was a stone weight of Iron by the relation of their own Generation, & three barrs of Iron to come over my face, and a peece of it was put in my mouth, which was so unreasonable big a thing for that place as cannot be well

> related, which was locked to my head, and so I stood their time with my hands bound behind me with the stone weight of Iron upon my head and the bitt in my mouth to keep me from speaking; And the Mayor said he would make an Example to all that should ever come in that name. And the people to see me so violently abused were broken into teares, but he cryed out on them and said, for foolish pitty, one may spoile a whole Citty. And the man that kept the prison doore demanded two-pence of every one that came to see me while their bridle remained upon me; Afterwards it was taken off and they kept me in prison for a little season, and after a while the Mayor came up againe and caused it to be put on againe, and sent me out of the City with it on, and gave me very vile and unsavoury words, which were not fit to proceed out of any mans mouth, and charged the Officer to whip me out of the Towne, from Constable to Constable to send me, till I came to my owne home, when as they had not any thing to lay to my Charge.[6]

The mayor's choice of punishment is clearly symbolic: the scold's bridle was traditionally used to punish nagging wives; here, it is used to display publicly that the woman speaking in the market-place has overstepped her permitted bounds.[7] When another Quaker, Sarah Tims, was imprisoned in Banbury that same year, she was reproved by Mayor John Austen, "*that sweeping the house, and washing the dishes was the first point of the law to her*".[8] Meanwhile, in Cambridge, Mayor William Pickering ordered the flogging of Quaker prophets Mary Fisher and Elizabeth Wilson, enraged at their rejection of his insistence that they should be at home with their husbands: "They told him: they had no Husband but Jesus Christ, and he sent them. Upon this the Mayor grew angry, called them Whores, and issued his Warrant to the Constable to whip them at the Market-Cross till the Blood ran down their bodies".[9]

What, then, did Digger theory have to say about women's position? Did the Digger focus on the importance of property enable them to recognize that the economic position of women and men was radically different, or did the dominant assumption that gender difference was both natural and divinely ordained also characterize Digger thinking? One startling answer appears in one of Winstanley's last works, *The Law of Freedom* (1652), where rape is defined as "robbery of a womans bodily Freedom".[10] The perception here that a woman has a right to her own bodily integrity, has an identity distinct from that of her husband or her father, is a striking rejection of the social and religious norms of the day. Just as Deuteronomy perceives rape not as a crime against the woman but as an offence against her father, to whom recompense must be paid by the rapist (Deut. 22.29), so English law gave legal recourse not to the raped woman, but to her husband.[11] As in other areas of Digger thought, Winstanley can be seen here to step outside mainstream cultural ideas. As property rights in general were rethought, male possession of women was challenged. At the same time, however, the nature of the discussion of rape in *The Law of Freedom* suggests that this perception has not been fully thought through. Rape, like other crimes, can only be proven in Winstanley's projected system if evidence is brought from two witnesses, a situation that was hardly likely to occur. What we see here, I want to suggest, is true more generally of Digger writings: the question of women's position not infrequently edges its way into the pamphlets, but is never given focused attention. The result is a body of work that never quite comes to terms with what its implications might be for the different situations of women and men.

An early example of the intermittent presence of the issue of male power over women is found in the radical Digger vision that:

> In the beginning of Time, the great Creator Reason, made the Earth to be a Common Treasury, to preserve Beasts, Birds, Fishes, and Man, the lord that was to govern this Creation; for Man had Domination given to him, over the Beasts, Birds, and Fishes; but not one word was spoken in the beginning, That one branch of mankind should rule over another.
>
> And the Reason is this, Every single man, Male and Female, is a perfect Creature of himself; and the same Spirit that made the Globe, dwels in man to govern the Globe; so that the flesh of man being subject to Reason, his Maker, hath him to be his Teacher and Ruler within himself, therefore needs not run abroad after any Teacher and Ruler without him, for he needs not that any man should teach him, for the same Anoynting that ruled in the Son of man, teacheth him all things.[12]

Here, the first of the two creation stories in Genesis 1 is alluded to, where "In the beginning" "man" is both male and female (Gen. 1.27), and has "dominion over the fish of the sea, and over the fowl of the air, and over every living thing that moveth upon the earth" (Gen. 1.28). The insistence that "not one word was spoken in the beginning, That one branch of mankind should rule over another" echoes and thereby implicitly rejects the divine curse on Eve, that "thy desire shall be to thy husband, and he shall rule over thee" (Gen. 3.16). Instead, an alignment is made with the New Testament promise that "there is neither male nor female: for ye are all one in Christ Jesus" (Gal. 3.28). People can rejoice in the promise of John's first epistle, that as God's anointed, "ye need not that any man teach you" (1 John 2.27). It is consistent with this that when, in *A Watch-word to the City of London and the Armie* (1649), the Diggers mobilize the metaphor of God's people being like a body, the body they imagine is non-hierarchical, one based on St Paul's vision of community in 1 Corinthians 12, not on the traditional political metaphor. For Diggers, "whole mankind was made equall, and knit into one body by one spirit of love, which is Christ in you, the hope of glory, even [as] all the members of man's body, called the little world, are united into equality of love, to preserve the whole body".[13]

This radical theology is akin to the Quaker beliefs spread by women and men like Dorothy Waugh, Sarah Tims, Mary Fisher and Elizabeth Wilson in the decade to come: each believer has an Inner Light to which they should turn for guidance; church ministers and even the Bible itself are irrelevant. Women could, even must, put their understanding of God's will as shown by their Inner Light before any demands that could be made of them by their husbands. *The True Levellers Standard Advanced* (1649), though, like other Digger pamphlets written before most female activism began, does not as it proceeds extend its analysis into questions of gender hierarchy. The Bible stories of oppression the Diggers cite are those of disputes between elder and younger brothers – Cain and Abel, Jacob and Esau, Ishmael and Isaac. Although they lament that in present-day England "The one looks upon himself as a teacher and ruler, and so is lifted up in pride over his fellow Creature: The other looks upon himself as imperfect, and so is dejected in his Spirit, and looks upon his fellow Creature of his own Image, as a Lord above him",[14] the direct echo here of Eve's relationship with Adam seems to pass unnoticed by the men who are making it. When in *A New-Yeer's Gift for the Parliament and Armie* (1650), therefore, Winstanley defines the characteristics of "kingly power" – the established hierarchies that must be overthrown for reformation to be complete – the parallels that might be seen between national and family power structures are not for him at issue. Instead, he deplores:

> the power of the Tithing Priests over the Tenths of our labours; and the power of the Lords of Mannors, holding the free use of the Commons, and wast Land from the poor, and the intolerable oppression either of bad Laws, or of bad Judges corrupting good Laws; these are branches of the Norman conquest and Kingly power still, and wants a Reformation.[15]

Just as *The True Levellers Standard Advanced* uses Bible language that applies to the relationship between husband and wife to talk about the need to abolish social rank, however, thereby perhaps prompting the reader to wonder whether women's position might not also be of significance, other Digger pamphlets also seem haunted by the possibility that these arguments for a great overturning might be extended to apply to men's relationship with the other sex. In *Fire in the Bush* (1650), for instance, Winstanley's reproof to upholders of the law of property directly alludes to Eve's relationship with Adam in Genesis 2.23, where Adam welcomes the newly created Eve as "bone of my bones, and flesh of my flesh". Addressing landowners, Winstanley challenges them: "you are that power that hedges some into the Earth, and hedges others out, and takes to your selves by the power of the killing sword; A liberty to rule over the labours and persons of your fellow-creatures, who are flesh of your flesh, and bone of your bone."[16]

Perhaps this sidestepping of the question of women's position, even as it continually introduces itself through the Bible passages to which the Digger pamphlets allude, is due in part to the fact that the assumed addressee of these texts is male. In *Fire in the Bush*, for example, God's promise in Acts 2.17 that in the last days before the great overturning "I will pour out of my Spirit upon all flesh: and your sons and your daughters shall prophesy" is the source of Winstanley's assumption that both "sonnes and daughters" can be inspired by Christ.[17] As Winstanley moves on to describe the characteristics of fallen humankind, however, and to envisage the new world that can be made through divine guidance, it is men he is talking to, and so only the male figure that is in his mind. Relating the state of affairs in contemporary England to Bible stories, Winstanley's examples are all of the doings of men. A particularly clear instance of this concentration on male experiences is the description given of the fallen Adam, who "eates and drinks excessively; cloathes himself vaine gloriously, or runnes into the immoderate use of women".[18] Eve becomes the mere object of male desire, or disappears, as if reabsorbed into her husband's side. Winstanley has nothing to say about the fallen Eve: she is not his concern. This eclipse of the female has two contradictory effects. On the one hand, as here, Digger writings are free from the practice of blaming women for the Fall, and from insisting on their consequent subordination. On the other hand, although Eve is spared condemnation, she is also absent from the envisioned restoration, as Christ "now … begins to appeare, to draw all men after him, to cast out the curse".[19] The Garden is being reclaimed not by both sexes, but by men alone.

Eve's disappearance is manifested in the pamphlets in various ways. We find, for instance, that Diggers are implicitly male. In *An Humble Request* (1650), despite the pamphlet's opening insistence that God's restoration is promised to "whole Mankind", it is a Digger's wife who has miscarried when kicked, not a Digger, and it is not families of Diggers, but Diggers with their wives and children who have been cast out of their homes.[20] In *A New-Yeers Gift*, when the case is made for confiscated crown lands to be redistributed to the common people, "the people" are defined in a way that is implicitly masculine. Since married women rarely had property rights, they were not usually taxpayers. The case made for land reform is blind to this, Winstanley arguing as if the whole nation consisted of a combination of soldiers and those whose taxes paid for the soldiers' maintenance. Echoing I Samuel 30, where the spoils of war after David's defeat of the Amalekites are divided between the soldiers and those unable to fight, Winstanley insists:

> And the Common-people, consisting of Souldiers, and such as paid Taxes and Free-quarter, ought to have the freedom of all waste and common land, and Crown-land equally among them; the Souldiery ought not in equity to have all, nor the other people that paid them to have all; but the spoyle ought to be divided between them that stay'd at home, and them that went to Warr; for the Victory is for the whole Nation.[21]

The phrase "them that stay'd at home" might reintroduce the ghost of women, but the definition "people that paid" has the effect of excluding them from "the whole Nation". In these ways, St Paul's silencing of women is re-enacted in Digger pamphlets which, though purporting to speak for "the Common-people", have men's experiences as their central point of reference, and also are signed only by men.

If part of the explanation for Eve's disappearance lies in the facts that men's experiences, not women's, are being thought about, and that men, not women, are the assumed addressees, another factor is the silent accepting of traditional definitions of male and female roles. The most frequently mentioned female figure in these texts is the earth itself, which is described as a mother with conventional maternal qualities. In the *True Levellers Standard Advanced*, for example, the demand is made to

> make the Earth a Common Treasury, without grumbling ... And hereby thou wilt *Honour thy Father, and thy Mother*: Thy Father, which is the Spirit of Community, that made all, and that dwels in all. Thy Mother, which is the Earth, that brought us all forth: That as a true

> Mother, loves all her Children. Therefore do not thou hinder the Mother Earth, from giving all her Children suck, by thy Inclosing it into particular hands, and holding up that cursed Bondage of Inclosure by thy Power.[22]

To see the land as "Mother Earth" is to redefine a traditional metaphor so as to argue against property ownership. At one level, this is a radical move, one designed to make a connection between traditional and revolutionary values. But at the same time, because the question of gender is left unexamined, the effect is a reconfirmation of established male and female roles. The masculine "Father" is the divine "Spirit of Community, that made all". The maternal Earth is defined by her love for her children. During Winstanley's first incursions on the heath to cut turf he was part of a mixed-sex group, women as well as men insisting on their common right.[23] Digger philosophy, by contrast, here defines the female as essentially different from the male, and as essentially maternal.

A further example of Diggers using traditional ideas in support of their demands for radical change is the use they make of the family model when arguing for democracy. What they propose is a nation which in many ways is structured like a large family, or an organic community made up of families who care for one another. This is a utopian vision that denies, of course, the real power differences between family members. This denial is shown nowhere more clearly than in *The Law of Freedom*, when the origins of good government are explained:

> *Adam* was the first Governor or Officer in the Earth, because as he was the first Father, so he was the most wise in contriving, and the most strong for labor, and so the fittest to be the chief *Governor* ... In the first Family, which is the Foundation from whence all Families sprang, there was the Father, he is the first link of the chain Magistracy. The necessity of the children that sprang from him doth say, Father, do thou teach us how to plant the Earth, that we may live, and we will obey. By this choyce, they made him not onely a Father, but a Master and Ruler. And out of this root springs up all Magistrates and Officers, To see the Law executed, and to preserve Peace in the Earth, by seeing that right Government is observed.
>
> For here take notice, That though the children might not speak, yet their weakness and simplicity did speak, and chose their Father to be their Overseer.[24]

Children do not, of course, choose their fathers, but Winstanley's interest here is not in the internal relationships of families, but in the large "family" that is the nation. As a result, the envisioned family-like structures of *The Law of Freedom* are unremittingly, if benignly, patriarchal. Fathers are to cherish, protect and educate their children, and also to beat them if they do not work. If the father is weak, or if he dies before the children are grown, it is not the mother who assumes responsibility and rights within the family, but other men from the father's trade organization.[25] Whilst the goal here might be to establish a society based on community responsibility and mutual support – the children of one guild member are to be treated as if they were the children of them all – the effect is also to remove or deny the actual independence of widows in mid-seventeenth-century England. In England in the 1640s, a widow had control of her property and children, and assumed many of her husband's guild prerogatives when he died.[26] The exclusion of this solution to the problem of paternal death from *The Law of Freedom* gives especial pause for thought, because Jerrard Winstanley himself served his seven-year apprenticeship under a widow, Sarah Gater: he knew full well that women could and did run both households and workshops.[27]

The reformation Winstanley envisages in *The Law of Freedom* has other shortcomings when it comes to the question of women's position. The most obvious blindspot is the one already mentioned: rape is radically defined as "robbery of a womans bodily Freedom",[28] but can only be proven if there are two witnesses available. The main framework of the law here has been designed to prevent malicious prosecution, but the implications of such provisos for crimes like rape have not been thought about. A similar tendency to work with a paradigm that is masculinist is betrayed in the plan that retirement will happen at the age of forty, when people "shall be freed from all labor and work, unless they will themselves".[29] At 40 years old, a wife and mother would inevitably be intensely engaged in child-rearing, and in the "sewing, kniting, spining of Lynnen and Woollen" planned as the work "all Maides shall be trained up in".[30] Though Winstanley intends girls, like their brothers, to be taught to read, far more intellectual energy is applied to working through how to abolish the constraints that limit male freedom and achievement than is used in relation to female lives. If a boy proves to have aptitudes different from those of the trade he is apprenticed to, structures are planned that will allow him to develop his talents, "that so the Spirit of knowledge may have his full growth in man, to finde out the secret in every Art". Girls, by contrast, are without pause dedicated to "easie neat works" like needlework and spinning.[31]

What then is to be made of the Digger position on women? All the cases I have cited of women being punished for stepping out of line post-date

Digger activism by five or six years, and that passage of a few years seems to have made a tremendous difference. Although Digger pamphlets are haunted by the possibility that their arguments for equality might be extendable to women, the case is never developed by them. Perhaps if the Digger community on George Hill had survived, these gender applications would have been developed. Instead, it was other women, elsewhere in revolutionary England, who went on to make the connection that if "no branch on mankind should rule over another", then the patriarchal family, too, had to be rethought.[32]

NOTES

1. T.E., *The Lawes Resolutions of Womens Rights* (1632), p.125.
2. Amy Erickson, *Women and Property in Early-Modern England* (London: Routledge, 1993).
3. In Ann Hughes (ed.), *Seventeenth-century England: A Changing Culture* (London: Open University, 1980), pp.28–9.
4. Thomas Gataker, *Marriage Duties Briefly Couched Together* (1620), pp.9–10.
5. Helkiah Crooke, *Microcosmographia* (1651), p.203; first published 1615.
6. Dorothy Waugh, in *The Lambs Defence Against Lyes* (1656), pp.29–30.
7. See D.E. Underdown, "The Taming of the Scold: The Enforcement of Patriarchal Authority in Early Modern England", in A.J. Fletcher and J. Stevenson (eds.), *Order and Disorder in Early Modern England* (Cambridge: Cambridge University Press, 1985).
8. Anne Audland *et al.*, *The Saints Testimony Finishing through Suffering* (1655), p.8; emphasis original.
9. Mabel Richmond Brailsford, *Quaker Women 1650–1690* (London: Duckworth, 1915), p.100.
10. Gerrard Winstanley, *The Law of Freedom in a Platform* (1652), in *Works*, pp.499–602; this reference, p.599.
11. T.E., *The Lawes Resolutions of Womens Rights* (1632), extracted in Kate Aughterson (ed.), *Renaissance Woman: Constructions of Femininity in England* (London: Routledge, 1995), p.157.
12. William Everard, Gerrard Winstanley, and others, *The True Levellers Standard Advanced* (1649), in *Works*, pp.245–66; this reference p.251.
13. *A Watch-word to the City of London and the Armie* (1649), in *Works*, pp.313–39; this reference p.323.
14. *Works*, p.253
15. *A New-Yeers Gift* (1650), in *Works*, pp.351–96; this reference p.357.
16. *Fire in the Bush* (1650), in *Works*, pp.443–97; this reference pp.492–3.
17. *Works*, p.463.
18. Ibid., p.483.
19. Ibid., p.488.
20. Ibid., pp.423, 433, 434; see also *A New-Yeers Gift* (*Works*, p.365), where the latter incident is described in similar terms.
21. *Works*, p. 371; see also the dedicatory epistle to *The Law of Freedom*, where the same case is made.
22. *Works*, p. 265.
23. See David Taylor, "Gerrard Winstanley in Cobham", in this volume.
24. *Works*, pp.536–8.
25. Ibid., pp.545, 549.

26. See Alice Clark, *Working Life of Women in the Seventeenth Century* (London: Frank Cass, 1968, first pub. 1919); Erickson, *Women and Property*.
27. J.D. Alsop, "Sarah Gater", in *New Dictionary of National Biography*. I am grateful to Professor Alsop for providing me with pre-publication details of his research.
28. *Works*, p.599.
29. Ibid., p.577.
30. Ibid., p.579.
31. Ibid., pp.579–80.
32. Recent work on women radicals includes Hilary Hinds, *God's Englishwomen: Seventeenth-century Radical Sectarian Writing and Feminist Criticism* (Manchester: Manchester University Press, 1996); Elaine Hobby, "'Come to Live a Preaching Life': Female Community in Seventeenth-Century Radical Sects", in Rebecca D'Monté and Nicole Pohl (eds.), *Female Communities 1600–1800: Literary Visions and Cultural Realities* (London: Macmillan, 1999); Phyllis Mack, *Visionary Women: Ecstatic Prophecy in Seventeenth-Century England* (Berkeley, CA: University of California Press, 1992).

"Furious divells?" The Diggers and Their Opponents

JOHN GURNEY

From 1 April 1649, when Winstanley and his companions began to dig on St George's Hill, until 19 April 1650, when the colony on Cobham's Little Heath was finally destroyed, the Diggers were subjected to a constant stream of physical assaults, economic boycotts and legal actions.[1] Winstanley's pamphlets tell us a good deal about the identity of the Diggers' most tenacious opponents, and about the tactics adopted by them in their attempts to drive the Diggers away. Our understanding of the dynamics of the conflicts in which the Diggers and their enemies engaged has undoubtedly benefited from Winstanley's determination to record the many instances of harassment suffered by the Diggers.[2] It is clear, however, that Winstanley's writings cannot on their own be relied upon to provide a full and convincing account of the actual motives of the Diggers' opponents. The Digger pamphlets, as has often been pointed out, served a polemical purpose, and their arguments were carefully designed to appeal to particular groups of readers.[3] We should not expect to find in them any persuasive explanation of why Walton freeholders, with their "snapsack boyes and ammunition drabs", or Cobham gentry with their "hired men and servants", should have worked so determinedly to smash the Digger colonies and to disperse Winstanley and his followers. We must look beyond Winstanley's writings if we are to seek to understand the motives of opponents such as John Taylor and William Starr, or the Cobham and Stoke d'Abernon inhabitants who were accused of destroying the colony in 1650.

Despite the forthright and combative tone of *The New Law of Righteousnes* and *The True Levellers Standard Advanced*, with their confident assertions that private property and oppression would shortly give way to universal community, most early newsbook reports of the digging on St George's Hill tended to portray the Diggers as harmless or deluded – as "feeble souls and empty bellies" – rather than as a threat to the social order.[4] The Council of State, in its letters to Lord Fairfax and the Surrey justices of the peace, also displayed a certain ambivalence, describing the Diggers as "ridiculous people" and conceding that "their actions hitherto have beene onely ridiculous", while warning that they "threten and give out that they will proceed to other of more dangerous consequence". Captain John Gladman, the first army officer to investigate the digging, dismissed it as "not worth the writing nor yet taking nottis of"; Fairfax's tolerant attitude when he met Winstanley and William Everard indicates that he too saw them as little threat.[5]

The one report to suggest that the Diggers had any violent intention was the "information" provided by Henry Sanders, when he first alerted the Council of State to the Diggers' activities on St George's Hill. It was Sanders who claimed that the Diggers threatened to "pull downe and levell all park pales, and lay open", to force the inhabitants of the locality to work with them, and to cut the legs off any cattle that were allowed to stray near the plantation.[6] Sanders was both a messenger and agent of Surrey's parliamentarian administration and a Walton yeoman. As an employee of the county committee, he had been active since at least 1645 in commanding the guard at Byfleet bridge, appraising sequestered goods and collecting arrears of taxes. In 1648 he had been involved in the arrest of those suspected of having participated in the Earl of Holland's rising in Surrey, while only a month before the digging began he had been responsible for bringing before the Council of State a Chertsey individual accused of illegally cutting the state's woods.[7] Sanders' report on the digging reflected the concerns of a minor state official charged with maintaining order locally, but it also showed the extent to which local inhabitants might fear the consequences for their community of the arrival of the Diggers. As Sanders pointed out, the Diggers' numbers were increasing steadily in the early weeks of April, and were expected to rise still further. They had also started firing the heath, burning at least ten acres of it, "which is a very great prejudice to the Towne".[8]

Brian Manning, in his detailed and perceptive analysis of the politics of the Digger movement, has highlighted the "genuine and unforced hostility locally towards the Diggers", and has suggested that had the Diggers been able to carry out their programme of communal cultivation they "would have as effectually deprived the local inhabitants of their common rights over the commons and wastes as any enclosing landlord".[9] The Diggers certainly failed to address the issue of the customary rights of manorial tenants to the commons, and in championing the right of access to commons of all poor people they broke with the tradition that access should be restricted to the tenants or inhabitants of a particular locality. Winstanley's response to the arguments of his opponents, both gentry and freeholders, that the commons rightfully belonged to the (local) poor, was to declare that the poor had effectively lost their proper share of the commons to their wealthier, more powerful neighbours. Lords of manors and freeholders, Winstanley declared, "make the most profit of the Commons, by your overstocking of them with Sheep and Cattle: and the poor that have the name to own the Commons have the least share therein; nay, they are checked by you, if they cut Wood, Heath, Turf, or Furseys, in places about the Common, where you disallow.'[10] In place of customary use-rights, the Diggers saw only the "mercinary wills of men" preventing the exploitation of England's commons and wastes for the benefit of the poor.[11]

We should, nevertheless, guard against exaggerating the impact that the St George's Hill Digger colony might have had on the local community. It is worth remembering that the Diggers only ever occupied a small part of Walton Heath, and even if their numbers had swelled as much as they hoped and their opponents feared, it is unlikely that their activities would have completely prevented Walton's inhabitants from enjoying the rights they claimed over their commons. St George's Hill was no doubt carefully chosen by Winstanley as the setting for the first Digger colony. Walton Heath extended to more than two thousand acres and, like the other sites suggested as possible locations for colonies, including Newmarket, Hounslow and Hampstead heaths, it was exceptionally large for a common so close to London.[12] The hill lay at some distance from the most populated parts of the parish of Walton, and was much more accessible to the settlements of Street Cobham and Church Cobham than it was to the village of Walton. Manorial control over the heath was lax, and was hampered by the fact that Walton's commons were shared between the Crown manors of Walton and Walton Leigh and extended into neighbouring parishes. Juries at manorial courts of survey were unable to state the bounds or even the extent of these "hethy & Sandy Groundes", because "the Comons lyeth in severall Lordships" which had rights of intercommoning. The commons were unstinted, and there was a history of squatting on the waste.[13]

It was unfortunate for the Diggers that Walton's inhabitants had a long tradition of resisting encroachments on their commons. Although Walton parishioners had on occasion been able to build cottages on the commons without hindrance, local attitudes were very different when it came to dealing with pressures from outside the parish. The Diggers, who included several inhabitants of the neighbouring parish of Cobham, were treated from the beginning as outsiders. Winstanley's detailed descriptions of the attacks on the Diggers on St George's Hill show clearly that large numbers of locals were involved in the campaign to disrupt the digging.[14]

Apart from Francis Drake, farmer of the manor of Walton, on whose behalf legal action was initiated against the Diggers in June 1649,[15] only two Walton opponents, John Taylor and William Starr, were actually mentioned by Winstanley by name. Taylor was accused of leading "above a hundred rude people" against the Diggers in the early days of the colony, and of carrying the Diggers to Walton and then Kingston. He and Starr were also said to have led the ritualized protest on 11 June, when four Diggers were badly beaten by a crowd of men dressed in women's clothing. In Winstanley's account of this attack, Taylor and Starr were portrayed as freeholders, who rode on horseback while their companions followed on foot; these freeholders and their fathers, Winstanley declared, had clearly acquired their lands "by murder, violence, and theft, and they keep it by the same power in regard they will not speak like men, but fight and devoure like beasts".[16]

Both Taylor and Starr had interests in that part of Walton parish which lay close to St George's Hill. John Taylor came from a family of carpenters and bricklayers – a family of prosperous rural artisans rather than large-scale agriculturists. His grandfather John, a carpenter who died in 1575, had succeeded in building a cottage unopposed on Walton Heath and had thereby gained unstinted access to the commons.[17] From wills, legal records and manorial documents it is evident that the Taylors' freehold tenements were small and that the family were not major landholders. John Taylor's elder brother Richard, a citizen and carpenter of London who died in 1624, had inherited from his father a cottage in Walton with one acre of land, while his brother William, another carpenter, had been left a cottage at Heron's Corner in Walton with two acres of land; the two tenements of John Taylor described in a Walton survey of 1651 each had less than an acre of land attached.[18] The Taylors appear to have gained their living not only from building work but also from sheep farming, an activity for which Walton's commons were well suited.[19] Their dependence upon the commons for a livelihood would have made them particularly sensitive to the threats posed by those who sought to follow them in encroaching upon Walton Heath.

William Starr fits much more closely Winstanley's picture of a rich freeholder. Starr had substantial holdings – some of which had been enclosed from the commons – at Painshill near St George's Hill, in one of the areas most directly affected by the digging, and this no doubt explains the leading role he took in the campaign against the Diggers.[20] His antagonism towards the Diggers may, however, also have owed something to the bitter and long-standing dispute between his father and his neighbour Robert Bickerstaffe, the father of the Digger Henry Bickerstaffe. Bickerstaffe was descended from a family of minor court officials, who had held freehold and copyhold property in Cobham since at least 1547, as well as several properties in the town of Croydon. Robert Bickerstaffe acquired the lease of the Queen's estate of Painshill Farm in Walton in 1630 through his half-brother Hayward Bickerstaffe, a page of the bedchamber, but he had already begun to hold land in the vicinity some years earlier.[21] The dispute between Bickerstaffe and James Starr, which involved conflicts over boundaries and rights of way, had not only led Bickerstaffe to challenge his neighbour in a series of financially damaging law suits in Kingston's Court of Record and in the Court of King's Bench, but had also led to violent confrontations in the fields around Painshill. Bickerstaffe was accused of ploughing up and blocking footpaths, encroaching upon Starr's lands, and impounding his cattle.[22] On at least one occasion Starr was attacked by Bickerstaffe and his servants. In November 1619, when Starr tried to prevent Robert Bickerstaffe carrying wood across his lands, Bickerstaffe's servants are said to have assaulted Starr, knocking him to the ground "that he colde not rise againe till he was holpe upp". A witness to this incident was the ten-year old William Starr, who two years later recounted in court how he had seen John Stephens alias Annis, one of Bickerstaffe's men, beating his father with his fists, his father "lyenge upon the ground & Stephens uppermost and after that Stephens was upp this deponent sawe two stones in Stephens his hand".[23] Henry Bickerstaffe was to become one of the most prominent Diggers, and he was well known to Starr. While it would be far-fetched to suggest that Starr was seeking in June 1649 to exact revenge for his family's humiliation at the hands of the Bickerstaffes, it is conceivable that his violent response to the Diggers bore some relation to the animosity he felt towards the Bickerstaffe family. At the very least the earlier incident does show how commonly disputes over land could lead to violent assaults of the kind experienced by the Diggers on St George's Hill.

The Diggers were driven off St George's Hill in the summer of 1649, and by late August they had settled on Little Heath in the neighbouring parish of Cobham.[24] Cobham's inhabitants also had long experience of dealing with encroachments on the manorial waste and unwelcome migrants: presentments at the manor court against tenants and other inhabitants who had received inmates were made on several occasions between 1610 and 1648, as were presentments against those who had built cottages or farm buildings on the waste. Inhabitants of neighbouring parishes were frequently presented for grazing their animals or cutting furzes on the commons belonging to the manor of Cobham.[25] In 1646 Winstanley himself was fined for digging peat on the waste.[26] Nonetheless, it is clear that patterns of opposition were far more complex in Cobham than they had been in Walton, due partly to the local origin of several of the Diggers. Cobham had a long tradition of social conflict, marked by a series of disputes between the lords of the manor, the Gavell family, and their tenants over such issues as entry fines, customary timber rights and rights to demise premises.[27] Winstanley, who in articulating the Digger programme drew skilfully on well-established languages of popular protest, succeeded in persuading at least some Cobham inhabitants to participate in the digging venture. The response to the Diggers in Cobham appears to have differed significantly from that seen in Walton, and it would seem that no immediate attempts were made to remove them forcibly from Cobham's Little Heath.

The move to Cobham marked a return to the parish where the ideas behind the Digger programme had first been developed. The reasons why the Diggers chose Little Heath are not known, but the possibility that they had secured some form of agreement with at least a section of the local community cannot be completely ruled out. Something similar does seem to have been the case at Wellingborough in Northamptonshire, where the Diggers, who all appear to have been locals, claimed the support of a number of their wealthier neighbours and local farmers when they started work on the town lands.[28] The Surrey Diggers, when they moved to Cobham, must have seemed less threatening to local inhabitants than when they had made their first appearance on St George's Hill. By the time the Diggers arrived in Cobham, local fears that their numbers might increase to several thousand would long have been dispelled. The Diggers had also reiterated their determination to avoid violent confrontation with their opponents.[29] In addition, Winstanley's demand for the withdrawal of wage labour, which had been central to the Digger programme in April, was less pronounced in the pamphlets and manifestos issued during the summer,[30] and he had come to adopt a much more conciliatory stance in relation to existing freehold property than he had shown in the earliest Digger pamphlets. In both *The New Law of Righteousnes* and *The True Levellers Standard Advanced*, he had argued forcefully that private property must be abandoned if the Restauration of Israel was to succeed.[31] His acknowledgement that privately worked enclosures could continue to survive unmolested alongside the communally cultivated common lands – at least in the short term – appears first to have been made when he and Everard were summoned before Fairfax on 20 April; the position was restated explicitly in June 1649, when Winstanley sought to reassure the Lord General that the Diggers would "keep within the bounds of our Commons, and none of us shall be found guilty of medling with your goods, or inclosed proprieties, unlesse the Spirit in you freely give it up".[32] The Digger pamphlets issued in June and July 1649 also emphasized the benefits to the wider community of the digging. In *An Appeal to the House of Commons*, for instance, Winstanley could stress the "profit of this business to the Nation", with its "quietting of the hearts of the poor oppressed that are groaning under burthens and straights", and argue that the Diggers sought "only to improve the Commons and waste lands to our best advantage, for the relief of our selves and others".[33] At a time of severe food shortage and high prices, the Diggers' aim of setting up self-contained communities to enable the poor to feed themselves might have had some appeal even for those who had little sympathy for Winstanley's communist ideals; the programme, shorn of some of its earlier, more militant language, would not have seemed particularly outlandish to those already familiar with the reforms proposed by more conventional thinkers such as John Jubbes or Peter Chamberlen.

Opposition to the Diggers in Cobham does not appear to have become intense until some weeks after they settled on Little Heath. Further arrests were made in mid October and two Digger houses were destroyed at the end of November.[34] It is clear that Winstanley believed that this opposition was largely gentry-led, rather than being an expression of popular hostility, and this is reflected in the tone of the pamphlets produced in the final weeks of the digging venture. As violence against the Diggers increased once more towards the end of 1649, Winstanley's arguments began to appear much less conciliatory than they had become during the summer. In pamphlets published in early 1650, he issued a direct challenge to the economic power of the gentry with his call for copyhold tenants to withhold their customary dues from landlords, and with his claim that tenants were now freed of all obligations to lords of manors.[35] This challenge was one that the local gentry could not afford to ignore, and almost certainly served to provoke them into yet more concerted action against the Diggers.

John Platt, the intruded minister of West Horsley, who had recently gained possession of the manor of Cobham through his marriage to Margaret, widow of Vincent Gavell, was identified by Winstanley as the Diggers' leading opponent in Cobham. His allies Thomas and Edward Sutton were members of a Cobham gentry family who held the impropriation of the living and had, during the sixteenth century, held the lease of the manor from Chertsey Abbey.[36] Sir Anthony Vincent, who was named by Winstanley as another of the Diggers' chief persecutors, was lord of the neighbouring manor of Stoke d'Abernon, but also had large property holdings in Cobham. The Vincents were closely connected to the Gavells through marriage, and had benefited from the long-standing financial difficulties of the latter family. Sir Anthony Vincent's father had acquired substantial portions of the Gavells' lands when parts of the demesne of the manor and outlying farms were sold off in 1610 to pay Francis Gavell's debts, and father and son had gained a reputation for exploiting Cobham's manorial resources when they held the wardships of Francis and Vincent Gavell.[37]

Winstanley's identification of his chief adversaries in Cobham as local gentry rather than, as in Walton, members of the middling sorts, gains some support from a draft indictment placed before the Grand Jury at the Croydon Assizes in July 1650. This was drawn up by the Diggers and their local sympathizers in an attempt to initiate legal proceedings against those they blamed for destroying the colony on 19 April.[38] The draft includes the names of Platt and Thomas and Edward Sutton, but the majority of those listed were not inhabitants of Cobham. Most were from Stoke d'Abernon and appear to have been, as Winstanley suggested in *An Humble Request*, tenants and servants of Sir Anthony Vincent.[39] They included Vincent's servants John Poore and William Davy, as well as Thomas Shore, whose father-in-law Nicholas Foster had been a servant of the Gavell family at Cobham.[40] There is a noticeable absence from the draft indictment, as there is from Winstanley's account of the April events, of the names of those members of Cobham's middling sorts who were most active at the time in parish and manorial affairs. Of the twenty men named in the draft, only Thomas Sutton, John Goose and Thomas Parrish had ever served on the homage at Cobham's manor court, and Parrish had only begun attending in 1642. Neither Sutton nor Goose had ever attended as regularly as, for instance, John Coulton, a Cobham yeoman who joined the digging on both St. George's Hill and Little Heath.[41]

As guardian of his wife's infant son Robert Gavell, John Platt was no doubt determined to protect what he saw as his established manorial rights against the Digger challenge. The threat posed by the Diggers to his rights to the wood growing on the commons seems to have particularly vexed him. The Diggers had challenged such rights in *A Declaration from the Poor Oppressed People of England*, when they laid claim to "Common Woods and Trees" and declared their intention of selling these woods to provide a stock for their community.[42] Winstanley and Platt were still discussing the question of cutting wood just days before the Little Heath colony was destroyed, and Platt seems even to have contemplated leaving the Diggers alone so long as his wood was undisturbed.[43] Vincent's hostility may have been prompted by similar concerns, if the Stoke Common from which the Diggers tried to take wood was the one in his lordship.[44] The threat posed by the Diggers to wood on the commons was always going to be of much greater concern to lords of manors than it was to the local tenantry.

The opposition of local gentry to the Diggers was not limited to the defence of their property interests, and this may explain why Platt was able, by late 1649, to gain wider support for his actions against the Diggers. Local opposition must, as Manning has suggested, have derived in part from hostility towards unorthodox opinions of the sort espoused by Winstanley.[45] Winstanley would have been well known locally for his radical religious views before the start of the digging; he had already published his most important religious tracts, and had very publicly come into conflict with the authorities in Kingston through his association with William Everard and the Kingston separatist John Fielder.[46] John Platt, as a Surrey minister as well as a manorial lord, is likely to have been especially offended by Winstanley's explicit rejection of orthodox belief and his opposition to tithes. Platt's followers are said to have cited the Diggers' refusal to attend church as one of the reasons for their attacks on the colony.[47] Support for Platt's stand against the Diggers would readily have come from Kingston's bailiffs and constables and from Platt's fellow ministers in the middle division of Surrey.[48]

Manning has also drawn attention to the accusation that the Diggers held partners as well as property in common.[49] While Winstanley vehemently denied this charge, and spoke out against "the Ranting practise", his acknowledgement that "there have been some come among the Diggers that have caused scandall" does suggest that not all his fellow Diggers shared his abhorrence of the sexual licentiousness so often ascribed to radical religious groups by their enemies.[50]

Another accusation supposedly made by Platt and rejected by Winstanley was that the Diggers were drunkards.[51] The possible connection between digging and drink is an intriguing one that has never been explored in detail. Several Diggers and their associates do appear to have had links with the brewing trade, and were therefore directly involved in activities that had long been targeted by moral reformers. The control of alehouses was one of the few activities of local government to have continued undisturbed in Surrey during the Civil War: Surrey alehouse keepers and victuallers were, for instance, summoned before justices of the peace to renew their licences in mid-1643, and in 1645 the county committee ordered Justices of the Peace to meet regularly to suppress superfluous alehouses and to punish the "notorious sins" of drunkenness, sabbath-breaking and neglect of monthly fasts.[52] Four Cobham residents, Elizabeth Perryer, Robert Jenman, Arnold Champion and Laurence Johnson, were presented before the manor court in 1642 for running common tippling houses.[53] Perryer was among those fined with Winstanley in 1646 for digging peat on the commons, while Johnson was the father-in-law of the Digger John Hayman, and was to take as his apprentice the son of another Cobham Digger, Daniel Freeland.[54]

The Bickerstaffe family's main freehold property in Cobham was the George Inn in Street Cobham, which was let by them during the 1640s to Richard Jenman, another of those fined in 1646 for digging peat.[55] The Digger Henry Bickerstaffe bought a tenement with malt houses in Kingston in October 1649, and may have operated as a malster.[56] His fellow Digger Urian Worlington alias Worthington, who had been a member of John Fielder's separatist group before he joined the digging, was another Kingston malster.[57] It is not certain whether the Thomas Ward who stood surety for Bickerstaffe in Kingston Court in June 1649 was the Cobham or Kingston resident of that name, but if it was the former, then he too was a victualler.[58] In 1653, he was to be presented at the Croydon Assizes together with Laurence Johnson and John Bradshaw of Cobham for running a common tippling house.[59]

Thomas Ward of Cobham was accused on 12 April 1650, just days before the destruction of the Digger colony, of having fought for the king during the Civil War.[60] Platt, who had been a strong supporter of parliament and was close to leading members of Surrey's county committee,[61] was said by Winstanley to have sought to persuade Fairfax that the Diggers were royalist sympathizers and were waiting for an opportunity to rise up in favour of Charles Stuart.[62] Such accusations would have been designed to play on the fears of the state authorities, who from the start of the digging had expressed concern that the gathering of large numbers of people on the commons might provide royalists with the chance to meet to raise an insurrection.[63] While there is absolutely no evidence to suggest that any Diggers had been anything other than committed parliamentarians during the war, it is true that Henry Bickerstaffe, for one, did have embarrassing kinship ties with a number of Surrey royalists, including members of the Lambert, Henn and James families. His uncle Hayward Bickerstaffe, as a page of the bedchamber, had been at Oxford during the Civil War, and had had his estate at Chelsham sequestered by the Surrey county committee. Hayward Bickerstaffe's son Charles was to be a leading royalist conspirator in Surrey in the 1650s: in 1659, for instance, he was to be responsible for gathering groups of armed men together in Holt Wood in Chelsham, before marching with them to a heath near Cobham where they were dispersed by the militia.[64]

The accusations of royalism may help to explain the hostility shown by some soldiers towards the Diggers in the autumn and winter of 1649, when they assisted John Platt in destroying Digger houses.[65] Another reason for their hostility may have been to do with the claim that the Diggers had begun to make to Crown lands as well as to commons and wastes. In May 1649, when the Diggers were visited by Fairfax, they were reported as seeking to justify their occupation of St George's Hill by stating that the site they had chosen was Crown land.[66] In December, after parliament had passed its act for the sale of the late king's lands, with the intention of settling soldiers' arrears, Winstanley argued for the first time in print that civilians who had paid taxes and free quarter during the wars had as much right to these lands as did soldiers: all the common people, both soldiers and civilians, "ought to have the freedom of all waste and common land, and Crown-land equally among them; the Souldiery ought not in equity to have all, nor the other people that paid them to have all".[67] The question of the disposal of Crown lands was of the greatest importance for members of the army in 1650; the Diggers' claim to these lands could be seen by soldiers as posing a direct threat to their attempts to secure their arrears.

Parliamentary surveys of Crown lands began taking place on estates near St George's Hill and Little Heath while the Diggers were present on the commons, and this no doubt provided a further reason for the authorities to treat sympathetically Platt's request that the Diggers be removed.[68] One of the most active Surrey surveyors was Captain John Inwood, who, as lessee of Cobham's manor house in 1649, would have had first-hand knowledge of the Diggers' occupation of the commons.[69] He and his fellow surveyors were busy at work in the parish of Walton in February, March and April 1650.[70] Sales of land in the area started in April, when Henry Bickerstaffe's brother Anthony purchased Painshill Farm, and they speeded up in the months following the departure of the Diggers.[71] The presence of the Diggers on or near Crown land must have been a source of alarm to those responsible for the sale of these lands; their concerns would almost certainly have increased when it became clear to them that new settlements were being set up, with the encouragement of the Surrey Diggers, on Crown and common land elsewhere in southern England and the Midlands. This visible spread of Digger influences beyond Surrey seems to have provided the spur for the Council of State to act swiftly to suppress Digger settlements over a wide area, and to ensure that no new colony stood a chance of being established.[72]

Despite the violence of the opposition encountered by Winstanley and his companions during the last few weeks of their venture, it seems likely that most of the Diggers who came from Cobham were able to return to the parish not long after their forced removal in April 1650; Winstanley himself is known to have returned by June 1652.[73] The accommodating attitude of the local community towards the returning Diggers may have reflected the tolerance often shown within early modern communities towards local dissenters.[74] In Cobham it may also have been connected with the genuine sympathy that some inhabitants do seem to have felt for the Diggers and their programme. The willingness of Winstanley and other former Diggers to participate in parochial and manorial administration during the 1650s is also likely to have contributed to their acceptance locally.[75] Practical considerations may, however, also have played a part. The Diggers of Iver in Buckinghamshire claimed in May 1650 that their Surrey counterparts had left their children on the parish when they were driven away.[76] If this were indeed the case, then it would clearly have been in the interests of the parish authorities to allow the Diggers to return home to take charge again of their children. An intriguing echo of the Iver Diggers' claim can be heard, much later, in Joseph Besse's account of the arrest of a Quaker in Walton in 1670:

> At one of those Meetings was a very poor labouring Man, who was fined, and for lack of other Goods they took away his Spade, whereby he was disabled to work to maintain his Motherless Children, who had no support but from his Labour; wherefore he took the youngest of them, an Infant, and carried it to the Parish-Officers to take Care of; Upon which they returned him the Child again, and his Spade to work for it.[77]

Did he – and they – remember the events that had shaken their community twenty years before?

NOTES

1. For the chronology of the attacks, see Brian Manning, *1649: The Crisis of the English Revolution* (London: Bookmarks, 1992), pp.130–32; Andrew Bradstock, *Faith in the Revolution* (London: SPCK, 1997), pp.74–7. For the date of the destruction of the colony, see John Gurney, "Gerrard Winstanley and the Digger Movement in Walton and Cobham", *Historical Journal* 37/4 (1994), p.788.
2. *Works*, pp.284, 295–6, 301, 319–22, 327–33, 360, 362, 365–9, 393, 395, 432–7; C.H. Firth (ed.), *The Clarke Papers*, II (London: Camden Society, 1894), p.216; Public Record Office (P.R.O.), SP18/42/144.
3. Cf. Christopher Hill, *Religion and Politics in Seventeenth Century England* (Brighton: Harvester, 1986), p.204.
4. *Works*, pp.184–203, 252–66; *Mercurius Pragmaticus (for Charles II)* (17–24 April 1649). Cf. *A Modest Narrative of Intelligence* 3 (14–21 April 1649), p.23; *The Moderate* 41 (17–24 April 1649). An exception was *Mercurius Pragmaticus* (17–24 April 1649).
5. *Works*, p.281; *The Speeches of the Lord Generall Fairfax, and the other Officers of the Armie, to the Diggers at St Georges Hill in Surrey*, [May] 1649; P.R.O. SP25/94, pp.93–4; *Clarke Papers* II, pp.211–12. Cf. James Holstun, "Rational Hunger: Gerrard Winstanley's *Hortus Inconclusus*", in Holstun (ed.), *Pamphlet Wars: Prose in the English Revolution* (London: Frank Cass, 1992), p.175.
6. *Clarke Papers* II, pp.210–11.
7. P.R.O. SP28/214 (unfoliated), SP28/244–5 (unfol.) (warrants of the Surrey county committee to Henry Sanders and others 1644–46); SP25/62/63; *Calendar of State Papers Domestic 1648–49*, p.180.
8. *Clarke Papers* II, pp.210–11.
9. Manning, *1649*, pp.130, 131.
10. *Works*, p.273. Cf. ibid., pp.334, 435, 506; Manning, *1649*, p.131.
11. *Works*, p.657.
12. P.R.O. E317/Surrey/55, p.10; *The Declaration and Standard of the Levellers of England* (1649). There was also talk of occupying Oatlands Park and parts of Windsor Forest.
13. P.R.O. LR2/226 ff. 259–60; LR2/197 ff. 6–9; E317/Surrey/55, pp.10, 12.
14. *Works*, p.392. For conflicts in Walton, see Gurney, "Digger Movement", pp.777, 780–81.
15. *Works*, pp.301, 319; Kingston Museum and Heritage Service KE1/1/14 nos.159–62.
16. *Works*, pp.295–8, 392. For a discussion of the incident, Christopher Kendrick, "Preaching Common Grounds", in William Zunder and Suzanne Trill (eds.), *Writing and the English Renaissance* (London: Longman, 1996), pp.217–21. Starr was to be a persistent opponent: *Works*, pp.331, 435.
17. P.R.O. E134/32 Eliz/E14, deposition of William Taylor.
18. P.R.O. Prob 11/118 f. 264; Guildhall Library 9051/6 f. 143v; Surrey History Centre (S.H.C.) 793/1; 3015 (unfol.), copy survey of Walton common fields Feb. 1650–51; M.E. Blackman (ed.), *Ashley House (Walton-on-Thames) Building Accounts 1602–1607* (Surrey Record Society XXIX, 1977), pp.23, 56–7, 70.
19. P.R.O. Prob 11/118 f. 264; *Calendar of Assize Records: Surrey, Surrey Indictments, Elizabeth I* (London: HMSO, 1980).
20. P.R.O. E134/9 Jas I/H7; Gurney, "Digger Movement", pp.777–8.
21. P.R.O. LR2/190 ff. 266, 270v; E317/Surrey/44, p.7; E134/9 Jas I/H7; National Library of Wales Wynnstay 161 f. 103v; *Abstracts of Surrey Feet of Fines 1509–1558* ed. C.A.F. Meekings (Surrey Record Society, 1946), p.68.
22. P.R.O. E134/9 Jas I/H7; E134/19 Jas I/T2.
23. P.R.O. E134/19 Jas I/T2, depositions of Elizabeth Dalton and William Starr.
24. *Works*, pp.317, 337.
25. S.H.C. K44/1/7–8; 2610/11/8/33, pp.36–7, 41–3; 4398/1/6, pp.9–10.
26. S.H.C. 4398/1/10; David Taylor, above.
27. Gurney, "Digger Movement", pp.785, 790–93.
28. *Works*, p.649. For the origin of the Wellingborough Diggers, see Northamptonshire Record Office 350P/645. The Iver Diggers were locals, and it is likely that the other known Digger

colonies were primarily local ventures: Keith Thomas, "Another Digger Broadside", *Past and Present* 42 (1969), pp.60–61, 65, 67–8.

29. *Works*, pp.256, 266, 281, 301; Manning, *1649*, p.127.
30. Timothy Kenyon, *Utopian Communism and Political Thought in Early Modern England* (London: Pinter, 1989), p.176; Gurney, "Digger Movement", p.780.
31. *Works*, pp.184–203, 252–66.
32. Ibid., pp.283, 305–6; *A Modest Narrative of Intelligence* 3 (14–21 April 1649); Manning, *1649*, p.116; Gurney, "Digger Movement", pp.779–80; Christopher Hill, *Liberty Against the Law* (London: Allen Lane, 1996), pp.285–6, 289, 295; J.C. Davis, *Utopia and the Ideal Society* (Cambridge: Cambridge University Press, 1991), pp.183–4. Winstanley's compromise position was perhaps not so clearly stated in *The True Levellers Standard Advanced* as Professor Davis suggests.
33. *Works*, pp.301, 303. Arguments of this sort were to be repeated in later appeals: see, for instance, *Clarke Papers* II, pp.218, 220.
34. *Works*, pp.360, 393; *Clarke Papers* II, p.216.
35. *Works*, pp.407–15; Hill, *Religion and Politics*, p.218; Manning, *1649*, p.130; Gurney, "Digger Movement", p.786.
36. Manning, *1649*, p.124; Gurney, "Digger Movement", pp.786–8.
37. P.R.O. SP15/40/48; S.H.C. 181/15/19; 2610/1/38/22; 4398/2/1.
38. P.R.O. ASSI 35/91/10, mm. 119–22.
39. *Works*, p.435.
40. For Foster, see London Metropolitan Archives DW/PA/7/11 f. 443; P.R.O. SP15/40/48. The identities of the accused are discussed more fully in Gurney, "Digger Movement", pp.788–90.
41. S.H.C. K44/1/9; 2610/11/8/33; 4398/1/4–10.
42. *Works*, pp.272–5; Christopher Hill, *The World Turned Upside Down* (London: Temple Smith, 1972), p.105.
43. *Works*, p.433; Gurney, "Digger Movement", p.787.
44. *Works*, p.392. Winstanley's "Stoke Common" may instead have been the Stokes Heath situated in the parish of Cobham. This belonged to the manor of Esher Waterville or Milbourne, which had been bought in 1628 by the Corporation of Kingston for the benefit of the town's poor.
45. Manning, *1649*, p.130.
46. Ibid., p.99; L. F. Solt, "Winstanley, Lilburne, and the Case of John Fielder", *Huntington Library Quarterly* 45/2 (1982); Gurney, "Digger Movement", pp.795–6.
47. *Works*, pp.433–4; Manning, *1649*, p.130.
48. Fielder's separatist group had already faced violent attacks from soldiers, watermen and apprentices in Kingston: John Fielder, *The Humble Petition and Appeal of John Fielder of Kingston* (1651), pp.12, 16–17, 21–2.
49. Manning, *1649*, p.131.
50. *Works*, pp.366–7, 399–403; Gerrard Winstanley, *Englands Spirit Unfoulded* (1650), ed. G.E. Aylmer, *Past and Present* 40 (1968), pp.14–15.
51. *Clarke Papers* II, p.217.
52. P.R.O. SP28/244 (unfol.), county committee warrant to the high constables of Elmbridge hundred, 29 May 1643; British Library Add. MS 71,534 f. 178.
53. S.H.C. 4398/1/9.
54. S.H.C. 4398/1/10; PSH/COB/1/1, p. 44; PSH/COB/5/1; on the peat-digging episode see David Taylor, "Gerrard Winstanley at Cobham", above.
55. P.R.O LR2/190 f. 266; C10/468/162; S.H.C. 2610/29/3; 4398/1/10.
56. S.H.C. K145/19. He sold it in 1652: K145/20.
57. S.H.C. 181/10/a–b; Fielder, *Petition and Appeal*, p.2.
58. Kingston Museum and Heritage Service KE/1/14.
59. P.R.O. ASSI 35/94/8; ASSI 35/94/12, m. 121; Gurney, "Digger Movement", p.792. Their names preceded that of Winstanley in the bill of presentments at the July 1653 Assizes.
60. P.R.O. SP19/22, p.37. Thomas Ward of Kingston was also a royalist; it is possible that they were the same person.

61. See, for instance P.R.O. SP28/334 f. 61.
62. *Works*, p.366; *Clarke Papers*, II, p.217; P.R.O. SP18/42/144.
63. P.R.O. SP25/94, pp.93–4.
64. P.R.O. SP23/186/890, 900; SP28/18 (unfol.), breviate of sequestrations in Surrey; *Mercurius Politicus* 583 (11–18 Aug. 1659), p.674; *Calendar of the Clarendon State Papers* IV, pp.328–55; David Underdown, *Royalist Conspiracy in England 1649–1660* (New Haven: Yale University Press, 1960), pp.280–81. Charles Bickerstaffe's son, born in 1661, was named Stuart, a clear indication of where the father's allegiances lay. For the political affiliations of Henry Bickerstaffe's brother Anthony, see Gurney, "Digger Movement", p.783.
65. *Works*, pp.368, 393; *Clarke Papers* II, p.216.
66. *The Speeches of the Lord Generall Fairfax.*
67. *Works*, p.371.
68. P.R.O. E317/Surrey.
69. John Platt had leased Cobham Court to him in 1647: T.E.C. Walker, "Cobham: Manorial History", *Surrey Archaeological Collections* 58 (1961), pp.49–50.
70. P.R.O. E317/Surrey/6, pp.44, 55, 61.
71. P.R.O. E121/4/8 (6). The purchase took place on 15 April, four days before the destruction of the colony.
72. Cf. Hill, *Religion and Politics*, p.206; Holstun, "Rational Hunger", p.175.
73. Gurney, "Digger Movement", p.794.
74. cf. Bill Stevenson, "The Social Integration of Post-Restoration Dissenters 1660–1725", in Margaret Spufford (ed.), *The World of the Rural Dissenters* (Cambridge: Cambridge University Press, 1995), pp.360–87; Christopher W. Marsh, *The Family of Love in English Society, 1550–1630* (Cambridge: Cambridge University Press, 1994), pp.188–96.
75. For Winstanley, J.S. Alsop, "Gerrard Winstanley: Religion and Respectability", *Historical Journal* 28/3 (1985), p.706.
76. Thomas, "Another Digger Broadside", pp.59, 65.
77. Joseph Besse, *A Collection of the Sufferings of the People called Quakers* vol. I (London, 1753).

"The Consolation of Israel": *Representations of Jewishness in the Writings of Gerrard Winstanley and William Everard*

CLAIRE JOWITT

On 20 April 1649 the Digger leaders Gerrard Winstanley and William Everard met with General Fairfax to explain their reasons for taking over the common land at St George's Hill earlier that month. After both refused to remove their hats, Everard acted as spokesperson for the movement, making a speech that was published within three days and widely reported in contemporary broadsheets.[1]

> Everard said, he was of the race of the Jews; that all the liberties of the people were lost by the coming in of William the Conqueror, and that ever since, the people of God had lived under tyranny and oppression worse than that of our forefathers under the Egyptians. But now the time of deliverance was at hand, and God would bring his people out of this slavery, and restore them to their freedom, in enjoying the fruits and benefits of the earth. And that there had lately appeared to him a vision, which bade him arise, and dig and plough the earth, and receive the fruits thereof; that their intent is, to restore the creation to its former condition.[2]

This essay uses Everard's extraordinary claim of Jewish self-identity as a way of exploring Digger beliefs about Jews. Everard's statement that "he was of the race of the Jews" is examined in relation to other contemporary Digger publications, specifically Winstanley's *Truth Lifting up its Head above Scandals* (written in response to Everard's imprisonment at Kingston in 1648), *The New Law of Righteousnes* (1649) and *The True Levellers Standard Advanced* (published at the same time as the meeting with Fairfax in April 1649) which was signed by fifteen Diggers, including Winstanley and Everard (whose name is first). Everard's "Jewishness" is also placed in the context of the snowballing mid-century debate over Jewish readmission in which – for the first time since the expulsion of Jews from England in 1290 – English theologians, politicians and writers seriously debated the merits of a native English Jewish population.[3] What this essay seeks to establish, then, is the extent to which Everard and Winstanley were using an historical Israelite identity as a metaphor for their own political, religious and social aims and situation. It also examines whether beliefs and knowledge concerning contemporary practising Jews – which were starting to be widely circulated in England for the first time in three hundred and fifty years – were implicated in this parallel and, if so, what this tells us concerning the Diggers' attitudes to Jews.

In the pamphlets *The New Law of Righteousnes* and *The True Levellers Standard Advanced*, in particular, an Israelite identity is important since – as we have already seen in Everard's speech – the Diggers used the captivity of the Israelites under the Egyptians as a parallel to that of the English people downtrodden by the legacy of William the Conqueror. In *The True Levellers Standard Advanced*, for example, this political point is made especially forcefully since the "plain-hearted people" under Norman rule are called the "poor enslaved English Israelites".[4] In other words, like the Israelites, 1640s Englishmen continue to be oppressed by a hostile foreign regime. Moreover, this tyranny over those described by Everard to Fairfax as poor "people of God" will soon end through the project of Digging, in the same way that the "the Babylonish yoke laid upon Israel of old, under Nebuchadnezzar" was finally ended and the men of Judah were allowed to return to Jerusalem. It appears, then, that Winstanley and Everard were using the idea of the "chosenness" of the Israelite nation by God as a way of claiming authority by precedent for the situation of the Diggers. The oppression of the English under the Norman yoke is thus rendered as merely the last in a series: 'Successively from that time, the Conquering Enemy, have still laid these yokes upon Israel to keep Jacob down: And the last enslaving Conquest which the enemy got over Israel, was the Norman over England'.[5] Thus the children of Israel's persecution by Egyptian or Babylonian enemies, and their subsequent freedom and position as God's chosen people, offers a model to Winstanley and Everard which emphasizes both divine support and the hope of the achievement of their aims for the contemporary "English Israelites" of the Digger movement. Noticeably, established beliefs about the role of contemporary Jews in ushering in the millennium through their mass conversion to Christianity are appropriated in this pamphlet and transposed onto the English people: "It is shewed us, That all the Prophecies, Visions, and Revelations of Scriptures, of Prophets, and Apostles, concerning the calling of the Jews, the Restauration of Israel; and making of that People, the Inheritors of the whole Earth; doth all seat themselves in this Work of making the Earth a Common Treasury."[6] Thus "the Jews" about to be called are, for Everard and Winstanley, the English populace to the project of digging.[7]

Everard's speech to Fairfax also represents the identification between Diggers and Israelites in terms of a symbolic familial bond: the Hebrews are described as "our forefathers". Significantly, this ancestry is not shared by those that have benefited from the imposition of the laws of William the Conqueror – "Kings, Lords, Judges, Justices, Bayliffs, and the violent bitter people that are Free-holders" – since English ruling classes are descended from the oppressive Babylonians in *The True Levellers Standard Advanced*.[8] However, in Winstanley's 1648 pamphlet, *Truth Lifting up its Head above Scandals*, the argument concerning a shared ancestry between Diggers and Jews is not developed. Written in support of Everard, who had been imprisoned, according to the preface, for "hold[ing] blasphemous opinions: as to deny God, and Christ, and Scriptures, and prayer", Winstanley, "being slandered as well as he", was moved to attempt a clear expression of the movement's religious creed.[9] Structured in terms of a dialogue between questions and answers concerning Digger beliefs, the central concern of the pamphlet is to rebut the idea that the Diggers – like the Jews – reject Christ. According to Winstanley, this misunderstanding has arisen because "I said that Jesus Christ at a distance from thee, will not save thee; and that this is not the humane flesh, but the Spirit in that body, that is the Saviour, and the Seed, that must bruise the Serpents head in mankind. And hence they say I deny Christ".[10] Consequently, Winstanley proceeds to describe his beliefs concerning Christ, specifically that Christ's "humane body was the Lambe that answered all the types of Moses Law: But that body tooke its name from the spirit that dwelt within it". Hence, he continues, it was not Christ's body that was important, rather "He was the spirit of meeknesse and humility, which saved humane flesh" and "when the same Anointing or Spirit that was sent downe into that body; is sent down into yours, changing your vile bodies and making them like that glorious body, killing all the cursed powers in the flesh; making your flesh subject to the Spirit; now you are become one with Christ, and with the Father, which is your salvation".[11] In this pamphlet only Moses amongst the Jews is represented positively since he correctly foretold the coming of Christ, but his "Law" was unable to recognize the essentially spiritual nature of the Messiah and hence "the Rulers of the Jewes slew him" and he "was killed by the curse" of "covetous, proud flesh" "that ruled in the Jewes".[12] Hence Jewish leaders are here represented as Christ-killers and it is those that practise this religion, rather than the Diggers, that, according to Winstanley, reject the spiritual salvation that Christ represented. As such, this hostile representation of Jewishness is significantly different from that offered in 1649 by *The True Levellers Standard Advanced*, or indeed *The New Law of Righteousnes* in which, as we shall see, Winstanley constructed a much more sympathetic view of Jewishness which attempted to emphasize similarities between Diggers and Jews rather than focusing on differences.

In *The New Law of Righteousnes* the similarities between the Hebrew nation and the Diggers are drawn out by Winstanley in an extended parallel.

The emphasis of the argument concerning the similarity between Diggers and Israelites is religious in this pamphlet rather than explicitly political as in *The True Levellers Standard Advanced*. The preface – dated 26 April 1648 (n.s.1649) – is addressed "To the twelve tribes of Israel that are circumcised in heart, and scattered through all the nations of the earth", and is signed "A waiter for the consolation of Israel, Jerrard Winstanley"; there is no direct mention of the oppression of the Norman Yoke.[13] Winstanley's preface is perhaps the clearest indication of what the Diggers understood by the category of "a Jew":

> You are the Abrahamites in whom the blessing remaines, that lives not now in the type, but enjoyes the substance of circumcision; For he is not a Jew, that is one outward in the flesh; but he is a Jew, that is one inward, whose circumcision is of the heart: Whether he be born of the nation of Jews extant in the world, or whether he be born of other Nations in whom the blessing remains; it is Abrahams promised seed that makes a Jew; and these are they of whom it is said, Salvation is of the Jews.
>
> What was that seed of Abraham, that is called the blessing?
>
> It is the Law and power of righteousnesse, which made Abraham to forsake his Isaac, his dearest relations in the flesh, rather than he would refuse the way of his Maker; and herein Abraham found peace: So that this King of righteousnesse, and this Prince of peace that ruled in Abraham, is the blessing of all Nations, for this shall save his people from their sins, and free them from all distempers of the unrighteous flesh. This is the one spreading power that shall remove the curse, and restore all things from the bondage every thing groans under.[14]

In language that is remarkably similar to that repeatedly employed by the Quaker leaders George Fox and Margaret Fell, Winstanley here ruminates on the Pauline distinction (Rom. 2: 28–9) between "inward" and "outward" Jewishness.[15] "Inward" Jewishness clearly represents a spiritual state imbuing those that possess it with "the Law and power of righteousnesse". "Outward" Jews are those that do not, as yet, hold this "blessing" and remain attached to ritualized and "fleshly" religious practices. Consequently, Abraham is celebrated for preferring and obeying his "Maker'[s]" command to sacrifice Isaac rather than privileging "fleshly" attachment to his earthly family. Hence Diggers, or "Inward Jews", represent a divinely chosen spiritual minority in captivity to the earthly majority of "Outward Jews" – the Reformed English Protestant Church and all other non-Diggers. Importantly, Winstanley makes clear that "the spreading power" of "Inward" Jewishness does not exclude those that currently practise the Jewish religion: "Whether he be born of the nation of Jews extant in the world, or whether he be born of other Nations in whom the blessing remains; it is Abrahams promised seed that makes a Jew; and these are they of whom it is said, Salvation is of the Jews." Hence contemporary Jews are a nation "in whom the blessing remains" and, for Winstanley, it is a question of patiently waiting until the process of transformation into a state of "Inward" Jewishness is made manifest:

> And this seed (Dear Brethren) hath lien hid in you, all the time appointed, and now is breaking forth. And the Nations shall know, That salvation or restauration rather, is of the Jews, that King of righteousnesse and Prince of peace, that removes the curse, and becomes himself the blessing, arises up in you, and fils, and will fill the earth, both man-kind, and the whole Creation, Fire, Water, Earth and Air, for the blessing shall be every where.[16]

Jews, similar to other non-Diggers, are included in this imminently expected change (described using the present tense of "arises") from "Outward" to "Inward" Jewishness since Winstanley confidently states "all" or "every man or woman, born of Jew or Gentile" "shall know that this almighty King of righteousness is our Saviour, and besides him there is none".[17] This pamphlet, then, is motivated by a universalist salvational ethic which extends to contemporary Jewry even though, since there was no Jewish population in England at this time to respond to Digger beliefs, Winstanley's schemes with regard to Jews appear highly unlikely to succeed. In other words, *The New Law of Righteousnes* expresses a theoretical inclusion of Jews within Digger ideas concerning universal salvation, but the pamphlet does not concentrate on steps for the practical realization of the conversion of the Jews, specifically that Christian-Jewish contact would need to be increased, most prominently by Jewish readmission into England.

Indeed, some other millenarians – including Henry Jessey, John Dury, William Erbery and Edward Nicholas – argued that in order for the Jews to be converted to Christianity – a prerequisite for the Second Coming – Jews must be readmitted into England to be proselytized since only exposure to Protestantism in its pure English interpretation would cause them to renounce their faith. As a result Edward Nicholas, for example, published *An Apology for the Honorable Nation of the Jews* in February 1648, which emphasized English Protestants' moral and religious responsibility to proselytize Jews and which could only be achieved through the latter's presence in England.[18] Readmission would thus effect "the glory of God, the comfort of those his afflicted people, the love of my own sweet native Countrey of England, and the freeing of my own soul in the day of account".[19] Furthermore, the Leveller Richard Overton in his 1645 text *The Arraignment of Mr. Persecution* – which he dedicated to the Westminster Assembly of Divines – argued that the problems facing contemporary Christians were caused by the policy of "our priests not to suffer a Jew by authority to live amongst them". Overton continues: "how then can we complaine of the vengance that is at this time upon us & our children, that have been so cruell, so hatefull, so bloody minded to them and their children? We have given them the cup of trembling, surely we must tast of the dregges: Hearken therefore no longer to those which teach this bloody doctrine of persecution."[20]

Nevertheless, as we shall see, in comparison to many contemporary Christian descriptions of Jews and Jewishness, Winstanley's are noticeably moderate in *The New Law of Righteousnes*, since the persecution Jews historically suffered under the Egyptians and Babylonians becomes empathetically transposed onto the Diggers – and more generally onto all those that are either poor or oppressed. This shared history of enslavement allows Winstanley to include contemporary Jews amongst the "blessed" who are about to understand and receive "the new law of righteousness". Winstanley here cuts across racial distinctions as Jews, as well as all non-Digger Christians, are about to be transformed into "Inward Jews". Hence in the preface to *The New Law of Righteousnes* Winstanley concentrates on the chosenness of the Israelites rather than focusing on the depravity of the Jews or their part in the death of Christ. This representation of Jews was considerably less hostile than that expressed in *Truth Lifting up its Head above Scandals* or in the work of other mid-century commentators including, for example, Thomas Browne in *Religio Medici* (1643), Clement Walker in *Anarchia Anglicana: Or, the History of Independency* (1649), and George Fox in *A Visitation to the Jews* (1656).[21] Browne, for instance, described the obstinacy of "the contemptible and degenerate issue of Jacob" who persist in "their own Doctrine" notwithstanding their past history of apostasy ("and so easily seduced to the Idolatry of their Neighbours") and Fox commented on the way the Jews "killed him [Christ], they cast him out, and delivered him up to the Gentiles to be mocked, scourged and crucified".[22]

However, the main body of the text of *The New Law of Righteousnes* does voice criticism of contemporary Jews, who are described as following "forms and customes of the Beast".[23] The argument of Winstanley's text is based on the notion of successive ages of divine revelation. After the Fall of the first "unrighteous Adam" into "the fleshes law" of "troubles, oppressions and complainings", Winstanley believes that God instigated a three-step timetable over "6000 years near hand expired; in every one of which he draws man-kind higher and higher into himself, out of the power of the Serpent or bondage".[24] God's "three methods in discovering this mystery" of the spirit were:

> The first Method is this: He was pleased to call forth Moses to be his servant, and in, by and through him, he reveals himself to lie under types, shadows, sacrifices; that man-kind by them might be led to see his Maker; And this was the Covenant of an outward testimony, which Moses, a man that was mixed with flesh and spirit, was Mediator of. And this [*sic*]
>
> Secondly did point out the Apostolical testimony which was to be manifested in aftertimes; and that was to acknowledge honour, and bear witnesse of the Lamb Jesus Christ, that was the substance of Moses. For the Apostles declare themselves to be witnesses of Christ, the great Prophet, that Moses said should come after him, to whom every man should hearken, and then leave the teachings of shadows, which they receive from him. Act. 3.22.
>
> Therefore say they, We eat and drank in his presence, we heard him speak, and saw his miracles, and bear testimony to the world, that the Rulers of the Jews slew him, and that he was raised from the dead by the Almighty power. And this single appearance of the man Christ Jesus (for herein the righteous Law dwelt bodily) was a more spirituall declaration then the former. And this types out [*sic*]
>
> The third Method of Divine discovery, which indeed doth finish the mystery; and herein the Lord takes up all into himself, even into the Spirit that governs the Creation; for he is in all, and acts through all.[25]

The Jewish religion as handed down by Moses represents, then, for Winstanley, the first stage in Man's recovery of the pre-lapsarian state of righteousness in which God originally created humanity. Moses was thus "mixed with flesh and spirit" and the "Mediator" of the "outward testimony" of the Covenant of God. Jesus, "the substance of Moses" and "a more spirituall declaration then the former" represents the second stage in this hierarchical conception of mankind's journey back to spiritual perfection. Significantly, Winstanley does not blame the whole Jewish nation for the murder of Christ, rather it is the "Rulers of the Jews" that "slew him" since, as he goes on to describe, "as Moses gave way to Christ ... Moses administration began to be silent and drew back" and "the worshippers in Moses ministration, envied and killed such as worshipped the Son of man".[26] The third and final stage in Man's recovery of righteousness, which according to Winstanley is occurring at the time of writing, is the generation of Christ in all people. Consequently, "as the ministration of Moses gave way to this [Christ after the flesh (in one single body)]; so this ministration is to give way to the inward teachings of Christ, and the spreading of the Spirit, in sons and daughters".[27] Just as those that continue to practise the Jewish religion despite the revelation of Jesus Christ (the "substance" of Moses' prophecy) are "corrupted" and of the "Beast", those that persist in worshipping the fleshly Christ are similarly misguided: "And therefore I must tell you that yet live in dipping, in water and observation of Gospel-forms and types, you live yet under the ministration of Jesus Christ after the flesh" and these Christians "should all cease and give way to the spirituall worship of the Father in the latter dayes".[28]

The hierarchical distinctions Winstanley establishes here represent a developmental model for the achievement of "Inward" Jewishness. Simultaneously Jewishness is both celebrated and despised. Jewishness is celebrated as an antecedent of the inward spirituality of the Diggers as the Hebrew people were chosen by God as the nation in which to locate his blessing. However, contemporary Jews, like contemporary non-Digger Christians, cling to fleshly practices until they convert to Digger spiritual beliefs. Consequently, whereas the pamphlet emphasizes theoretical universal salvation rather than offering a methodology for the realization of these aims, Winstanley also demonstrates little interest in the practices of contemporary Jews. On the one hand, this means that in this pamphlet he does not imbue Jews with the type of stereotypical anti-Semitic characteristics described by other Christian writers of the time. George Sandys in *A Relation of a Journey Begun An: Dom: 1610* described Jewish women as "for the most part ... goggle-eyd", a description later echoed by Robert Burton in his encyclopaedic *The Anatomy of Melancholy*, who also comments on the "goggle-eyes" of Jews of both sexes as well as the *foetor Judaicus* – the distinctive, unpleasant Jewish odour.[29] Indeed, Burton's description of contemporary Jews as "sottish, ignorant, blind, superstitious, wilful, obstinate, and peevish" concluded with the judgement that "they be scarce rational creatures".[30]

But Winstanley's lack of interest in contemporary Jews also meant he had little understanding or knowledge of real Jewish practices or customs. In the late 1640s such information was increasingly becoming available in England as contact between continental Jews and English Christians increased both by letter and through personal acquaintance, and published accounts of Jewish practices by Jews were also printed in English for the first time. For example, the Venetian rabbi Leon Modena, from the beginning of the seventeenth century until his death in 1648, corresponded with, preached before, or was acquainted with English Christians including, amongst others, the Cambridge Hebraist John Lightfoot, the bibliophile Samuel Slade, the member of Parliament and English ambassador at the Hague William Bowell, the English ambassador of Venice Henry Wotton, the Protestant bishop in Ireland William Bedell, and the travelogue writer Thomas Coryat.[31] Indeed, in *Coryat's Crudities* the author describes a visit to the Venetian ghetto and an encounter with an unnamed rabbi – who could easily be Modena – whom he attempts to proselytize until the rabbi becomes, understandably, somewhat "exasperated" and the debate descends into the two "earnestly bickering".[32] Furthermore Modena's *Historia De Gli Riti Hebraici*, written "at the request of an English nobleman, who intended to give to the King of England" and published in Italian in Venice in 1616, was then translated into French and published in Paris in 1637, before finally appearing in an English edition, *The History of the Rites, Customes, and Manner of Life, of the Present Jews*, translated by the impecunious royalist hymn-maker and musician Edmund Chilmead in 1650.[33] Modena's text – which was intended for a Christian readership – sought to diffuse hostility between Jews and Christians by relating to its readers accurate details about Jewish rites thus correcting the kind of hostile misinformation in circulation in countries such as England where there was, officially at least, no native Jewish population.[34] Consequently, Modena carefully states his own position in the preface as a way of not alienating his Christian readership:

> in my Writing, I have kept my self exactly to the Truth, remembering my self to be a Jew, and have therefore taken upon Mee the person of a Plain, Neutral Relater onely. I do not deny, but that I have endeavoured to avoid the giving occasion to the Reader of deriding the Jews, for their so many Ceremonies: neither yet have I at all taken upon me to defend, or maintain them: for as much as my whole Purpose is to give a bare Relation of them onely, and no way to perswade any to the observing of them.[35]

Moreover, contemporary radical interest in Jewishness is further revealed by the fact that in 1647–48, Parliament, in a unprecedented gesture, ordered that £2000 from the dean and chapter lands at Cambridge and £500 from receipts at Goldsmiths' Hall be used to buy shipments of Hebrew books. The purchase was organized by the Hebraist John Selden and Modena's correspondent John Lightfoot and was swiftly satirized in the Royalist newspaper *Mercurius Pragmaticus* (28 March–4 April 1648). The purchase by Selden – described as so familiar with Hebrew that "hee had been one of the Bricklayers of old Babel" – was lampooned as a waste of money, with Jewish writers described as "the first founders of our modern Pharisies, and the primitive Christians of this last seven years Edition".[36] In other words, Royalists here identify Jewish writings as the influences on and originators of Parliament's (the "modern Pharisies") desire to kill Charles/Christ.

Winstanley's texts, by contrast, appear completely uninformed concerning this growing body of information concerning Jews and Jewishness. The circulation of such information contributed to the debate about Jewish readmission which many other radical writers and groups supported, and in turn led to the Whitehall Conference on Jewish readmission in December 1655. Winstanley's texts ossify Jews into their Biblical incarnation, and a Hebrew identity is thus rendered as merely a useful tool or metaphor by which to signal both chosenness and persecution. Unlike, for example, the Baptists Joanna and Ebenezer Cartwright (or Cartenright), whose experiences and contacts with the thriving Jewish community in Amsterdam led them to petition Fairfax about Jewish readmission to England, Winstanley appears to have had no active interest in contemporary Jewish concerns. The Cartwrights' *The Petition of the Jewes* was presented to Parliament's Council of War on 5 January 1648 (n.s.1649) and was published the following year.[37] The presentation of the petition was intended to coincide with the parliamentary debate concerning what forms of religious toleration the government would allow, and hence Jewish readmission was discussed. Though the resulting bill, the "Agreement of the People" (approved 15 January 1648–49) only granted toleration to groups who "profess faith in God by Jesus Christ", thus excluding Jews, nevertheless the Cartwrights' petition reveals the way in which some nonconformists actively engaged with Jewish issues and showed knowledge of contemporary Jewry.[38] The Cartwrights' pamphlet, for instance, recognizes the mercantile benefits the readmission of European Jewry into England would engender, since Amsterdam merchants had thriving trade connections with Jews and non-Jews in many areas: "the inhumane cruel Statute of banishment made against, may be repealed, and they under the Christian banner of Charity, may again be permitted to *trade* and dwell amongst you in this Land, as now they do in the Nether-lands".[39]

In conclusion, Digger interest in Jewishness must be seen as limited. To reach firm conclusions about William Everard's attitudes to Jewishness is problematic because it is impossible to know what exact share he had in *The True Levellers Standard Advanced* since it is signed by so many Diggers, and he appears to have left the movement some time in the late spring or early summer of 1649. Broadsheets for May 1649 report that Everard was involved in the Leveller rebellion in the army which was put down in that month at Burford.[40] Furthermore, it has also been argued that by August 1649 William Everard was staying with the English Behmenist John Pordage of Bradfield near Reading in Berkshire.[41] In Pordage's *Innocencie Appearing* (1655) – where Pordage sought to set the record straight against the accusations of heresy which had led him to be examined in 1651 by the Committee for Plundered Ministers and by magistrates in 1654 – he describes a vision of the "conjuror" William Everard he experienced in his bedroom in 1649.[42] Everard's connection with the Kabbalist-orientated Pordage – who claimed in *Innocencie Appearing* to have benefited from discussions with a rabbi concerning the question of whether Adam was both male and female – is suggestive, then, that Everard might have had a broader interests in Jewish issues and learning than Winstanley.[43] But, though Pordage appeared to have had personal contact with practising Jews, there is no direct evidence that Everard himself had such meetings and, furthermore, Pordage's interest was in Jewish mysticism rather than either orthodox Jewish texts and beliefs or issues of concern to contemporary Jewry such as readmission to England.

For Winstanley, it was the history of Biblical Hebrew oppression that inspired the repeated construction of metaphors of an Israelite identity. Digger salvation thus did not exclude contemporary Jews, but the developmental model concerning a divine timetable evolved in *The New Law of Righteousnes*, which saw Jewishness as a primitive and corrupt version of inward Digger godliness, does not encourage interest in either seventeenth-century Jewish religious practices, or issues of concern to contemporary Jewry. But Winstanley is rarely explicitly antagonistic or militantly hostile to Jews. He makes it clear that the Jewish people as a whole were not responsible for Christ's death, identifying only obstinate Jewish leaders as culpable. Indeed, he continued to use metaphors of Israel's chosenness in many later pamphlets. For example, in a letter "To My Lord Generall and His Councell of Warr", dated 8 December 1649, Winstanley uses early Israelite practices of non-monarchic, elected government as an example that English Republicans would be well advised to emulate. Writing to ask that Fairfax grant the "poore commoners this quiett freedome to improve the common land for our livelyhood", he expresses the hope that "there will not bee any kingly power over us, to rule at will and wee to bee slaves, as the power has bin, but that you will rule in love as Moses and Joshua did the Children of Israell before any kingly power came in, and that the Parliament wilbee as the Elders of Israell, chosen freely by the people to advise for and assist both yow and us".[44] In this example, then – as in *The True Levellers Standard Advanced* – an Israelite model is used as a positive political example that the English government should consider.[45] Indeed, in his last work, *The Law of Freedom in a Platform* (1652), Winstanley still used similar images. In the opening dedication to Cromwell, for example, he praises the General using Israelite references: "God hath honored you with the highest Honor of any man since Moses time, to be the Head of a People, who have cast out an Oppressing Pharaoh".[46] In this text, "Israels Commonwealth" in which "They had no Beggar among them" is represented as a time of "brotherly freedom" before the establishment of the tyranny of "oppressing Kings".[47] What this text seeks to do, then, is warn Cromwell against failing to live to up his radical promises: "But if they who profess more Righteousness and Freedom in words then the Kings government was, and yet can find no government to ease the people, but must establish the Kings old Laws, though they give it a new name; I will leave the sentence, worthy such a profession and such a people, to be given by the heart of every rational man."[48] Politically at least, if not in terms of religious practices, the Jews continued to offer a model of successful non-monarchic government which Winstanley urged the English to emulate.

NOTES

For comments on earlier drafts of this essay I am grateful to Andrew Bradstock, Carola Scott-Luckens, Andrew Hadfield, Sarah Prescott and Diane Watt. I should like to dedicate this article to Carola, whose generous advice not only makes her an excellent reader of my work but also a splendid friend.

1. *The Declaration and Standard of the Levellers of England delivered in a Speech ... by Mr. Everard* (London: G. Laurenson, 23 April 1649); this is copied in Bulstrode Whitelock's, *Memorials of the English Affairs*, 4 vols. (Oxford, 1853), III, p.18, as well as appearing in L.H. Berens, *The Digger Movement in the Days of the Commonwealth* (London: Simpkin, Marshall, Hamilton, Kent & Co, 1906), p.37. Broad-sheet accounts include: *A Modest Narrative of Intelligence* (14–21 April), E.551 (9); *A Perfect Diurnal* (16–23 April), E.529 (18); *A Perfect Summary of an Exact Diary of some Passages of Parliament* (16–23April), E.529 (19); *The Impartial Intelligencer* (18–25 April), E.529 (20); *Continued Heads of Perfect Passages in Parliament* (20–27 April), E. 529 (23); *The Kingdome's Faithfull and Impartiall Scout* (20–27 April), E.529 (22); *Mercurius Pragmaticus* (17–24 April), E.551 (12); *The Moderate Intelligencer* (19–26 April), E. 552 (4). For a discussion of the politically motivated differences in the broadsheets' accounts of the meeting see D.W. Petegorsky, *Left-wing Democracy in the English Civil War: Gerrard Winstanley and the Digger Movement* (Stroud: Alan Sutton, 2nd edn. 1995 (original 1940)), p.163–6. For a summary of the Digger movement see G.E. Aylmer, "The Religion of Gerrard Winstanley", in J.F. McGregor and B. Reay (eds.), *Radical Religion in the English Revolution* (Oxford: Oxford University Press, 1984), pp.91–120.
2. Whitelocke, *Memorials of the English Affairs*, p.18.
3. On the history of the Jews in England see David Katz, *Philo-Semitism and the Readmission of the Jews to England 1603–1655* (Oxford: Oxford University Press, 1982); David Katz, *The History of the Jews in England 1485–1850* (Oxford: Oxford University Press, 1994); James Shapiro, *Shakespeare and the Jews* (New York: Columbia University Press, 1996).
4. *The True Levellers Standard Advanced* in *Works*, p.259. All subsequent references are to this edition. See Claire Jowitt, "Radical Identities? Native, Americans, Jews and the English Commonwealth", *The Seventeenth Century* 10 (1995), pp.101–19, at pp.104–5.
5. *The True Levellers Standard Advanced* in *Works*, p.259.
6. Ibid., p.260.
7. See Christopher Hill, "Till the Conversion of the Jews", in Richard Popkin (ed.), *Millenarianism and Messianism in English Literature and Thought 1650–1982* (Leiden: Brill, 1988), pp.12–26.
8. *The True Levellers Standard Advanced* in *Works*, p.259.
9. *Truth Lifting Up Its Head Above Scandals* in *Works*, p.103.
10. Ibid., p.112.
11. Ibid., pp.112–13.
12. Ibid., pp.123, 113.
13. *The New Law of Righteousnes* in *Works*, pp.149, 154.
14. Ibid., p.150.
15. Margaret Fell describes how Fox in 1652 interrupted the minister at St Mary's Church, Ulverston, and exhorted each member of the congregation to become a "Jew inward"; "His

first words were: 'He is not a Jew that is one outward; neither is that circumcision which is outward: but he is a Jew that is one inward; and that is circumcision which is of the heart'... he went on to rebuke those that understood the Scriptures only of themselves, without the illumination of the Spirit of Christ ... This opened me so, that it cut me to the heart." See Isobel Ross, *Margaret Fell: Mother of Quakerism* (London: Longmans, Green, 1949), p.11. For a fuller discussion of contact between Quakers and Jews and Quaker appropriation of Israelitish metaphors see Judith Kegan Gardiner, "Margaret Fell Fox and Feminist Literary History: A 'Mother in Israel' Calls to the Jews", *Prose Studies* 17 (1994), pp.42–56; Bonnelyn Young Kunze, *Margaret Fell and the Rise of Quakerism* (London: Macmillan, 1994), pp.211–28; Richard Popkin, "Spinoza's Relations with the Quakers in Amsterdam", *Quaker History* 73 (1984), pp.14–29; Claire Jowitt, "'Inward' and 'Outward' Jews: Margaret Fell, Circumcision and Women's Preaching", *Reformation* 4 (1999) pp.139–67.

16. *The New Law of Righteousnes* in *Works*, p.152.
17. Ibid., pp.153, 151. For an argument that the religious language in the Digger pamphlets should be taken seriously see Andrew Bradstock, "Sowing in Hope: The Relevance of Theology to Gerrard Winstanley's Political Programme", *The Seventeenth Century* 6 (1991), pp.189–204.
18. See B.S. Capp, *The Fifth-Monarchy Men: A Study in Seventeenth-Century English Millenarianism* (London: Faber & Faber, 1972); see also Katz, *The Jews in the History of England*, pp.112–13.
19. Cited by Katz, *Philo-Semitism and the Readmission of the Jews*, pp.181–2.
20. Richard Overton, *The Arraignement of Mr. Persecution* (London: Martin Claw Clergie, 1645), D3v. I am grateful to Eliane Glaser for this reference.
21. Thomas Browne, *Religio Medici*, in *The Prose of Sir Thomas Browne*, ed. N.J. Endicott (New York: Anchor Books, 1967), pp.1–90; Clement Walker, *Anarchia Anglicana, Or, The History of Independency. The Second Part* (London: 1649), pp.60–62. For a discussion of these texts see David Katz, *Philo-Semitism and the Readmission of the Jews*, pp.169–70, 178–9. George Fox, *A Visitation to the Jews*, in *The Works of George Fox*, 8 vols. (New York: AMS Press, 1975), IV, pp.53–75. For a discussion of the violence of Fox's language see David Loewenstein, "The War of the Lamb: George Fox and the Apocalyptic Discourse of Revolutionary Quakerism", *Prose Studies* 17 (1994), pp.25–41.
22. Browne, *Religio Medici*, p.32; Fox, *A Visitation to the Jews*, *Works*, IV, p.54.
23. *The New Law of Righteousnes* in *Works*, p.163.
24. Ibid., pp.159–60. This trinitarian schema, originally developed by Joachim of Fiore (1135–1202), was perceived as considerably more radical than the one of seven dispensations which Winstanley discussed in his first pamphlet *The Mysterie of God, Concerning the whole Creation, Mankinde, To be Made known to every man and woman, after seven Dispensations and Seasons of Time are passed over* (1648). This is discussed more fully in Andrew Bradstock, *Faith in the Revolution: The Political Theologies of Mntzer and Winstanley* (London: SPCK, 1997), pp.110–15. See also Holstun, this volume (above).
25. *The New Law of Righteousnes* in *Works*, p.160.
26. Ibid., pp.161, 163.
27. Ibid., p.162.
28. Ibid.
29. George Sandys, *A Relation of a Journey begun An: Dom: 1610* (London, 3rd edn. 1632), p.149.
30. Robert Burton, *The Anatomy of Melancholy*, ed. H. Jackson (London: Everyman, 1972), I, pp.211–12; III, pp.361–2. For a fuller discussion of Christian anti-Semitic descriptions of Jews in the period see Shapiro, *Shakespeare and the Jews*, pp.13–31.
31. For further details concerning Modena's connections with English Christians see Cecil Roth, "Leone da Modena and England", *Transactions of the Jewish Historical Society of England* 11 (1928), pp.206–25; idem., "Leone da Modena and his English Correspondents", *Transactions of the Jewish Historical Society of England* 17 (1953), pp.39–43; see also Howard E. Adelman, "Modena: Autobiography and the Man", in Mark Cohen (ed.), *The Autobiography of a Seventeenth-Century Venetian Rabbi: Leon Modena's Life of Judah* (Princeton: Princeton University Press, 1988), pp.19–49.

32. Thomas Coryat, *Coryat's Crudities* (London, 1611), excerpted in Roth, "Leone da Modena and England", pp.217–21, (pp.220, 221). The traveller William Lithgow also described the Jewish communities that he observed in Jerusalem in *The Total Discourse of the Rare Adventures and Painefill Peregrinations of Long Ninteene Yeares Travayles from Scotland* (1632).
33. Leon Modena, *The Life of Judah*, p.146; *The History of the Rites, Customes, and Manner of Life, of the Present Jews, throughout the World. Written in Italian by Leo Modena, a Rabbine of Venice. Translated into English, by Edmund Chilmead, Mr. of Arts, and Chaplain of Christ-Church* (London: John Martin, 1650); on Edmund Chilmead see *DNB*, IV, pp.257–8.
34. For a discussion of crypto-Jewish communities in England prior to readmission see David Katz, *The History of the Jews in England*, pp.107–44.
35. "The Authors Preface", *The History of the Rites, Customes, and Manner of Life, of the Present Jews, throughout the World*, C5r–v.
36. For further details see Katz, *Philo-semitism and the Readmission of the Jews*, pp.175–6.
37. Joanna Cartwright, *The Petition of the Jewes* (London: George Roberts, 1649), E.537 (17).
38. See Katz, *Philo-semitism and the Readmission of the Jews*, pp.177–82.
39. Joanna Cartwright, *The Petition of the Jewes*, A3r; for a fuller discussion of the economic implications of Jewish readmission see Edgar Samuel, "The Readmission of the Jews to England in 1656 in the Context of English Economic Policy", *Jewish Historical Studies* 31 (1988–90), pp.153–69.
40. See *Works*, pp.103–4; see also Aylmer, "The Religion of Gerrard Winstanley", pp.97–8, 100–101.
41. In the preface to *Truth Lifting up its Head above Scandals* Winstanley describes Everard as "the Redding Man" so it is possible that his acquaintance with Pordage – who had been a curate in Reading prior to becoming rector at Bradfield – was of long standing. See *Truth Lifting up its Head* in *Works*, p.103; see also Nigel Smith, *Perfection Proclaimed: Language and Literature in English Radical Religion 1640–1660* (Oxford: Oxford University Press, 1989), p.189.
42. John Pordage, *Innocencie Appearing* (London, 1655), p.68. For a fuller discussion of this text see Smith, *Perfection Proclaimed*, pp.205–14.
43. Cited by Smith, *Perfection Proclaimed*, pp.206–7.
44. *Two Letters to Lord Fairfax* in *Works*, p.349. This letter is also reprinted in *The Clarke 45.* For further details see Andrew Bradstock, *Faith in the Revolution*, pp.91–2.
47. Ibid., pp.524, 525, 528.
48. Ibid., p.528.

Civil Liberty in Milton, the Levellers and Winstanley

WARREN CHERNAIK

Despite the valiant efforts of Christopher Hill in *Milton and the English Revolution* to forge links between Milton and the "popular radical traditions" of the seventeenth century, Milton and Winstanley are still, in the conventional view, sharply contrasted as elitist and radical democrat.[1] Though few Miltonists would put this contrast in such crudely reductive terms as Aers and Kress, scornfully discussing Milton as "a leisured intellectual who never in his life *had* to work for a living", twentieth-century critics frequently find an element of "class prejudice" in Milton's insistence that "they who adhere to wisdom and truth" are necessarily "few": "Milton plainly claims to represent an intellectual elite, ''above the vulgar pitch'', propagators of "truth" in lesser mortals. Unlike Winstanley, he does not show any signs of having reflected on the social basis of this self-proclaimed elite and on its relationship to the powerful commercial and landed classes in England."[2] In my view – and here I largely agree with the position argued by Sharon Achinstein in *Milton and the Revolutionary Reader* – Milton, Winstanley and such Leveller pamphleteers as Walwyn, Overton and Lilburne, while observing the decorum of addressing particular audiences in differing circumstances, share in a common project: the creation of a public sphere of discourse which, by its very existence, challenged the hegemony of traditional ruling elites.[3]

The polemical writings of Milton, Winstanley and the Levellers are part of an unprecedented explosion of the printed word, much of it in the form of unlicensed pamphlets, during the period of the English Revolution. Indeed, the sheer bulk of the Thomason Collection in the British Library is stupefying – more than 22,000 pamphlets, bound in 2,272 stout volumes, as testimony of Milton's unsleeping "pens and heads ... sitting by their studious lamps, musing, searching, revolving new notions and idea's".[4] In its title alone, Richard Overton's *A Defiance against all Arbitrary Usurpations* (1646) illustrates the "transformation from a closed political arena into an open one": by making one's thoughts public in print, contemplation can be turned into action. Like his fellow Leveller John Lilburne, Overton characteristically presents his own situation as representative, potentially "every man's case": his pamphlet, according to its title page, has been "published by his friends for the publick benefit of all the Free-born people of England".[5] Licensing restrictions, Overton argues, as Milton had done three years earlier, though in markedly less aggressive terms, are injurious to the "publick good": "Yea, and this persecuted means of unlicensed Printing hath done more good to the people, then all the bloodie wars; the one tending to rid us quite of all slavery; but the other onely to rid us of one, and involve us into another."[6]

Milton's stance in the exordium to *Areopagitica* is that of the private citizen offering "publick advice", exercising the right of "free born men" to "speak free" to those in positions of authority in the state.

> They who to States and Governours of the Commonwealth direct their Speech ... or wanting such accesse in a private condition, write that which they foresee may advance the publick good; I suppose them as at the beginning of no meane endeavour, not a little alter'd and mov'd inwardly in their mindes: Some with doubt of what will be the successe, others with feare of what will be the censure.[7]

Though unlike Milton's tract it does not emphasize the state of mind of the private petitioner, uncertain of how his offering will be received by those wielding power, William Walwyn's *The Compassionate Samaritane* (1643), a plea for liberty of conscience addressed "To the Commons of England", assumes a similar stance at the outset:

> To you whom the People have chosen for the managing of their affaires, I present this necessary Treatise without boldnesse and without feare: for I am well assured, that as it is mine, and every mans duty, to furnish You with what we conceive will advanse the Common good ... so likewise it is, Your duty, to heare and put into execution, whatsoever to Your judgments shall appeare conducing to those good ends and purposes.[8]

Walwyn speaks of reciprocal duty (the duty of the representative body to hear, the duty of every citizen to furnish material for consideration – "I shall make bold as a Common of England to lay claim to that priviledge, being assured that I write nothing scandalous, or dangerous to the State"), where Milton foregrounds the vulnerability of the single, unprotected man, aware at all times of "the very attempt of this addresse thus made, and the thought of whom it hath recourse to".[9] Yet both proceed on the assumption that "the publick good" is or should be the common concern of those holding public office and those subject to civil authority who make their thoughts public in print.

Milton's contrast of "the old and elegant humanity of Greece" and "the barbarick pride of a *Hunnish* and *Norwegian stateliness*", or, a few sentences earlier, the contrast between "the magnanimity of a trienniall Parliament" and "that jealous hautinesse of Prelates and cabin Counsellours that usurpt of late" serves several functions.[10] In accordance with standard classical rhetorical principles, Milton uses judicious praise (which he carefully distinguishes from base "Courtship and flattery") to predispose his immediate audience toward receiving his advice sympathetically, while at the same time he sets both good and bad examples of the exercise of political authority before them, suggesting that they too are able to "abstain ... distinguish, and ... prefer that which is truly better". The eminence of the "High Court of Parlament", Milton suggests, is not the "bad eminence" of the "barbaric" tyrants of the "gorgeous East" (or in this case, the frozen North), nor are they subject to the petty jealousies of courtiers and prelates who would advance themselves above their fellow men, denying any common bond.[11] The implicit ideal of responsible, "milde and equall" government, "civill and gentle greatnesse" (recognizing the "greatnesse" while counselling those occupying high office to be "civill and gentle") is stated more fully in *The Readie and Easie Way* in the contrast of a king who "must be ador'd like a Demigod, with a dissolute and haughtie court about him" and "a free Commonwealth" where "they who are greatest" are "not elevated above their brethren; live soberly in thir families, walk the street as other men, may be spoken to freely, familiarly, friendly, without adoration".

It is possible that, as Nigel Smith suggests, the classical colouring so prominent in *Areopagitica* (beginning with the title and the Greek quotation on the title page) has republican implications, in invoking "the image of society in which individual virtue can flourish".[12] Again and again, Milton associates the practice of pre-publication censorship with popery and tyranny, contrasting the "ancient and famous Commonwealths" of Greece and Rome, where such "tyranny over learning" was unknown, with the inordinate presumption of would-be tyrants who, like "the Popes of *Rome* engrossing what they pleas'd of Politicall rule into their owne hands, extended their dominion over mens eyes".[13] In setting forth, later in *Areopagitica*, "the manifest hurt" licensing can do as "discouragement and affront" to learning, Milton appeals in part to patriotism, praising "the art, the wit, the grave and solid judgement which is in England" and presenting the imposition of licensing restrictions as "an undervaluing and vilifying of the whole Nation". In visits to "other Countries" and in particular Italy, Milton says: "I have sat among their lerned men ... and bin counted happy to be born in such a place of *Philosophic* freedom, as they suppos'd England was, while themselvs did nothing but bemoan the servil condition into which lerning amongst them was brought."[14] Here again praise is mixed with warning: freedom is something which must be strenuously defended, and which can easily be lost.

In his exordium, Milton defines civil liberty in terms of freedom of access, the willingness of those in power to listen to the grievances of those who seek redress. "For this is not the liberty which wee can hope, that no grievance ever should arise in the Commonwealth, that let no man in this World expect; but when complaints are freely heard, deeply consider'd, and speedily reform'd, then is the utmost bound of civill liberty attain'd that wise men looke for."[15] The "plainest advice", Milton argues, is "a kinde of praising", since in the well-ordered commonwealth "private persons are hereby animated to thinke ye better pleas'd with publick advice, then other statists have been delighted heretofore with publicke flattery".[16] In stating his central proposition, that Parliament be "willing to repeal [an] Act of your own setting forth ... by judging over again that Order which ye have ordain'd *to regulate Printing*", Milton suggests that Parliament not only should be open of access but that it should recognize "the voice of reason" and respond accordingly: "there can no greater testimony appear, than when your prudent spirit acknowledges and obeyes the voice of reason from what quarter soever it be heard speaking."[17] Walwyn uses a similar formula in addressing Parliament at the beginning and the end of *The Compassionate Samaritan*, reinforcing his argument with Biblical allusions immediately recognizable to his intended audience. His rhetorical strategy is to credit those he is addressing with the attributes he hopes to find in them – reason, compassion, "justnesse" – reminding them that power should be exercised responsibly.

> There are none left, to play the good Samaritanes part but Your selves, who as You have power; will, (I make no question) be willing too, when You have once well considered the matter, which this small Treatise will put You in mind to doe.
>
> The greatest glory of authority is to protect the distressed; and for those that are Judges in other mens causes to beare themselves as if the afflicted mens cases were their owne ... That so this Parliament will prove themselves loving Fathers to all sorts of good men, bearing equall respect to all, according to the trust reposed in them, and so inviting an equall affection and assistance from all: That after Ages may report of them, they did all these things, not because of the importunity of the people, or to please a party, but from the reason and justnesse of them, which did more sway with them, than a Petition subscribed with Twenty thousand hands could have done.[18]

Both Walwyn and Milton argue the fundamental equality of all persons before God ("bearing equall respect to all" – the equivalent phrase in Winstanley, repeated over and over again, is "without respect of persons") and the sovereignty of "the gift of reason" implanted in man by God and enabling him "to be his own chooser".[19] But, as a comparison of the two titles would suggest, Walwyn's characteristic analogies are Biblical rather than classical, and his arguments, far more than those in *Areopagitica*, are explicitly aimed at defence of Separatists, urging "that as well particular and private Congregations, as publike, may have publike protection." The idea that Parliament's authority rests on "the trust reposed in them", expressed in Walwyn's peroration, is never explicitly stated in *Areopagitica*, though the doctrine of popular sovereignty, with political power a derivative and revocable trust, is central to *The Tenure of Kings and Magistrates*: "It being thus manifest that the power of Kings and Magistrates is nothing else, but what is only derivative, transferr'd and committed to them in trust from the People, to the Common good of them all, in whom the power yet remaines fundamentally, and cannot be tak'n from them, without a violation of their natural birthright."[20]

In the digression in praise of Parliament in *An Apology* (1642), Milton again lists "the generall concourse of suppliants, the free and ready admittance, the willing and speedy redresse in what is possible" as signs of a restored commonwealth, aware of the importance of civil liberty as well as liberty of conscience. Yet Milton's encomium in the *Apology* presents the actions of the Long Parliament in remedying the "afflictions of this kingdome" as directly inspired by God, whose divine will is enacted through their means. In this attempt "to reach the height of their prayses" with an answerable style, Milton risks not only flattery (since one can hardly say that "greatest likelihoods are brought that such things are truly and really in those persons to whom they are ascribed") but the very identification of earthly power and divine power he argues against elsewhere:

> It will not seem much otherwise, then as if some divine commission from heav'n were descended to take into hearing and commiseration the long remedilesse afflictions of this kingdome ... Therefore the more they seeke to humble themselves, the more does God by manifest signes and testimonies visibly honour their proceedings; and sets them as the mediators of this his coven'nt which he offers us to renew ... Such acceptation have their prayers found with him, that to them he hath bin pleas'd to make himselfe the agent, and immediat performer of their desires; dissolving their difficulties when they are thought inexplicable, cutting out wayes for them where no passage could be seene.[21]

A passage in *Areopagitica* in some respects comparable presents not accomplishment, but "human capacity" or potential, not the immediate miraculous intervention of God in ways that ignore the ordinary processes of nature but the activities of ordinary citizens in their daily lives. Milton begins with a direct address to Parliament, characterizing them as members of the body they represent: "Lords and Commons of England, consider what Nation it is wherof ye are, and wherof ye are the governours: a Nation not slow and dull, but of a quick, ingenious, and piercing spirit, acute to invent, suttle and sinewy to discours, not beneath the reach of any point the highest that human capacity can soar to."[22] The element of "patriotic fervour ... expressed in resonant apocalyptic terms" has been noted by Michael Wilding and others: the claim that England as a nation has been specially chosen as "separate to God, / Design'd for great exploits" is characteristic of Puritan revolutionary thought of the Civil War period. In *Areopagitica*, far more than in *An Apology*, the millennial hope is advanced as "propending" – an inclination, a possibility offered, a beginning ("some rousing motions", as Milton later puts it in *Samson Agonistes*):[23]

> Yet that which is above all this, the favour and the love of heav'n we have great argument to think in a peculiar manner propitious and propending towards us. Why else was this Nation chos'n before any other, that out of her as out of *Sion*, should be proclaim'd and sounded forth the first tidings and trumpet of Reformation to all *Europ*? ... Now once again by all concurrence of signs ... God is decreeing to begin some new and great period in his Church, ev'n to the reforming of Reformation it self: what does he then but reveal Himself to his servants, and as his manner is, first to his English-men?[24]

Throughout the "mansion house of liberty" passage, Milton suggests the distinct possibility that the prophetic hopes will not be fulfilled, that "we mark not the method of [God's] counsels, and are unworthy", that Parliament, choosing wrongly and ignoring the advice offered, will fail to show "a little generous prudence, a little forbearance of one another, and some grain of charity".[25] The aim of Milton's persuasive rhetoric here is to counteract those who "counsell ye to such a suppressing",[26] to convince his immediate audience to share his transformative vision. The passage is in its implications profoundly egalitarian: learned men "sitting by their studious lamps", artisans busily hammering away at the forge, soldiers in the field all labour in their chosen vocation, with no distinctions of rank, each seeking to serve "beleaguer'd Truth" in a different way.[27] If we compare this passage to the equally celebrated peroration of *The Readie and Easie Way* (a tract which is optimistic only in its title), we find in the earlier text none of Milton's notorious elitism or scorn for "the general defection of a misguided and abus'd multitude";[28] instead, the writer presents himself as one of many "labourers" in a common cause. The powerful rhetoric of the *Areopagitica* passage seeks to enlist the reader in that cause: the opening imperative "Behold", the immediacy and propulsive force of the drumroll of present participles (which make "reading" and "musing" forms of action), the urgency of the rhetorical questions, the interwoven metaphors of warfare and harvest, all point the reader in the direction of hope rather than fear, making the millennium seem imminent rather than a distant promise providing consolation in adversity.

> Behold now this vast City: a City of refuge, the mansion house of liberty, encompast and surrounded with his protection; the shop of warre hath not there more anvils and hammers waking, to fashion out the plates and instruments of armed Justice in defence of beleaguer'd Truth, then there be pens and heads there, sitting by their studious lamps, musing, searching, revolving new notions and ideas wherewith to present, as with their homage and their fealty the approaching Reformation; others as fast reading, trying all things, assenting to the force of reason and convincement. What could a man require more from a Nation so pliant and so prone to seek after knowledge. What wants there to such a towardly and pregnant soile, but wise and faithfull labourers, to make a knowing people, a Nation of Prophets, of Sages, and of Worthies. We reck'n more than five months yet to harvest; there need not be five weeks, had we but eyes to lift up, the fields are white already.[29]

A significantly different view of civil liberty, and in particular the readiness of access and responsiveness of those exercising power in the state, can be found in a number of pamphlets by Richard Overton, Walwyn's associate among the Levellers, and the "true leveller" Gerrard Winstanley, written during the 1640s. *A Remonstrance of Many Thousand Citizens, and other Free-born People of England, To their owne House of Commons* (1646) follows the same conventions of direct address as *Areopagitica* and *The Compassionate Samaritane*. Unlike these two pamphlets, it is presented as a collective utterance, rather than the work of an individual author writing "from his private house" (in this respect it resembles Winstanley's *A Declaration from the Poor Oppressed People of England* (1649), with forty-five names, including Winstanley's, subscribed at the end). The only name the *Remonstrance* bears on its title page is that of John Lilburne, not the author but a private citizen whose civil liberties, the pamphlet argues, have been violated by "Illegal and Barbarous Imprisonment". The *Remonstrance*, like several of the works I have been discussing, uses the language of trust in outlining the relationship between those in power and "the Universality of the People", but it does so in a markedly confrontational, assertive way:

> Wee are well assured, yet cannot forget, that the cause of our choosing you to be *Parliament-men*, was to deliver us from all kind of Bondage,

> and to preserve the Common-wealth in Peace and Happinesse: For effecting whereof, we possessed you with the same Power that was in our selves, to have done the same; For we might justly have done it our selves without you, if wee had thought it convenient ... But yee are to remember, this was only of us but a Power of trust, [which is ever revokable, and cannot be otherwise,] and to be imployed to no other end, then our owne well-being ... As ye well know, Wee are your Principalls, and you our Agents; it is a Truth which you cannot but acknowledge.[30]

In stating the principle of popular sovereignty at the outset, the *Remonstrance* makes it clear where in its view the ultimate power should lie, citing its axioms as self-evident. Like other radical pamphlets of the period, including those of Winstanley, it uses a vocabulary of bondage and freedom, tyranny and deliverance: one tyrant and oppressor has simply replaced another, as for Milton "*New Presbyter* is but *Old Priest* writ large": "For if you or any other shall assume, or exercise any Power, that is not derived from our Trust and choice thereunto, that Power is no lesse than a usurpation and an Oppression, from which we expect to be freed, in whomsoever we finde it; it being altogether inconsistent with the nature of *just Freedome*, which yee also very well understand."[31] The counsel offered in the *Remonstrance* is for Parliament no longer to perpetuate itself ("Ye have now sate full five yeeres, which is four yeeres longer then wee intended"), but instead to call new elections, and to reform its behaviour toward the civil liberties of its citizens. Throughout the pamphlet, the second-person address holds forth the possibility (theoretical at least) that Parliament will recognize the justice of these severe criticisms and moderate its behaviour accordingly.[32] Overton particularly emphasizes a failure of civility, a wilful separation of the members of Parliament from their fellow citizens and equals:

> Wee can scarcely approach your Door with a Request or motion, though by way of Petition, but yee hold long debates, whether Wee break not your *Priviledges* ... Yee now frequently commit mens Persons to Prison without shewing Cause; Yee examine men upon *Interrogatories* and *Questions* against themselves, and Imprison them for refusing to answere ... Ye have listned to any Counsells, rather than to the voice of us that trusted you: Why is it that you have stopt the Presse; but that you would have nothing but pleasing flattering Discourses, and go on to make your selves partakers of the *Lordship over us*, without hearing anything to the contrary ... Yee are extreamely altered in demeanour towards us, in the beginning yee seemed to know what Freedome was; made a distinction of honest

> men, whether rich or poor, all were welcome to you, and yee would mix your selves with us in a loving familiar way, void of Courtly observance or behaviour.[33]

In Overton's *An Appeale From the degenerate Representative Body the Commons of England assembled at Westminster: To the Body Represented* (1647), with the author identified boldly on the title page as "Richard Overton, Prisoner in the infamous Goale of Newgate, for the Liberties and Freedomes of England", there is no longer even the fiction that the Parliament is capable of listening to counsel and reforming itself. Overton begins by conceding that there are no historical precedents for his defiance of Parliament's authority. "It is confessed, that our *English Histories* and *Records* of the *Actions* and *Transactions* of our *Predecessours*, both of ancient and late times, (so far as I can understand) do not afford me any example or president for any APPEALE from Parliaments to people, neither is there any such liberty provided in th *Letter* of our law." In his justification, he cites the principle of trust: those who abuse the power they have forfeit their right to power, which then reverts to the hands of those who entrusted it:

> A*ll betrusted powers if forfeit, fall into the hands of the betrusters* ... and where such a forfeit is committed ... disoblegeth from obedience ... While the *Betrusted* are *dischargers* of their *trust*, it remaineth in their hands, but no sooner the *Betrusted* betray and forfeit their *Trust*, but (as all things else in dissolution) it returneth from whence it came, even to the hands of the *Trusters*.[34]

As proof that Parliament has turned oppressor, Overton cites some of the same abuses mentioned in the *Remonstrance*, but in stronger and more vivid, concrete terms, creating a miniature drama, complete with dialogue and stage directions. In the *Appeale*, Overton accuses the two Houses of Parliament, "Traytors to their Trust", of being deaf to the complaints of the common people (like Winstanley, he is "confident, that it must be the poore, the simple and meane things of this earth that must confound the mighty") and of treating "the *Rights and freedomes* of the *people*" with contempt. Parliament has now become "they", rather than being addressed as "you":

> This is their course, in stead of Relief for oppression, themselves do *oppresse*, and which is worst, then *stop the* mouthes of the oppressed ... shut their doores and eares against the cry of the people, both of Country and City ... Yet these very men contrary to their many Oathes, Covenants, Declarations, Vowes and Protestations, call the Petitioners *Rogues, Villains, seditious, factious fellowes*, and bid a *pox of God on them*, offer to draw their Swords at them, life up their *Canes* at them

> in a menacing manner, shake them by the shoulders, and otherwise abuse them, and not only so; but imprison some of them.[35]

In another passage filled with vivid particularizing detail Overton describes his own arrest and brutal treatment, "most incivilly and inhumanely dragged to *Newgate* headlong through the streets upon the stones through all the dirt and the mire", to remain in prison without redress for several months.[36] Like Lilburne in a number of his pamphlets, Overton seeks to make the reader "a present audience" – in Joan Webber's words, "dramatizing events taking place in his own city, on familiar streets, among his neighbors".[37] As Lilburne does in *London's Liberty in Chains discovered* (1646), Overton lays particular stress on the incivility of the "unnaturall and cruell" treatment of his wife, as innocent victim of her husband's persecutors. The conduct of the officers of the state is made to appear even more "barbarous" when directed at a woman "with her tender infant of half a years of age in her armes" (and one "of godly conversation", untainted by "incivility or immodesty"), whom they drag "headlong upon the stones ... reviling and abusing her with the scurrilous names of Whore Strumpet, &c".[38] Lilburne in a comparable passage overtly evokes standards of courtesy and civility, illustrating their violation with authenticating local detail which makes the reader an eye-witness:

> [The officer] without any more adoe, laid violent hands upon her, and endeavoured to throw her down the next staires, which are three or four steps ... but being not content with this, he followed her into the Court of Requests-chamber, and took her by the throat, as if he would have throtled her, and would have drag'd her away as a prisoner ... a piece of unmanlike cruelty and barbarism, which will be in future ages, a badge of shame.[39]

At several points in *London's Liberty in Chains discovered*, Lilburne addresses his audience of London citizens directly, reminding them "how, and by whom your Rights and Liberties have been invaded, and how you are inslaved".

> This briefe relation, thus made unto you, may bee a sufficient discovery of the intentions and sinister ends of your great *Masters*, to continue you still under an enforced slavery and subjection ... Look but upon your industrious *Neighbour-Nation*, the Netherlands ... if wee will but tread in the same steps, each one labouring in his place to preserve the common Liberties and Lawes of the Kingdome, which makes us indeed true free-men, without seeking, or endeavouring to Lord it thus (as we now do) one over anothers faith; your Brethren, together with you, and all the Commons of *England*, have an equall

> interest, and property in the Law, being all of us free-born *Englishmen*.[40]

The slippage here from "you" to "wee" and "us" is significant, since the author's strategy, like Milton's in *Areopagitica*, is to enlist himself (or his authorial persona) and those he is addressing in a common cause, "each one labouring in his place".

Overton's appeal to the people in defiance of the power that has imprisoned him without due process of law has a no less practical side. On the title page he directs the *Appeale* "in especiall" to "His Excellency, Sir *Thomas Fairfax* (Captaine Generall) and to all the Officers and Souldiers under his Command", and at the end of the pamphlet, with a markedly more conciliatory, even deferential tone, addresses the army (from its "most excellent Generall" to its "Gentleman Souldiers"), announcing that he will offer "my person and my cause unto your defensive protection" and redefining "the people" as the Army: "to make my humble address and appeale unto this Army, as to the *naturall Head* of the *Body naturall* of the people at this present."[41] At this particular moment in the struggles for power between the rival forces of Army and Parliament in the late 1640s, then, Overton firmly aligns himself with the Army – though in 1648 and 1649, he and other Leveller leaders would be deeply suspicious of the Army greandees as potential tyrants and oppressors.

Winstanley's pamphlets on behalf of the Diggers are all based on the assumption that words must be subordinate and ancillary to action, and all employ the decorum of direct address, appeals aimed at one or another of the various groups contending for power in the shifting political circumstances of 1649–52.[42] *A Declaration from the Poor Oppressed People of England*, addressed to "you that call yourself lords of manors and lords of the land", seeks to challenge rather than persuade, using the second-person address as a declaration of hostilities, distinguishing the enlightened from the unenlightened, the propertiless from the propertied.

> The King of righteousness, our maker, hath enlightened our hearts so far as to see that the earth was not made purposely for you to be lords of it, and we to be your slaves, servants and beggars; but it was made to be a common livelihood to all, without respect of persons ...
>
> Therefore we are resolved to be cheated no longer, nor be held under the slavish fear of you no longer, seeing the earth was made for us as well as you ... If we lie still and let you steal away our birthrights, we perish; if we petition we perish also, though we have paid taxes, given free-quarter and ventured our lives as much as you.[43]

All Winstanley's other pamphlets in defence of the actions of the Diggers are pleas for support, urging those in positions of power to recognize their common cause with the ordinary people, with whose aid and on whose behalf they had overthrown the monarchy. Here for example is *An Appeal to the House of Commons*:

> The cause is this: wee amongst others of the common people ... have ever been friends to the Parliament ... You of the gentry, as well as we of the comonalty, all groaned under the burden of the bad government and burdening laws under the late King Charles ... We looked upon you to be our chief council, to agitate business for us ...
>
> Stop not your ears against the secret mourning of the oppressed ... lest the Lord see it and be offended and shut his ears against your cries, and work a deliverance for his waiting people some other way than by you.[44]

Again it is "you" and "we", but as allies in the war recently fought (*A New-Yeers Gift* begins "Gentlemen of the Parliament and Army: you and the common people have assisted each other to cast out the head of oppression which was kingly power seated in one man's hand"), as active agent and body represented, as ears to listen and voice to speak out. The Biblical echoes in the last of these passages from the *Appeal* suggests that supplication can modulate into warning: in a single paragraph, Winstanley can juxtapose practical arguments from mutual interest ("you and we joined purse and person together in this common cause") and heightened passages of exhortation, addressed to those who are wilfully deaf and will not hear. In these pamphlets, Winstanley's stance again and again is that of the Old Testament prophet urging repentance before it is too late:

> Let not pride blind your eyes, that you should forget you are the nation's servants.
>
> O that there were a heart in you to consider of these things, and act righteousness, how sweetly might you and the people live together. If you grant this freedom we speak of, you gain the hearts of the nation; if you neglect this, you will fall as fast in their affections as ever you rise. I speak what I see, and do you observe; slight not that love that speaks feelingly, from the sense of the nation's burdens.[45]

The voice of inspired prophecy, warning against man's iniquities, is clearly present in the preface to *A Watch-word to the City of London and the Armie* (1649), where he speaks of himself as having had a vision in a trance, with a "voice within me [which] bade me declare it all abroad": "I have declared this truth to the Army and Parliament, and now I have declared it to thee likewise, that none of you that are the fleshly strength of this land may be left without excuse, for now you have all been spoken to."[46] Winstanley, as a passage in *A New-Yeers Gift* illustrates, interpreted the

Sermon on the Mount and the prophecies of Isaiah literally: the apocalyptic transformation he envisioned would exalt the humble and topple the mighty from their seats. Lawyers interested only in "the lodging of ... estates in [their] purse", hireling clergymen who "deceive the people by a shew of holiness or spiritual doctrine, as they call it, difficult to be understood by any but themselves", rich landowners who live off "the fruit of other men's labours, not their own" are all part of a corrupt system which must be swept away. "For I tell you and your preachers, that Scripture which saith *The poor shall inherit the earth*, is really and materially to be fulfilled. … And I see the poor must first be picked and honoured in this work, for they begin to receive the word of righteousness, but the rich generally are enemies to true freedom."[47]

Winstanley in addressing those in positions of power – Fairfax, Cromwell, the Army, the Parliament – presents himself not simply as a private citizen but as a poor man, dressed in humble garments, working with his hands, one whose language is simple, unadorned and direct, and who speaks the truth on behalf of those, like him, who can "hardly get bread, but with great difficulty": "I tell you this is a sore evil, and this is truth; therefore think upon it, it is a poor man's advice, and you shall find weight in it, if you do as well as say."[48] In addressing *The Law of Freedom* to the victorious Cromwell, "head of a people who have cast out an oppressing Pharaoh", in 1652, he uses a series of striking metaphors which, though self-deprecatory in tone, equate poverty and humble birth with the capacity to illuminate. Cromwell is praised by implication as one able to recognize the truth under the "clownish" outward trappings: "And now I have set the candle at your door, for you have power in your hand, in this other added opportunity, to act for common freedom if you will: I have no power ... Though this platform be like a piece of timber rough hewed, yet the discreet workmen may take it and frame a handsome building out of it." "It is like a poor man that comes clothed to your door in a torn country garment, who is unacquainted with the learned citizens' unsettled forms and fashions; take off the clownish language, for under that you may see beauty."[49]

Yet when Winstanley uses direct address in the eloquent and moving peroration of *A New-Yeers Gift*, it does not appear to reflect the expectations that any person or group with "power in [its] hand" will provide succour for the downtrodden and oppressed. Indeed, the apocalyptic vision here leaves little scope for human agency or for the gradual, piecemeal remodelling of society and correction of abuses. Instead, hope is deferred to the time of the Second Coming, fervently awaited, when everything will be miraculously transformed and the dreams of the oppressed and powerless will finally come true.

> And this shall be your misery, O you covetous oppressing tyrants of the earth, not only you great self-seeking powers of England but you powers of all the world. The people shall all fall off from you, and you shall fall on a sudden like a great tree that is undermined at the root ... You or some of you hate the name Leveller, and the chiefest of you are afraid and ashamed to own a Leveller, and you laugh and jeer at them. Well, laugh out, poor blind souls: the people and common soldiers both lets you alone, but they laugh in their hearts at you ...
>
> The time is very near that the people generally shall loathe and be ashamed of your kingly power, in your preaching, in your laws, in your counsels, as now you are ashamed of the Levellers. I tell you Jesus Christ who is that powerful spirit of love is the head Leveller; and *as he is lifted up, he will draw men after him*, and leave you naked and bare, and make you ashamed in yourselves.[50]

When Milton speaks of civil liberty in *The Readie and Easie Way*, he associates it once more with the open access of ordinary citizens to those in power, adding that "civil rights" (undefined) should be protected and that the ideal state should be meritocratic, allowing equality of opportunity, and (of course) a republic rather than a monarchy: "The other part of our freedom consists in the civil rights and advancements of every person according to his merit: the enjoyment of those never more certain, and the access to these never more open, than in a free Commonwealth."[51] Yet it is curious that both Milton in *The Readie and Easie Way* and Winstanley in *The Law of Freedom*, in formulating detailed blueprints for a utopian society, restrict freedom severely, and show a marked distrust for the common people, praised so extravagantly in their earlier tracts. The "free commonwealth" proposed in *The Readie and Easie Way* is extremely remote from egalitarian democracy, with a severely limited franchise and power vested in a perpetual Senate – a "general councel of ablest men" chosen by this limited electorate, with its members, once elected, to hold office until death.[52] Distrustful of "the noise and shouting of a rude multitude" so foolish as to desire a return of monarchy, Milton goes so far as to urge compulsion on those who differ from his opinion of "the main end of government": "Is it just or reasonable, that most voices against the main end of government should enslave the less number that would be free? More just it is doubtless, if it com to force, that a less number compell a greater to retain, which can be no wrong to them, thir libertie, then that a greater number for the pleasure of thir baseness, compell a less most injuriously to be thir fellow slaves."[53] This argument for the forcible rule of the enlightened minority over the unregenerate majority, added in the second edition of *The Readie and Easie Way*, has been much discussed by critics, most of whom see the passage as sharply contrasting with the advocacy of liberty in Milton's earlier writings.[54]

Winstanley's imagined ideal commonwealth, presented to Cromwell in 1652, resembles *The Readie and Easie Way*, Harrington's *The Commonwealth of Oceana* (1656), and other writings of the decade following the abolition of the monarchy – "seeing England is declared to be a free commonwealth and the name thereof established by law", Winstanley writes, "surely then the greatest work is now to be done" – in its concern with the settling of the state on republican principles. Corns has seen *The Law of Freedom* as a gradualist document, showing a willingness to "compromise" in the hope that "partial implementation" of reforms might be an attainable end.[55] Yet the model of government Winstanley sets out in *The Law of Freedom* is extraordinarily authoritarian, with a multitude of laws (though no lawyers), a complicated bureaucracy of overseers, task-masters, peace-makers, police and executioners in each parish, punishing offenders with whips, forced labour, "short diet", imprisonment and (for repeated offences) death, insisting on unquestioning obedience of children to parents, and giving to this very unfree commonwealth the power to assign all citizens to one or another labour or trade, allowing no one to live idle or "neglect the duty of his place": "if there were not power in the hand of officers, the spirit of rudeness would not be obedient to any law of government but their own wills."[56] Twentieth-century scholars have disagreed over the extent to which the emphasis on "the subjection of men to the secular discipline of the state" in *The Law of Freedom* is compatible with, or can be predicted from, Winstanley's earlier writings. In an interesting essay, J.C. Davis, arguing that "Winstanley always had a respect for power and ... was never an anti-authoritarian", sees *The Law of Freedom* as the logical culmination of Winstanley's earlier political writings. Corns, who emphasizes the politics of Winstanley's address to Cromwell "as a potential patron or agent of revolutionary change", nevertheless finds in *The Law of Freedom* an element of "pessimism which partly subverts his purpose".[57] Hill, whose treatment of *The Law of Freedom* I find generally persuasive, characterizes this work, the longest and most elaborate of Winstanley's political pamphlets, as the product of "bitter experience", predicated on the failure of the Digger experiment: "the heyday of the Revolution was over, and with it Winstanley's optimistic confidence."[58]

Barbara Lewalski has argued convincingly for the basic consistency of Milton's political views in the pamphlets written in the rapidly changing circumstances of 1659–60, seeing *The Readie and Easie Way*, in its two versions, each "endeavoring to deal directly with existing conditions", as illustrative of Milton's "practical attempt to rescue the Puritan cause, if possible, from the ever-increasing perils besetting it". Hill similarly argues that "the perpetual oligarchy recommended in the tract was far from being Milton's ideal solution: it was the only remedy he could think of to check the Gadarene rush to monarchy".[59] Nevertheless, even if the conviction that "only those who have attained inner freedom can properly value or long maintain political liberty" ("For who loves that must first be wise and good", in the words of Sonnet XII) remained a central Miltonic doctrine throughout his career, the authoritarian cast of the argument in favour of compulsion in *The Readie and Easie Way* does appear to limit the scope of civil liberty to an extraordinary degree. What underlies the deep pessimism of this passage, as of the far more attractive, eloquent passage which ends *The Readie and Easie Way*, is, as Arthur Barker suggests, a "sense of God's desertion", an awareness that no one is listening.[60] The conventions of direct address, of counsel freely offered and received, have broken down, and all that is left is prophetic lament, a farewell to liberty: "they may permitt us a little Shroving-time first, wherin to speak freely, and take our leaves of Libertie."[61] Though Milton in his peroration allows for the possibility of a saving remnant, "sensible and ingenuous men" not immune to rational persuasion, the passage is permeated with the awareness that all is lost, and that the hope of experiencing a revival of liberty must be deferred indefinitely:

> Thus much I should perhaps have said though I was sure I should have spoken only to trees and stones; and had none to cry to, but with the Prophet, *O earth, earth, earth*! to tell the very soil it self, what her perverse inhabitants are deaf to. Nay though what I have spoke should happ'n (which Thou suffer not, who didst create mankinde free, nor Thou next, who didst redeem us from being servants of men!) to be the last words of our expiring libertie. But I trust I shall have spoken perswasion to abundance of sensible and ingenuous men; to som perhaps whom God may raise of these stones to become children of reviving libertie; and may reclaim, though they seem now chusing them a captain back for *Egypt*, to bethink themselves a little and consider whither they are rushing.[62]

NOTES

All references to Milton's prose are to *Complete Prose Works* (New Haven and London: Yale University Press, 1953–82); subsequent references to *CPW*. Quotations from *Paradise Lost* and other poems by Milton are from *The Poems of John Milton*, ed. John Carey and Alistair Fowler (London: Longman, 1968).

1. Christopher Hill, *Milton and the English Revolution* (London: Faber and Faber, 1977), pp.69–116, 95. In arguing for the "affinities" between his ideas and those of his radical contemporaries (p.115), Hill sees Milton as "living in a state of permanent dialogue with radical views which he could not wholly accept, yet some of which greatly attracted him" (pp.113–14).
2. David Aers and Gunther Kress, "Historical Process, Individual and Communities in Milton's Early Prose", in Francis Barker *et al.* (eds.), *1642: Literature and Power in the Seventeenth Century* (Colchester: University of Essex, 1981), pp.294–5; *Eikonoklastes*, *CPW*, III, p.348. More sophisticated and nuanced accounts which emphasize Milton's intellectual, social and religious elitism include Michael Fixler, *Milton and the Kingdoms of God* (London: Faber and Faber, 1964), pp.160–69; and Annabel Patterson, "'Forc'd Fingers': Milton's Early Poems and Ideological Constraint", in Claude J. Summers and Ted-Larry Pebworth (eds.), *"The Muses Commonweal": Poetry and Politics in the Seventeenth Century* (Columbia: University of Missouri Press, 1988), pp.16–22.
3. Sharon Achinstein, *Milton and the Revolutionary Reader* (Princeton: Princeton University Press, 1994), pp.8–16 and *passim*. In arguing for Milton as a writer who, like Lilburne and other Leveller pamphleteers, encouraged his readers "to think of themselves in new ways", as "active and informed participants in the political process" (pp.32, 42), Achinstein draws on the ideas of Jürgen Habermas, *The Structural Transformation of the Public Sphere*, tr. Thomas Burger (Cambridge: Polity Press, 1992), esp. pp.25–6.
4. *Areopagitica*, *CPW*, II, p.554; *Catalogue of the Pamphlets ... collected by George Thomason, 1640–1661*, 2 vols. (London, 1908), I, xxi; Achinstein, *Milton and the Revolutionary Reader*, pp.1, 13–14.
5. Richard Overton, *A Defiance against all Arbitrary Usurpations* (1646), Thomason tracts E353 (17), title page; Achinstein, *Milton and the Revolutionary Reader*, p.10. On Lilburne's self-presentation as "both an ordinary man and a symbol of all men", see Joan Webber, *The Eloquent "I": Style and Self in Seventeenth-Century Prose* (Madison and London: University of Wisconsin Press, 1968), p.58; on printing as a form of action, see ibid., p.15.
6. Overton, *Defiance*, p.26.
7. *CPW*, II, ed. Ernest Sirluck, pp.485, 486, 488.
8. *The Compassionate Samaritane* (1644), in Jack R. McMichael and Barbara Taft (eds.), *The Writings of William Walwyn* (Athens and London: University of Georgia Press, 1989), p.100.
9. Ibid., p.100; *CPW*, II, p.487.
10. *CPW*, II, pp.488–9.
11. Ibid., pp.486–7, 488–9, 514–15; *Paradise Lost*, II, pp.1–6. On the persuasive strategies of *Areopagitica*, see the excellent discussion by Sirluck in *CPW*, II, pp.172–8.
12. *The Readie and Easie Way to Establish a Free Commonwealth* (2nd edition, 1660), *CPW*, VII, ed. Robert W. Ayers and Austin Woolrych, p.425; *CPW*, II, 488–9; Nigel Smith, "*Areopagitica*: Voicing Contexts, 1643–5", in David Loewenstein and James Grantham Turner (eds.), *Politics, Poetics, and Hermeneutics in Milton's Prose* (Cambridge and New York: Cambridge University Press, 1990), p.116.
13. *CPW*, II, pp.493, 501, 539.
14. Ibid., II, pp.530, 535, 537–8.
15. Ibid., II, p.487.
16. Ibid., II, p.488.
17. Ibid., pp.490–91.
18. *The Writings of William Walwyn*, pp.100, 123–4. The general parallel with *The*

Compassionate Samaritane is pointed out in *CPW*, II, p.490. Sharon Achinstein points out how Lilburne uses a similar rhetorical strategy in his successful defence against the charge of treason: "By claiming the jury was comprised of reasonable men, he was urging that they act reasonably to acquit him; by expressing their identity as his 'peers' and 'brothers', he was enjoining them to act in consort with him" (Achinstein, *Milton and the Revolutionary Reader*, p.50).

19. *CPW*, II, p.514.
20. *The Writings of William Walwyn*, p.124; *CPW*, III, p.202.
21. *CPW*, I, pp.922, 926–7. I have discussed this passage at some length in "Christian liberty in Marvell and Milton", in R.C. Richardson and G.M. Ridden (eds.), *Freedom and the English Revolution* (Manchester: Manchester University Press, 1986), pp.53–5.
22. *CPW*, II, p.551.
23. *Samson Agonistes*, 31–2, 1382; Michael Wilding, "Milton's *Areopagitica*: Liberty for the Sects", in Thomas N. Corns (ed.), *The Literature of Controversy* (London: Frank Cass, 1987), pp.20–21. Cf. Hill, *Milton and the English Revolution*, pp.179–84; and David Loewenstein, *Milton and the Drama of History* (Cambridge: Cambridge University Press, 1990), pp.37–9, 42–7.
24. *CPW*, II, pp.552–3.
25. Ibid., II, pp.553–4.
26. Ibid., p.559.
27. Cf. Wilding, "Milton's *Areopagitica*", pp.21–5.
28. *CPW*, VII, p.463.
29. CPW, II, pp.553–4. David Loewenstein, in discussing this passage, comments on "Milton's sense of the resurgent, almost tangible energy of the regenerate body politic" in describing "the teeming city preparing itself for war" (*Milton and the Drama of History*, p.46).
30. Don M. Wolfe (ed.), *Leveller Manifestoes of the Puritan Revolution* (New York and London: Thomas Nelson and Sons, 1944), pp.112–13; *LFOW*, p.108; *Areopagitica, CPW*, II, p.489.
31. *Leveller Manifestoes*, p.113; "On the New Forcers of Conscience under the Long Parliament", p.20. Joseph Frank, in *The Levellers* (New York: Russell and Russell, 1969), pp.81–5, characterizes the Remonstrance as "in both matter and manner an explosive document", with a tone which is a "mixture of threatening belligerence and optimistic idealism".
32. Overton uses a similar approach in *An Arrow against All Tyrants* (1646), Thomason tracts E356 (14), which once again begins with a clear statement of the principles of popular sovereignty and delegated powers held in trust (pp.3–4). The pamphlet concludes with an eloquent plea to the House of Commons, attempting to shame them into behaving in accordance with their trust as "Commissioners, and lawfull Deputies": "Therefore now step in or never, and discharge your duties to God and to us, and tell us no longer that such motions are *not yet seasonable, and wee must still wait* ... For shame, let never such things be spoken, far less recorded to future generations" (p.15).
33. *Leveller Manifestoes*, pp.127, 120–21, 123, 126.
34. Ibid., pp.156–7, 162.
35. Ibid, pp.168, 170, 188.
36. Ibid., 164.
37. Webber, *The Eloquent "I"*, pp.74–5.
38. *Leveller Manifestoes*, p.165.
39. *London's Liberty in Chains discovered* (1646), Thomason tracts E 359 (17), p.33.
40. Ibid., pp.9–11.
41. *Leveller Manifestoes*, pp.156, 184. Frank points out that, as in the arguments of the Levellers in the Putney Debates that year, the New Model Army, directly addressed in *An Appeale*, is presented as "the only instrument potentially willing and able to execute the will of the people" (*The Levellers*, p.125).
42. On Winstanley's "shrewd grasp of realpolitik" in addressing his pamphlets in defense of the Diggers to potential allies within the Army and Parliament, see Thomas N. Corns,

Uncloistered Virtue: English Political Literature, 1640–1660 (Oxford: Oxford University Press, 1992), pp.165–9.

43. *LFOW*, pp.99, 104.
44. *An Appeal*, in *LFOW*, pp.111, 114–15.
45. *A New-Yeers Gift* in *LFOW*, pp.161, 167; *An Appeale*, in *LFOW*, pp.114, 118. On the use of the language of Old Testament prophecy in Winstanley's writings in defence of the Diggers, see Christopher Hill, *The Religion of Gerrard Winstanley*, Past and Present Supplement, no. 5 (Oxford, 1978), pp.29–32; and George M. Shulman, *Radicalism and Reverence: The Political Thought of Gerrard Winstanley* (Berkeley and Los Angeles: University of California Press, 1989), pp.75–6, 99–107.
46. *A Watch-word*, in *LFOW*, pp.127, 129.
47. *The Law of Freedom in a Platform: Or, True Magistracy Restored*, in *LFOW*, pp.279, 287, 298; *New-Yeers Gift*, in *LFOW*, p.203; *A Watch-word*, in LFOW, p.149.
48. *A New-Yeers Gift*, in *LFOW*, p.168.
49. *The Law of Freedom*, in *LFOW*, pp.275, 285–6.
50. *A New-Yeers Gift*, in *LFOW*, pp.203–4.
51. *CPW*, VII, p.458.
52. *CPW*, VII, p.432.
53. *CPW*, VII, pp.442, 455.
54. See, for example, Arthur Barker, *Milton and the Puritan Dilemma* (Toronto: University of Toronto Press, 1942), pp.270–73; and Austin Woolrych's discussion of this passage in *CPW*, VII, pp.211–12, 215–18. A notable exception to this critical consensus is Francis Barker in *The Tremulous Private Body: Essays on Subjection* (Ann Arbor: University of Michigan Press, 2nd edn. 1995), pp.38–47, who argues that the ideology underlying *Areopagitica* is itself authoritarian, representing "a fresh form of control" in constituting a pattern of subjectivity "which is already internally disciplined, censored, and thus an effective support of the emergent pattern of domination" (pp.41–2); a similar view of *Areopagitica* as "severely repressive" is advanced, less subtly, in John Illo, "Areopagiticas Mythic and Real", *Prose Studies* 11 (1988), pp.1–23.
55. *The Law of Freedom in a Platform*, in *LFOW*, p.313; Corns, *Uncloistered Virtue*, pp.172–3. The opening sentence of *The Law of Freedom*, chapter I, identifies the overriding necessity of "these days" as "to find out where true freedom lies, that the commonwealth of England might be established in peace" (p.249). On Harrington, Marvell, and other writers who proposed a non-monarchical settlement between 1652 and 1656, see my discussion in Warren Chernaik and Martin Dzelzainis (eds.), *Marvell and Liberty* (London: Macmillan, 1999), pp.202–6.
56. *The Law of Freedom in a Platform*, in *LFOW*, pp.288–9, 324–337, esp. 332–3.
57. J.C. Davis, "Gerrard Winstanley and the Restoration of True Magistracy", *Past and Present* 70 (1976), pp.76–93, esp. 78, 84; Corns, *Uncloistered Virtue*, pp.172–3.
58. Introduction to *LFOW*, p.41. For further statements of the view that *The Law of Freedom* is "the fruit ... of Winstanley's defeat" and for this reason represents a sharp break from the pamphlets written at the time of the Digger experiment, see Hill, *Religion of Winstanley*, pp.44–5, 49; and Shulman, *Radicalism and Reverence*, pp.213–22, 232–7, 242.
59. Barbara Kiefer Lewalski, "Milton: Political Beliefs and Polemical Methods, 1659–60", *PMLA* 74 (1959), pp.191–202, esp. 194–5; Hill, *Milton and the English Revolution*, p.200. Cf. Corns, *Uncloistered Virtue*, pp.279–92.
60. Sonnet XII (On the Same), 12, Lewalski, "Political Beliefs", p.199; Barker, *Milton and the Puritan Dilemma*, p.261. For a similar view, see Hill, *Milton and the English Revolution*, pp.199–207; and Mary Ann Radzinowicz, *Toward "Samson Agonistes"* (Princeton: Princeton University Press, 1978), pp.82–3, 163–4: "The second edition of *The Readie and Easie Way* was written when there was no doubt in Milton's mind that the Good Old Cause had failed: it marked the end of all hope."
61. *CPW*, VII, pp.408–9.
62. Ibid., VII, pp.462–3. James Holstun, in *A Rational Millennium: Puritan Utopias of*

Seventeenth-Century England and America (New York and Oxford: Oxford University Press, 1987), pp.247–65, sees the second edition of *The Readie and Easie Way* “not as political proposition for the present but as polemical defiance of the future”, addressed not to any immediate audience but to posterity, and characterizes the work, especially its final paragraph, as “fundamentally pessimistic” (pp.256, 262). Corns, though he finds the generic term “jeremiad”, central to Holstun’s argument, of limited usefulness, also emphasizes the “undertone of sadness” and “frail confidence” in Milton’s peroration (*Uncloistered Virtue*, pp.283–5).

Communism, George Hill and the Mir*: Was Marx a Nineteenth-Century Winstanleyan?*

JAMES HOLSTUN

Despite the recent academic vogue of a "three kingdoms" theory of the English Civil War and culturalist theories of early modern nation formation, it is harder to find comparatist analyses of English radicalism now than it was twenty or fifty or a hundred years ago. G.P. Gooch begins his *English Democratic Ideas of the Seventeenth Century* (1898) with a chapter on the continental Reformation.[1] So does Lewis H. Berens, in *The Digger Movement in the Days of the Commonwealth* (1906), which also includes "The Twelve Articles of the German Peasantry" of 1525 as an appendix.[2] And in *Winstanley: Socialisme et Christianisme sous Cromwell* (1976), as in so much of his work, Olivier Lutaud emphasizes the international dimensions of the English Revolution – in itself, and in its reception.[3] He concludes with some of the ways in which Winstanley has been remembered and forgotten, tracing the rebirth of modern interest in Winstanley to Russia, where the liberal historian M.M. Kovalevskii discussed Winstanley in his *Precursors of English Radicalism* (1892) even before Gooch's discussion or Eduard Bernstein's.[4]

Why this precocious Russian interest? The liberal Kovalevskii, like his radical Narodnik countrywomen and men, had been roused by the precarious revolutionary potentials set free when the serfs gained nominal emancipation in 1861. This was the epoch, says Lutaud,

> when young enthusiasts, despite brutal repression, began 'to go to the people'; when one becomes conscious of a strange similarity between the problems of old England and of Alexander II's Russia: the problem of government and the struggle against absolutism, the problem of religion and the critique of clerical orthodoxy, and above all the problem of society and the real emancipation of a peasantry eager for land. The *commune* of Surrey encounters the *mir*.[5]

As a proper noun, *mir* does indeed name the accident-prone Russian space station. But as an improper noun, it means *earth*, *universe*, *peace* and *the Russian peasant commune*, an institution that survived into the twentieth century. Where mere traces of communal agriculture survived in Britain and Western Europe, these Russian communes held three-fifths of the arable land in European Russia in the 1870s.[6] Though under a sustained capitalist assault comparable to that experienced by smallholding peasants in early modern England, they continued to manage land, government and social welfare services collectively, and their members held most of their lands and worked some of them in common.

These multiple meanings put me in mind of Gerrard Winstanley, the great communist prose poet of English improper nouns. In *The Breaking of the Day of God* (1648), Winstanley seems to be thinking of the *mir* when he says, "by earth, I understand mankind; all sects and nations, as they are considered one flesh, or one earth; of which all of us are made even one created humanity".[7] In *A New-Yeers Gift to the Armie*, he speaks of "two Earths, in which the Spirit of Love declares himself. ... the Living Earth, called *Mankinde*", and "the great Body of Earth in which all creatures subsist".[8] When Winstanley and the Diggers desanctified St George's Hill as George Hill, they also resanctified it by unhorsing George, changing him from a knight to a farmer working the earth – a *georgos* tilling *gea*. That one word *mir*, in fact, contains my thesis in this paper: in the commune of European Russia or Winstanley's Surrey, the people freely intermix with the earth and each other; in communist utopia, the immediate producers will associate freely and peacefully because they jointly control the means of production.

By moving between Surrey in the 1640s, Russia in the 1870s and (implicitly) the present and future, I may already have set off some warning bells. Anglophone literary critics are paying more attention to Winstanley as one of the great English visionary writers, but historical materialists who also want to understand him as a theorist of communism have a tougher row to hoe. Richard Schlatter says that Winstanley was "not a proto-Marxist or a creator of humanistic utopias" but a "religious mystic".[9] Paul Elmen dismisses marxist readings of Winstanley, then observes that "far from being a secular program, Winstanley's vision of a new heaven and a new earth was not unlike John's on Patmos" – an observation presumably meant to etherealize Winstanley, not remind us of John's curses at the merchants of Babylon.[10] David Mulder finds even Elmen too much of a modernizer, and accuses him of foisting onto Winstanley an anachronistic Salvation Army ethic.[11] John R. Knott, Jr. argues that, while digging "may look like striking progressive social theory, anticipating some of the central concerns of marxism", it "can better be understood as a profound nostalgia for an idealized life of perfect simplicity and 'plain-heartedness'".[12] In "The Economic and Social Thought of Gerrard Winstanley: Was He a Seventeenth-Century Marxist?" Winthrop Hudson answers, predictably, "no", then adds, dumbfoundingly, that the Diggers "did not conceive of their venture as a means of effecting social change or as a way of gaining desired ends".[13]

The examples could be multiplied. Such caveats are always offered up as a fresh and cheeky response to the dogmas of some cloth-eared communist orthodoxy, even though they are always pretty much the same, and even though it is hard to find anyone who has uttered the much-refuted phrase. So in order to breathe some fitful life into this battered red straw man, I shall say the words:

> Winstanley was almost a seventeenth-century marxist. After throwing off the religious mystifications of his earlier writings, he began to develop a crude but workable materialist theory of English society. If only he had lived long enough to work out the dialectic of production that governs all historical development – or even to read Marx! But in the meantime, we can strip off the religious husk of his prophecies and get to their materialist kernel.

Now that is a stupid thing to say – not completely stupid, but stupid enough, and I do not intend to spend any time at all celebrating how close Winstanley came to being a marxist, or lamenting his failure to make it all the way.

But what is a marxist? Anti-communists who try to enclose Winstanley in a distant past are a little too quick to assume the simplicity of the answer to that question, as if the marxist tradition were a non-contradictory whole unified by choral reverence towards its founding prophet. But Marx himself once sounded a dissonant note when he told his Franco-Cuban son-in-law, Paul Lafargue, "One thing for sure – I'm no marxist".[14] So if Winstanley was not a marxist, and Marx was not a marxist, maybe they were similar sorts of non-marxist?

That is what I want to suggest. Because I am not only a marxist interpreting Winstanley, but a winstanleyan interpreting Marx, I sometimes find myself itching to say this:

> Marx was almost a nineteenth-century winstanleyan. After throwing off the Smithian mode-of-production narrative that governed his earlier theory of history, he began to develop a rough but fascinating theory of a transition from the peasant commune to democratic communism that would skip the stage of proletarian destitution. If only he had lived long enough to synthesize his studies of the *mir* – or even to read Winstanley!

That, too, is not completely stupid, but it is not quite right, either. What I really want to say is something more like this: Marx and Winstanley were not marxists, or even winstanleyans, but *communists* – a term eminently worth cancelling and preserving. They grounded their vision of society in the concept of the mode of production, their vision of history in class struggle, and their vision of utopia in the vernacular traditions of peasant communism criticized and transformed by a programme of communist improvement.[15] I shall talk first about Marx as a nineteenth-century winstanleyan (emphasizing his "regressive" interest in peasant communism), then about Winstanley as a seventeenth-century marxist (emphasizing his "progressive" interest in communist improvement), then about the problems of anachronism that these awkward expressions conjure up. This will lead me into a few concluding words about the surprising but rather strong affinities among, on the one hand, stagist dialectical materialism, capitalist modernization theory, and the anticommunist history of ideas that tries to enclose Winstanley in a distant past; and on the other, Winstanley's agrarian communism, Marx's vernacular communism, and the liberation theology that struggles to break down these historicist enclosures.

So, to begin with, was Marx a nineteenth-century winstanleyan? That is to say, did he ever suggest that pre-capitalist social forms (such as smallholding and the peasant commune) might become something other than fetters on progress and human liberation? Could they become the basis for an advanced communism, allowing pre-capitalist peoples to skip the phase of proletarian expropriation and misery? John Gray voices the anticommunist received wisdom: "In fact, along with many other nineteenth-century thinkers, Marx despised the social and technological immobility of peasant societies. He viewed the abolition of peasant farming as an indispensable prerequisite of economic progress and regarded the capitalist factory as the model on which farming should in the future be based".[16] And indeed, in much of Marx's work, and even more of Engels', we find the stagist modernization narrative that they inherited from Adam Smith.[17] This narrative describes a fixed sequence of productive modes, stretching from primitive communism to slavery to feudalism to capitalism to advanced communism, and driven forward by the self-developing forces of production, or by *homo œconomicus*' natural-born inclination to truck and barter. In this narrative, capitalism creates itself by reaching into its own past and using some "proto-capitalist" agent (markets, merchants, cities, technology) to break the pre-capitalist "fetters" keeping it from being born. The most one can do is accelerate or retard this inevitable sequence, so class struggle must be relentlessly forward, and any attempt to hold onto pre-capitalist social forms (like a common, or peasant smallholdings) would retard the predestined process of global proletarianization that must precede the communist utopia.

This philosophy of history frequently entails a certain contempt for the country and the witless yokels inhabiting it – as if the country were somehow "past", the city "present". In *The Conditions of the Working-Class in England* (1845), Engels describes pre-industrial peasants and artisans much as Hegel described dispirited Egypt and Asia:

> They were comfortable in their silent vegetation, and but for the industrial revolution they would never have emerged from this existence, which, cosily romantic as it was, was nevertheless not worthy of human beings. In truth, they were not human beings; they were merely toiling machines in the service of the few aristocrats who had guided history down to that time.[18]

In *The Communist Manifesto* (1848), Marx and Engels condemn capitalism for creating the suffering of the proletarian city, but they also emphasize its modernizing and progressive quality, which made "barbarian and semi-barbarian countries dependent on the civilized ones, nations of peasants on nations of bourgeois, the East on the West" and "rescued a considerable part of the population from the idiocy of rural life".[19] "Idiocy" may retain the relatively neutral Greek sense of "private, personal, separate", but that does not eliminate the condescension. In *The Eighteenth Brumaire* (1852), Marx depicts smallholding French peasants as a "sack of potatoes" without class-consciousness, and he blames the survival of Louis Napoleon's regime on their sullen reluctance to part with their smallholdings.[20] Even as late as the first volume of *Capital* (1867), Marx quotes without revision a passage from *The Communist Manifesto* which depicts the holders of small property ("the lower middle-classes, the small manufacturers, the shopkeepers, the artisan, the peasant") as reactionary fetters who "try to roll back the wheel of history", which will inevitably break free and crush them, however tragically.[21]

Raymond Williams traced this kind of city-centred modernization narrative to what he mordantly called an "urban idiocy – the idea that food grows in shops".[22] But it has been subject to a powerful critique by contemporary "political marxists" like Robert Brenner and Ellen Meiksins Wood.[23] And in his later writings, Marx himself abandoned it for a theory of historical transition emphasizing the relations of production rather than the autonomously developing forces, historically particular class struggles rather than the universal and inevitable unfolding of a developmental sequence. In *The Grundrisse* (1857–58), Marx mocks this Smithian modernization theory and, implicitly, his younger self: "Production, as distinct from distribution, etc., is to be presented as governed by eternal natural laws independent of history, and then *bourgeois* relations are quietly substituted as irrefutable natural laws of society *in abstracto*. This is the more or less conscious purpose of the whole procedure".[24] Marx's new theory of history brought along with it a new respect for, even fascination with, peasant smallholders who retain the means of production. *The Grundrisse* contains a striking, lyrical meditation on small production that synthesizes English social history and German dialectics in a fashion recalling and developing the communist phenomenology of the *1844 Manuscripts*. Marx argues that man is originally socialized as a "*species being, a tribal being, a herd animal* – though by no means as a *zoön politikon* in the political sense". Before capitalism, both primitive communists and individual smallholders were collective individuals:

> individuals related not as workers but as proprietors ... The individual is placed in such conditions of gaining his life as to make not the acquiring of wealth his object, but self-sustenance, his own reproduction as a member of the community; the reproduction of himself as proprietor of the parcel of ground and, in that quality, as a member of the commune.[25]

The same utopian relationship inheres in the more individualized peasant, yeoman or "free working petty landowner or tenant", and in the guildsman, whose "labour itself is still half the expression of artistic creation, half an end-in-itself", and whose very mastery implies ownership of the means of production.[26] Through the laws and customs of the guild, even the subordinate apprentice or journeyman enjoys a certain "co-possession" of the means of production.[27] In such pre-capitalist modes of production, the laborer does not appear for Marx "merely as a working individual in this abstraction", but has

> an *objective mode of existence* in his ownership of the land, an existence which is *presupposed* to his activity and not a mere result of it, and which is as much a precondition of his activity as his skin, his sense organs, which, though he also reproduces and develops these in his life process, are nevertheless presupposed to this reproduction process – this relation is instantly mediated by the naturally evolved and more or less historically developed and modified being of the individual as a *member of a community* – his naturally evolved being as part of a tribe, etc.

When capitalist primitive accumulation dissolves these communal relationships, this Marx of the *Grundrisse* emphasizes not the natural or economistic *inevitability* of the change, but its political *violence*, which produces a truly isolated "idiot" in the form, not of the peasant, but of the capitalist wage labourer: "The individual here can never appear so thoroughly isolated as he does as mere free worker."[28]

Marx developed these thoughts in his late studies of the primitive commune among the Iroquois and in Ireland, North Africa, South Asia and particularly in Russia.[29] He taught himself Russian by reading statistical reports and the works of Russian historians, political theorists and radicals. He read Kovalevskii's *Communal Landownership and the Causes, Course and Consequences of its Disintegration* (1879) in Russian, and the two met frequently in London, where Kovalevskii was conducting his research.[30] He studied intensively and with admiration the works of N.G. Chernyshevskii, then in internal exile. In his *Critique of Philosophical Prejudices against Communal Ownership*, Chernyshevskii had invoked Hegel and Schelling to argue that "In its form, the higher stage of development resembles the source from which it proceeds" – that is, that advanced communism might preserve and develop the traditional communism of the *mir*, not extirpate it: "Thus communal ownership is necessary not only for the well-being of the agricultural class, but also for the progress of agriculture itself. It appears the only full and rational way of combining the farmer's gain with improvement of the land, and productive methods with conscientious execution of work."[31] Indeed, Chernyshevskii thought that the remnants of communal agriculture in the Urals might make it possible for peasants there to adopt large-scale mechanized agriculture, and avoid the impoverishment incumbent on parcellized individual holdings.[32] Marx wrote to Engels that *The Situation of the Working Class in Russia* by Flerovskii (V.V. Bervi) was "the first work to tell the truth about Russian economic conditions", and calls it "the most important book published since your work on the *Condition of the Working-Class*". He admires the absence of "mysticism about the land" and "nihilistic extravagance", and the willingness to present "the family life of the Russian peasants ... the awful beating-to-eath of their wives, the drinking, and the concubines".[33] In their studies, Marx and Engels were equally contemptuous of Russian liberals heralding capitalist "progress" as Russia's salvation, and of Slavophile ethnic chauvinists celebrating the *mir* as a timeless emanation of the Russian world-soul. They reminded the former of the rigours of primitive accumulation in the West, the latter of the global ubiquity of the ancient commune. But they also saw a possible third way among socialist Narodniks (including Chernyshevskii and the People's Will party), whose anti-Tsarist violence and vision of a progressive peasant communism formed an early "Third Worldist" socialism.[34]

When using Marx to consider the Russian situation in the 1870s, Russian radicals and liberals drew on Marx's earlier vision of Smithian modernization theory in the first volume of *Capital*. In 1877, writing in the journal *Otechestvennye Zapiski*, N.K. Mikhailovskii responded to an earlier Russian review of *Capital*, and claimed that Marx had prophesied that Russia would have to undergo the process of primitive capitalist accumulation that had savaged Europe, and particularly England. This was not an altogether unreasonable reading, given that the Narodnik Marx was known only to his correspondents. But the next year, Marx responded that "The chapter on primitive accumulation does not pretend to do more than trace the road by which in Western Europe the capitalist economic order emerged from the entrails of the feudal economic order". He attacked Mikhailovskii for transforming "my historical sketch of the genesis of capitalism in Western Europe into a historico-philosophical theory of general development, imposed by fate on all peoples, whatever the historical circumstances in which they are placed". He rejected any impulse to employ such a theory apart from a discussion of particular political circumstances. Comparing the expropriation of peasants in early modern Europe and in ancient Rome, he notes that the former became proletarians, the latter slaves:

> Thus events strikingly analogous, but occurring in different historical milieux, led to quite disparate results. By studying each of these evolutions on its own, and then comparing them, one will easily discover the key to the phenomenon, but it will never be arrived at by employing the all-purpose formula of a general historico-philosophical theory whose supreme virtue consists in being supra-historical.[35]

In February 1881, Marx received a letter from the Narodnik V.I. Zasulich, who had attempted to assassinate the Tsarist Governor of St Petersburg, and who was then exiled in Zurich.[36] She asked Marx his opinion of those marxists who invoked his authority against the *mir*, calling it "an archaic form condemned to perish by history, scientific socialism, and, in short, everything above debate". Marx eventually sent her a short letter in which he called the *mir* "the fulcrum for social regeneration in Russia" – a bold enough statement. But in three long drafts for this letter, he went even further, calling arguments for the necessary destruction of the *mir* an attempt by Russian liberals to "naturalise capitalist production in their own country and, consistent with themselves, transform the great mass of peasants into simple wage-earners".[37] Such arguments merely repeat the ideological apologies of other imperialist and capitalist powers. "Sir Henry Maine", Marx says, "who was a keen collaborator of the British Government in carrying out the violent destruction of the Indian communes, hypocritically assures us that all the government's noble efforts to support the communes were thwarted by the spontaneous forces of economic laws!"[38] These comments significantly revise Marx's pronouncements of the 1850s, notorious among postcolonial critics, about the progressive and modernizing force of British rule in India. While he does not explicitly reject that earlier view, he now finds that the suppression of communal land ownership in India "was nothing but an act of English vandalism, pushing the native people not forwards but backwards".[39]

What threatens the commune – in India or Russia – is "neither historical inevitability nor a theory; it is the oppression by the State and exploitation by capitalist intruders":

> A certain kind of capitalism, nourished at the expense of the peasants through the agency of the State, has risen up in opposition to the commune; it is in its interest to crush the commune. It is also in the

> interest of the landed proprietors to set up the more or less well-off peasants as an intermediate agrarian class, and to turn the poor peasants – that is to say the majority – into simple wage-earners. This will mean cheap labour! And how would a commune be able to resist, crushed by the extortions of the State, robbed by business, exploited by the landowners, undermined from within by usury?[40]

The remnants of the communal structure in fact helped the state wring taxes from the emancipated serfs, and the "combination of destructive influences, unless smashed by a powerful reaction, is bound to lead to the death of the rural commune".[41] As the English agrarian "middling sort" split between yeoman freeholders and capitalist tenant farmers on the one hand, distressed copyholders and wage labourers on the other, so Russian peasants were splitting between wealthy kulaks and expropriated agrarian wage laborers.

But Marx was hopeful about the possibility of a reaction. The "rural idiocy" of French peasants reappears as the "isolation of rural communes, the lack of connexion between the life of one and the life of another", which leads to "a central despotism over and above the communes". But whereas Marx earlier proposed the political dispossession of French peasants and their submission to the necessities of stagist history, he now proposes the political reorganization of the Russian communes. The peasants who were previously "fetters" on the development of productive forces are now the victims of "government shackles". But it would be an "easy matter" to replace the top-down governmental *volost* administration with "an assembly of peasants elected by the communes themselves, serving as the economic and administrative organ for their interests" – a bottom-up reorganization reminiscent of Winstanley's *The Law of Freedom*.[42] A revolutionary project could reverse primitive accumulation and restore wealth for communal development. Marx takes a classic "stagist" bit of evidence and reverses its force: the near-extirpation of the commune elsewhere does not mean that events must follow the same course in Russia. Rather, because of the *mir*'s "contemporaneity with western production", it may "appropriate the latter's *positive acquisitions* without experiencing all its frightful misfortunes".[43] The communes could then form the basis for large-scale mechanized agriculture.[44] As late as the introduction to the second Russian edition of *The Communist Manifesto* (1882), Marx and Engels suggested that "the present Russian common ownership of land may serve as the starting point for communist development" if a Russian revolution ignites "a proletarian revolution in the West, so that the two complement each other".[45] In his Preface to the third volume of *Capital* (1894), Engels said that Russia "was to play the same role in the part dealing with ground rent that England played in Book I in connection with industrial wage labour", though Marx died too early to synthesize his work.[46]

These letters and drafts sit uneasily inside Marx's canon. Both Plekhanov and Lenin knew the letter to *Otechestvennye Zapiski*, sided strongly with Marx, and savaged Mikhailovskii in later quarrels, but both thought that a capitalist dynamic had begun irreversibly to eat away at the commune from within, making it useless as a utopian model for future society.[47] In his writings on the Narodniks and the agrarian question, Lenin distinguished between the "old Narodniks" of Chernyshevskii's generation, who "went among the people" espousing a "well-knit doctrine evolved in a period when capitalism was still very feebly developed in Russia", and contemporary Narodniks, whom he saw combining a reactionary Slavophile mystification of the commune with a liberal programme of reform that would accelerate its capitalist destruction.[48] David Ryazanov, the first editor and publisher of the letter and drafts to Zasulich, found them sceptical about any transition from the commune to advanced communism.[49] Christopher Hill describes the *mir* with sympathy but fundamentally follows Lenin's analysis.[50] Eric Hobsbawm observes flatly that Marx's idea of an alternate Russian road to socialism was unmarxist in itself, rejected by Russian marxists, and discredited in any case by the destruction of the communes.[51] Raymond Williams's interviewers in *Politics and Letters* insist that "Any revolution initially based on a peasantry has to pass through a proletarianization to create the conditions for a democratic socialism thereafter".[52] Dorothy Atkinson sees the *Gemeinschaft* of the communes fated to replacement by the *Gesellschaft* of rational, Soviet modernization.[53]

But others have convincingly challenged this sort of teleology. Perplexingly, Williams' interviewers add that Marx thought the communes capable of "a direct growth into socialism", and that "Modern research on the immediate post-revolutionary years in Russia tends to uphold him".[54] Richard N. Hunt says: "When combined with the theory of Oriental despotism and the *Grundrisse*'s flexibility concerning variant roads out of the primitive tribal community, it seems to leave in ruins the picture of Marxism as a rigid unilinear schema obliging all peoples to tread the same stepping stones."[55] Teodor Shanin ranks Russian revolutionary populism as an influence on Marx with Engels' more familiar triad of German dialectical philosophy, French utopian socialism, and English political economy.[56] Derek Sayer and Philip Corrigan take a more reserved view, but still acknowledge the importance of the *mir* in Marx's thought.[57] Jean-Paul Sartre, that ferocious critic of stagist dialectical materialism, denounces as "Marxist formalism" and even "Terror" the Stalinist impulse to reduce the movement of history to an unwitting pursuit of a predetermined goal. The letter to Mikhailovskii "clearly shows that, for Marx, the history of the noncapitalist and pre-capitalist societies of the past *is not over and done with*" – a temporally paradoxical phrase with both a retrospective meaning (*these societies* are not finished), and a prospective one (neither is *their history*).[58]

Despite Hobsbawm's argument, Marx's late interest in this "regressive" social form found striking historical confirmation in the twentieth-century communist revolutions. Though the commune was eventually destroyed or disappeared into the collective farm, it played a crucial role in the outbreak of the first communist revolution. On 23 April 1885, Engels wrote to Zasulich that Russia's revolutionary potential lay partly in its combination of various modes of production, "from the primitive commune to modern big industry and high finance, and where all these contradictions are forcibly pent up by an unheard-of despotism".[59] We could trace this argument forward to the "law of uneven and combined development" which Trotsky believed solved the "fundamental riddle of the Russian Revolution": "In order to realize the Soviet state, there was required a drawing together and mutual penetration of two factors belonging to completely different historical species: a peasant war – that is a movement characteristic of the dawn of bourgeois development – and a proletarian insurrection, the movement signalizing its decline. That is the essence of 1917."[60] Shanin says that Marx's contact with Russian populism allowed him to break free of a social Darwinist model of teleological social evolution, and to connect with the revolutionary traditions of the twentieth-century Third World, which have drawn from residual, pre-capitalist social formations in struggling to create a post-capitalist democracy of direct producers: "It has been the integration of marxism with the indigenous political traditions which has underlain all known cases of internally generated and politically effective revolutionary transformation of society by socialists".[61] Isaac Deutscher asks, "Even if the Marxists were right in Russia, are the Narodniks not vindicated in China?" Mao's communists were defeated in the cities, then withdrew into the countryside, where they had a much stronger base among the peasantry than did the Narodniks, and eventually proved victorious. And the Soviet Union actually played the role in China's revolution that Marx hoped Western Europe would play in Russia's: a political ally and repository of technological knowledge that would make it possible for a mainly peasant nation largely to bypass some of the horrors of primitive accumulation.[62] In 1973, Raymond Williams commented, "The 'rural idiots' and the 'barbarians and semi-barbarians' have been, for the last forty years, the main revolutionary force in the world".[63] On 1 January 1994, the day when NAFTA came squalling into the world to celebrate the completion of the west wing of the global capitalist New Jerusalem, the Zapatistas of Chiapas, Mexico, launched something that looked for all the world like a peasant rebellion in defense of agrarian use rights, articulating their anti-capitalist project in a series of ideologically self-conscious manifestos reminiscent of those produced by sixteenth-century German peasants. Ça ira.

Was Winstanley a seventeenth-century marxist? That is to say, did he ever move significantly beyond a nostalgic and traditionalist critique of the depredations worked by capitalist enclosure, to a progressive and communist critique? Like Marx, Winstanley reveals a nostalgic sense of *something lost* through his very critique of expropriation and alienation. But also like Marx, Winstanley fused that nostalgia with a vision of progressive improvement in a communist project that denies the modernizing inevitability of the capitalist present. Any form of social and cultural history genuinely opposed to the teleological false binaries of modernization theory should be alive to the existence of "third ways", even if they suffered defeat. Just as Marx imagined a revolutionary communist Narodism as a third way beyond Slavophile paternalism and capitalist liberalism, so Winstanley imagined communist Digging as a third way beyond feudal paternalism and capitalist improvement. Like Sartre's Marx, Winstanley believed that the history of the non-capitalist and pre-capitalist societies of the past was not yet over and done with. He saw the pre-capitalist common as the material and existential foundation for a post-capitalist society that would incorporate the genuine achievements of capitalist improvement without its oppressions.

I want to emphasize four aspects of Winstanley's progressive communism. First, he grounded his theory of society and history in a concept of the mode of production and class struggle. This terminology may seem anachronistic at first, but I believe it will seem more appropriate when we contrast Winstanley's theory of society with some contemporary alternatives. First, he is not much of an anti-papist – he spends remarkably little time bashing Rome. Nor is he much interested in the difference between king and parliament, for a post-regicidal parliamentarian landlord or evicting soldier exercises "kingly power", which "is like a great spread tree, if you lop the head or top-bow, and let the other branches and root stand, it will grow again and recover fresher strength".[64] He has no particular interest in status designations or subdivisions: old gentry, new gentry and yeoman freeholder alike are all exploiters.[65] His anti-normanism remains quite metaphoric, and never degenerates into credulous philo-saxonism.[66] He is not a traditionalist, for he has little interest in *restoring* an earlier paternalist social order, actual or imagined. Neither is he a Harringtonian republican, for he does not share in Harrington's economistic vision of revolution as the adjustment of the political "superstructures" to the relatively fixed economic "foundations". No less than Hartlibian schemes of capitalist improvement, Harrington's republicanism would leave existing relations of production largely untouched.

One might choose to characterize Winstanley as the proponent of a traditional "moral economy" – one who emphasizes its binary, *moral* dimensions (the rich exploiting the poor), rather than its structurally specific economic dimensions.[67] There is some truth here, for Winstanley's work comprises an entire poetics of metaphoric ethical binaries: the struggle of Jacob and Esau, common preservation and self-preservation, carnal imagination and godly Reason, common field and enclosure, power of love and kingly power.[68] Carlo Ginzburg says that such binary classifications reveal the "totally dichotomous view of the class structure, typical of a peasant society".[69] And of course, it is hard these days to view any binary with anything other than condescension, since so much anti-communist social theory, from deconstruction to historical revisionism, has pilloried the very idea of the binary, with all its conceptual kin (opposition, struggle, contradiction, conflict).

But perhaps such rustic dichotomies are not only *typical of peasants*, but also, in important ways, *true*. They reveal a particular form of situated practical and theoretical consciousness appropriate to the daily life and the class project of the Diggers and of surplus producers throughout the world and throughout history. Moreover, those ideologists who struggle to complicate and problematize such binary relationships out of existence are to be found, with striking regularity, among the ruling class appropriators of surplus, or their apologists among the professional-managerial class. We would also do well to remember that Marx's most mature "structural" conception of the mode of production, which he works out in the third volume of *Capital*, incorporates a binary moral economy: "The specific economic form, in which unpaid surplus-labour is pumped out of direct producers, determines the relationship of rulers and ruled, as it grows directly out of production itself and, in turn, reacts upon it as a determining element."[70] For Winstanley as for Marx, the mode of production is the historically specific relationship, both structural and ethical/political, between an exploiting class of surplus extractors (including kings, lords of manors, capitalist tenants, wealthy freeholders, lawyers, Councils of State and tithing clergy) and an exploited class of surplus producers (including distressed copyholders, wage labourers, small tradesmen and the poor). For Winstanley as for Marx, this relationship is both powerful and mutable: "And all the strivings that is in mankind, is for the earth, who shall have it; whether some particular persons shall have it, and the rest have none, or whether the earth shall be a common treasury to all without respect of persons."[71] For Winstanley as for Marx, the history of all hitherto existing society is the history of the pitched battle between the lamb and the dragon.[72]

Second, Winstanley develops a dialectical psychology that insists on the value of moving through a phase of alienation. In *Fire in the Bush*, he goes beyond mere moral denunciation of the "imaginary power" of acquisition by tracing three stages of consciousness. First comes the "plain-hearted state", which is peaceful but malleable, unstable and infantile: "you need not look back six thousand years to find it; for every single man and woman passes through it." This time is "the image of God, but not the strength and life of God; it is wise, but not wisdom itself". He associates it with the strength of Peter and Nathanael, which "proved weakness", and calls it "the first time of the Beast, or self, which is full of peace, while a man is in it; but it is a state like wax, flexible and easy to take any impression".[73] Next comes the "time of the curse" implied by the immoderate use of "the creatures" (material objects) – a time which forms the "second estate of mankind".[74] Here, the acquisitive Adam

> fears where no fear is: he rises up to destroy others, for fear, lest others destroy him: he will oppress others, lest others oppress him; and he fears he shall be in want hereafter; therefore he takes by violence, that which others have labored for. … For Imagination begins to tell the soul; if thou enjoyest not fullness of all objects, thou wilt want and starve for food, and so presently fear of poverty takes the throne and reigns; and fear bids thee go, get what thou canst, by hook or by crook, lest thou want, and perish, and die miserably.[75]

This sympathetic account, which suggests Sartre's analysis of seriality, is all the more remarkable given its publication in March 1650, when sustained attacks from without threatened the Cobham commune, and when Winstanley's words may have described defecting Diggers.[76] Finally comes the "third estate of mankind ... the day of Christ, or the rising up", and restoration from this state of bondage. This is more than the restoration of the first stage: "Now no man hath, or can have true peace, till he be able to see this clear distinction within himself; he that sees nothing but one power, nor never saw any other but one power in him, that man as yet is a slave to the Devil."[77] In his focus on the weakness and underdevelopment of the original, "unfallen" state, and the necessity for a progress through the others, he insists so strongly on the happiness of the *felix culpa* that it becomes no fault at all – a Pelagian progress, or perhaps a Romantic phenomenology of consciousness in the mode of Hegel or Wordsworth, or Chernyshevskii's belief that advanced communism would cancel and preserve the primitive commune.[78]

Third, Winstanley formulates a progressive dialectical theory of enclosure and depopulation which is structurally quite distinct from that of reactionary neofeudal paternalists. Where the latter see the tumults produced by primitive accumulation and sectarian ferment as the signs of a Babel-like confusion, or a violated moral economy, Winstanley sees them as signs of an imminent emancipation: "Before you live you must die, and before you be bound up into one universal body, all your particular bodies and societies must be torn to pieces."[79] This dialectical optimism, which sees the positive revolutionary potential in the breakdown of a unified church and a traditional social order, brings Winstanley surprisingly close to the ideologists of capitalist improvement. But finally, he is a communist improver. He sees the commons themselves expanding as a result of the people's victory in the Revolution. As Marx envisions the *mir* redeemed through a primitive accumulation in reverse, so Winstanley imagines the expansion of the commons when the common people regain those crown, deans, bishops, chapter and forest lands that they helped to liberate during the war.[80] And a programme of labour withdrawal will extend this liberation by turning all enclosures into commons. Distressed copyholders and wage labourers will continue leaving the land being taken from them and inhabit the commons.[81] When enough of them leave, agrarian capitalist rentiers and farmers would have to work their own fields, and the distinctions among landlord, tenant and labourer – among enclosure, small-holding and common field – will disappear. A quantitative increase in anti-paternalist depopulation will lead dialectically to a qualitative change in forms of land tenure. The God of the commons will safeguard the strike fund underwriting an agrarian general strike.

Fourth, and finally, Winstanley offers a progressive theory of improvement, which distinguishes oppressive capitalist relations of production from the potentially emancipatory forces of production that arise within them. One of the most striking things about Winstanley's utopian vision, particularly in *The Law of Freedom*, is how far it is from anything like a version of simplifying pastoral. Winstanley's utopia certainly promises no withering away of politics. With its vision of a complex governmental structure, its reformed system of education, and its coordinated programme of practical scientific research and development, it suggests not so much the utopian pastoralism of Morris's *News from Nowhere* as Raymond Williams' critique of that pastoralism for its radical "discontinuity" from Morris's England: "Because what the representation of discontinuity typically produces is a notion of social simplicity which is untenable. The extent to which the idea of socialism is attached to that simplicity is counter-productive. It seems to me that the break towards socialism can only be towards an unimaginably greater complexity."[82] Winstanley's utopia intimately engaged the most advanced scientific work of his day – notably, the Hartlibian enlightenment that provided a millenarian prelude to the culture of capitalist improvement that would define so much of England's future. Nigel Smith says that, in *The Law of Freedom*, Winstanley is "nothing more than a neo-Hartlibian projector".[83]

But if Winstanley is indeed a Hartlibian projector, he is also something more. True enough, Winstanley sounds awfully like Bacon or Hartlib or Plattes or Child when he proclaims that "To know the secrets of nature, is to know the works of God", or when he describes utopian tree science as "the right ordering of woods and timber trees, for planting, dressing, felling, framing of timber for all uses, for building houses or ships. And here all carpenters, joiners, throsters, plow-makers, instrument makers for music, and all who work in wood and timber, may find out the secret of nature, to make trees more plentiful and thriving in their growth, and profitable for use".[84] At first, this passage sounds as though it could come straight from *The New Atlantis*. But Bacon's idea of "profitable for use" entails a new force of technocratic domination in Salomon's House, leaving material production as invisible, unmentionable and *declassé* as in any courtly pastoral, while Digger improvement mixes research and artisanry. Winstanley forbids a new priesthood of "traditional knowledge" or contemplation: "he that only contemplates and talks of what he reads and hears, and doth not employ his talent in some bodily action, for the increase of fruitfulness, freedom, and peace in the earth, is an unprofitable son." For researchers and improvers as well as lawyers and clerics, "he is a monster who is all tongue and no hand".[85] *Fire in the Bush* attacks the secrecy and class privilege that reappears inside the Hartlibian Enlightenment: "For this is the vine that shall overspread the Earth, and shall be confined no longer within a college, or private university chamber, or under a covetous, proud, black gown, that would always be speaking words: but fall off when people begin to act their words."[86] Like Bacon, Winstanley proposes "deserved honor" for "every one who finds out a new invention"; but he also sees communism, not Bacon's kingly subsidies and patronage, calling forth a host of mute inglorious Bacons through a fourierist liberation of the (vocational) passions: "And certainly when men are sure of food and raiment, their reason will be ripe, and ready to dive into the secrets of the Creation, that they may learn to see and know God (the spirit of the whole creation) in all his works; for fear of want, and care to pay rent to task-masters, hath hindered many rare inventions."[87] In *The Law of Freedom*, Winstanley was a communist improver. As Marx imagines a *mir* that will appropriate the positive achievements of capitalist production without undergoing its "frightful misfortunes", so Winstanley imagines a commune that will appropriate the achievements of Baconian and Hartlibian improvement without submitting to its capitalist will to power.[88]

Could such a thing have been possible? Perhaps not, though we should be a little nervous about our own Whiggish and mechanical-materialist stagism, which identifies improvement itself with a particular regime of exploitation:

> Whether small-scale agricultural production was incapable of innovation is a matter for debate not only among historians but also among those concerned with surviving modern (especially Third World) peasantries. One might suggest that the question is not

> necessarily blocked by the fact that England, pioneer of industrial capitalism, did happen to develop, to begin with, an agrarian capitalism based on the destruction of the peasantry.[89]

Both Chernyshevskii and Marx believed that the Russian peasant commune could incorporate mechanized agriculture and other technologies of improvement. And any sincere critic of the Whig theory of history should be very nervous about the leap from saying "the state and the gentry crushed the Diggers" to saying "the Diggers couldn't have succeeded".

Now of course, all this comparison of Winstanley and Marx may raise suspicions that I suffer from what the revisionist historian Kevin Sharpe calls "that most dangerous of historical ailments, anachronism; from, that is, the translation into early Stuart England of the ideas and politics of a later age".[90] Conversely, Lotte Mulligan and Judith Richards warn those who would turn to Gerrard Winstanley for help in understanding poverty today that they fall into "not merely a methodological fallacy, but something like a moral error".[91] In response, I would hasten to emphasize that there are significant differences between the two. Winstanley chronically underestimated the need for armed struggle in effecting a communist revolution, while Marx and many of his followers chronically underestimated the importance of religion as a revolutionary ideology.[92] And a detailed structural comparison of Digger and Narodnik communism would certainly reveal a host of significant differences. But such a study would not and should not override the remarkable resonances of these two moments – resonances which are intelligible, not miraculous. Both projects grew from the experience of peasant small production – a remarkably widespread and resilient form of production. Both arose in a revolutionary moment which unleashed a sustained capitalist assault on pre-capitalist peasant holdings. In this regard, seventeenth-century England resembles seventeenth-century Russia considerably less than it does nineteenth-century Russia – and late twentieth-century Chiapas. And both writers were constituitively inorganic intellectuals who addressed the resulting conflict in part out of their own experience of migration and dislocation: Winstanley's from small-town Lancashire to metropolitan London to rural Surrey; Marx's from small-town Trier to revolutionary Paris to capitalist Victorian London.

The worst sort of anachronism, the worst sort of teleological or Whig history, is not that which uses present day ideas to understand the past, or vice versa; indeed, I doubt that any moderately ambitious project in historical writing could avoid either. Much worse is that form of teleology that claims that certain persons, peoples, and cultures were extirpated because of a natural and inevitable process of modernization. In this essay, I have suggested that we should refrain from identifying this sort of modernization narrative with the marxist theory of history as class struggle.[93] The identification frequently depends on a strategic slippage among three quite distinct statements:

1. A theory of history as inevitable modernization accompanies some marxist theories of history as class struggle.
2. A theory of history as inevitable modernization accompanies all marxist theories of history as class struggle.
3. A marxist theory of history as class struggle accompanies all theories of history as inevitable modernization. So anticommunist opponents of the former are automatically innocent of the latter.

I take the first statement to be demonstrably true and unlikely to be challenged by anyone who sees communist utopia as the place where workers control the means of production, and associate freely and creatively on the basis of that control. Democratic communists in particular should shudder at the thought of some misty-eyed but stiff-lipped emissary of Stalin or the Shining Path hurrying on the "inevitable" modernization of tribal peoples, peasants, and other small producers who maintain some immediate, non-market access to the means of production, and their reintegration, if they survive, inside an authoritarian state capitalism. In a horrifying irony, such small producers are to be evicted from a place that strangely resembles the communist utopia, and transferred to a place that strangely resembles the capitalist dystopia. Like the history of capitalist primitive accumulation, that of Stalinist agrarian collectivization was "written in the annals of mankind in letters of blood and fire".[94]

As my discussion of Marx on the *mir* indicates, I take the second statement to be demonstrably false, but all too familiar. In a recent essay, the brilliant post-revisionist historian Peter Lake groups marxism and Christopher Hill with capitalist modernization theorists lauding the "benefits of modernity, the controllability of the historical process, the benign capacity of the state to intervene and shape the economic and social development of the nation" – a staggering distortion of Hill's work, with its elegiac and sympathetic attention to the lived experience of a series of lost causes, and its scholarly but bone-deep hatred of the capitalist state.[95] In his Preface to *Liberty Against the Law*, Hill declares, "My aim is – with the help of ballads and other forms of popular literature, to rescue the landless ex-peasantry from posterity's enormous silence" – and the rest of his massive oeuvre bears eloquent witness. Hill echoes E.P. Thompson's Preface to *The Making of the English Working Class*, which criticizes the reformist socialism that ransacks the past for forerunners of the welfare state:

> It reads history in the light of subsequent preoccupations, and not as in fact it occurred. Only the successful (in the sense of those whose

> aspirations anticipated subsequent evolution) are remembered. The blind alleys, the lost causes, and the losers themselves are forgotten. I am seeking to rescue the poor stockinger, the Luddite cropper, the 'obsolete' hand-loom weaver, the 'utopian' artisan, and even the deluded follower of Joanna Southcott, from the enormous condescension of posterity.[96]

Indeed, from Rodney Hilton on the Peasant Rising of 1381 to Hill on the Diggers to J.M. Neeson on early nineteenth-century commoners, the "British" marxist historians (they seem to be increasingly North American) have focused on the creative practical consciousness of peoples *not yet* modernized and proletarianized, defending them from the enormous condescension of modernizing history, whether capitalist or dialectical materialist.

I take the third statement to be neither true in itself, nor properly derivable from the second statement, but still implicit in a good deal of writing by anti-communist historians. The problem is that, however fervently they spurn Whig teleology on the level of politics or popular self-determination, they tend to embrace it on the level of economy, whether they simply take the contemporary capitalist world system for granted, or actively reproduce some version of Smithian modernization theory. Like Tory landlords in the Restoration happily availing themselves of the latest techniques in enclosure and agricultural improvement, revisionist historians who denounce the Whig theory of political history happily avail themselves of an implicitly Whiggish theory of capitalist improvement – one that suggests a certain contempt for the (urban and rural) yokels who resist it. Anthony Fletcher, for instance, traces the English Revolution to sheer, cross-class cultural stupidity: the Puritan fear of popery clashed with the monarchist fear of parity in an "abnegation of reason" and a "curious mixture of folly and idealism", which derives in turn from "the imaginative poverty of the seventeenth century", when "people were made scapegoats for processes, which lacked the capacity to conceive of and weigh in the balance alternative political systems, which took a highly traditional view of the world as a place of 'limited good' where no one can prosper save at someone else's expense".[97] John Walter and Keith Wrightson trace early modern dearth and famine not to exploiting middlemen (the favourite enemy of the misrecognizing poor), but to "a marketing system as yet insufficiently developed to iron out regional inequalities of distribution" – an argument Irish revisionist historians have also found handy when working up a blame-free account of the Famine. Mark Kishlansky complains that Christopher Hill's history from below focuses on "cranks, crackpots, screwballs and fanatics, the nutters and kooks who appear in the wake of every genuine movement for social reform and who become the principal barrier to lasting change".[98] Kevin Sharpe, too, laments the "tired old marxist preoccupation with nascent popular movements" such as the Diggers, and worries that a "vast scholarly industry" has wasted "too many pages ... on endeavors to find meaning in the writings of the civil war's madmen", on "minor sects and crackpots". Winstanley's partisans have overlooked the benefits of enclosure, "which were not merely the invention of Tory apologists".[99] At its absolute worst, modernizing Whiggery turns peasant suffering into capitalist necessity and a sort of brisk eugenics.

But there is one last objection to comparing Winstanley and Marx: is not Winstanley a fundamentally religious thinker, and Marx a fundamentally secular one? Here, we run into a "secularization" controversy with remarkable parallels to that over "modernization". Once again, there are admittedly some "secularizers" on the left. George Juretic has argued for Winstanley's progress out of a self-mystifying religious ideology into revolutionary, secular rationality.[100] Though himself critical of Juretic, Christopher Hill does say that Winstanley's communism became "less theological and more materialist", and that he changed "from a religious to a social and political thinker".[101] These arguments have been effectively answered by Andrew Bradstock, who has shown their unstated (and untenable) assumption that millenarianism and socialism are mutually exclusive.[102]

But surprisingly enough, just as we find that opponents of "Whiggish" social or political history turn out to be fervent Whigs when it comes to economic history, so we find that some defenders of the "essentially religious" quality of seventeenth-century writers like Winstanley work from an implicit version of the secularization model. Conrad Russell says that

> in the normal seventeenth-century structure of authority, it was normal to find religion and politics as closely intertwined as economics and politics are today ... It does not help that the word 'religion' has slowly changed its meaning with the retreat of the State from religious enforcement, and that what takes place outside the South African Embassy may sometimes be nearer to seventeenth-century meanings of 'religion' than what takes place inside St. Martin-in-the-Fields.[103]

This feels reasonable and humane at first, but less so later. For just as economy formed part of the twist back then (as a tithe-hating Baptist, or Milton, or Winstanley, would zealously insist), so too did religion in 1990 (as the anti-racist nun outside the embassy would gladly have asserted).

Jonathan Clark accuses new leftists ("the Class of '68") of utterly ignoring "one auxiliary discipline which the revisionists were to find of immense importance in the understanding of early-modern England: theology. ... The undervaluation of ... ecclesiastical phenomena is a reflection of modern assumptions that religion is a small, specialized and insulated area of national life". He celebrates history's "renewed attention to religion *as religion* rather than as a sublimation of something else".[104] But can one imagine any phrase more alien to William Laud, or William Prynne, or William Walwyn, or any other seventeenth-century person, than "religion as religion"? It suggests the turf-consciousness of a shrinking orthodoxy in a modern state or an unpopular university department – indeed, precisely a "small, specialized and insulated area of national life" – not that totalizing and world-transforming immanent force of seventeenth-century English society. The generally meagre revisionist account of early modern religion as religion recalls a lesson learned by at least some literary critics, with a painful sense of years wasted in celebrating poem as poem or text as text: the reflexive noun intended to ring in an autonomous academic discipline more frequently sounds its death-knell, or a tinkling announcement of its retirement into ineffectual private life.

In his essay "The Religious Context of the English Civil War", John Morrill argues that "The English civil war was not the first European revolution: it was the last of the Wars of Religion".[105] This statement is troublesome not because it brings religion up, but because it shuts religion down. In separating religion and revolution, religion and modernity, Morrill implicitly denies the social and political vision driving such religious revolutionaries as the fourth-century Donatists and Circumcellions in Augustine's North Africa, the fourteenth-century peasants in John Ball's England, and the seventeenth-century poor in Winstanley's Surrey.[106] At the same time, it muffles the ideology of religious transcendence driving many "modern" revolutionary movements, whether we view that transcendence as superhuman or superindividual. Here, think of those righteous radical Dissenters in London and Belfast during the 1790s, John Brown's abolitionists and Hung Hsiu-Ch'ün's Taipings during the 1850s and 1860s, Antonio Conselheiro's millenarian communist cowboys in the Baía of the 1890s, and the liberation theologians of pan-Africa, from Nat Turner to Desmond Tutu to Jean-Bertrand Aristide.[107] The peasant rebellion – the most globally widespread and important form of social revolution in both the modern and the pre-modern world, and almost always fired by religious ideology – also muddies up Morrill and Russell's binary history. Ernst Bloch – that committed communist prophet of the continuing history of pre-capitalist forms – even finds "a constant, unwritten essence of Joachim of Fiore" in Bolshevik Russia:

> Several great peculiarities were thus able to spring up in Christo-romantic fashion on Bolshevist soil; the indisputable Bolshevik and equally indisputable chiliast Alexander Blok gave an indication of

> this, thoroughly in the Joachite spirit. When in Blok's hymn, the 'March of the Twelve', that is, of the twelve Red Army soldiers, a pale Christ precedes the revolution and leads it, this kind of presence of the Spirit is just as remote from the western Church-combines as it finds the eastern Church at least theologically open to it.[108]

The idea of some fundamental divide between pre-modern wars of religion and modern secular revolutions appears only inside a feebly credent or a feebly non-credent version of the history of ideas supplementing capitalist modernization theory, and it threatens to suck the life out of both sides of the divide.

If we wish to assert that Winstanley is a "fundamentally religious thinker", we need to be clear about what we mean by "religious", and resist the temptation to allow all visions of religion to collapse into each other. Lotte Mulligan, John K. Graham and Judith Richards criticize Hill and others for scanting Winstanley's religious language, for "minimizing the part theology played in his theories of social and moral change", for failing to see that Winstanley's God is transcendent as well as immanent, and for ignoring his belief that the world would be transformed not by the action of people but by a literal second coming.[109] Christopher Hill has answered this argument rather effectively, pointing out the widespread seventeenth-century belief that Christ might return not in person but in the collective persons of his revolutionary sons and daughters.[110] It is not all that clear that Winstanley believed in any conventional *first* coming, much less a second: "And here you may see the deceit of imagination and fleshly wisdom and learning; it teaches you to look altogether upon a history without you, of things that were done 6000 years ago, and of things that were done 1649 years ago."[111] "Theology" is a troublesome ally, particularly if one intends the formal university discipline of that name, for Winstanley refers to the "City Divinity" as "that great City Babylon" and proposes to execute professional ministers.[112] Too often, abstract claims for the fundamentally theological quality of Winstanley's writing smooth over the ferocity of his religious anti-clericalism.

But even if we mean an internally coherent religious idea system existing prior to social change, significant problems remain: only a desiccated version of the history of ideas can set an absolute opposition between "religion" and "society". Any sociologist of religion, whether theist, agnostic or atheist, would find that nonsensical – analogous to a rigorous opposition between apples and fruit (or fruit and apples), and particularly unhelpful for Winstanley, for whom "community of ownership in the earth and the resurrection of Christ are interchangeable concepts", while "True religion, and undefiled, is to let every one quietly have earth to manure, that they may live in freedom by their labors".[113] In the Preface to

Several Pieces, his 1649 reissue of his first five works, all of them dating from before the Digger commune, he insists on both the spiritual origin of his Digger revelation, and its distance from his early works: "And therefore though some have said I had done well if I had left writing when I had finished *The Saints Paradice*: surely such men know little of the spirit's inward workings; and truly what I have writ since or before that time, I was carried forth in the work by the same power, delivering it to others as I received it, and I received it not from books nor study."[114] As Lutaud has pointed out, Winstanley's failure to revert to a quietist waiting upon God in *The Law of Freedom*, after the repression of the Digger commune, is a phenomenon worth remarking.[115]

We can see an alternative approach to political theology in superb recent work on Winstanley by Andrew Bradstock, Lewis Daly and Christopher Rowland – all of whom contextualize him with religious struggles for social justice in Reformation Europe on the one hand, contemporary Latin America on the other. All of them, therefore, fall into that "moral error" diagnosed by Mulligan and Richards. So does Christopher Hill when he concludes *The English Bible* with "A Note on Liberation Theology" and brief discussions of Gustavo Gutiérrez and Leonardo Boff.[116] No doubt, atheist historical materialists who take the sociology of religion seriously and theist liberation theologians who take political theology seriously will continue to disagree about the ultimate context for understanding Winstanley's project. While the former will see "religion" as an important subset of the totality of "society", the latter may well see "society" as an important subset of "religion". But they come together in their resolute resistance to seeing "society" and "religion" as separate spheres, whether the separation is structural ("theology" vs. "society") or temporal ("a religious epoch" vs. "a secular epoch"). And they are both *teleological*, in the sense that anyone imagining a future distinct from the present, less savaged by suffering and oppression, is teleological. But their teleology (Marx's too, and Winstanley's) is the teleology of hope and struggle, not of Whig complacency, not of modernizing certitude. For both groups focus on class struggle, whether they see that struggle as Christ rising in sons and daughters, or the political struggle of the direct producers, or both.

Indeed, we may need to trace this liberation theology back past Boff, Winstanley and Christ to the Ancient Near East, making use of the discipline of "theology" that Jonathan Clark invokes but leaves in the lurch. Contemporary seminaries, departments of religion and departments of theology have little use for any absolute distinction between "religion" and "society" – neither in pastoral training nor in historical and academic study, where the concepts of "the sociology of religion" and "liberation theology" provoke controversy but not anathemas. Building on the work of George

Mendenhall, Norman Gottwald has argued that a theology of liberation and a Canaanite peasant rebellion underlie the Hebrew Scriptures themselves. He has built up a complex argument, thoroughly grounded in Ancient Near Eastern philology and archaeology, that the events recounted in Exodus, Joshua and Judges began as a peasant and slave revolt led by *hapiru* outcasts (the word may be cognate with "Hebrew").[117] Later, the court of King David redacted accounts of this rebellion through a sort of monarchical Whig historiography, producing the account we have today of an ethnic migration culminating in imperial conquest and nation formation. If Gottwald is right – if Yahwism is the liberation theology of Canaanite peasants – then Gerrard Winstanley may be something more than a peasant allegorist who boldly conflated the kingdom of God and the communal ownership of the earth. We face the arresting possibility that he produced the least allegorical reading of the Hebrew Scriptures in seventeenth-century England. We will have to consider for its truth value, and not just for its imaginative power, his claim that "The glory of Israel's Commonwealth is this, they had no beggar among them".[118]

NOTES

Thanks to Andrew Bradstock, Lew Daly, Barbara Foly, Simon Joyce, Dina Kuzminers, Chris Rowland, Carola Scott-Luckens, Ed White, and everyone who participated in "Diggers 350" in April 1999. Some of my arguments here derive from my *Ehud's Dagger: Class Struggle in the English Revolution* (London: Verso, 2000).

1. G.P. Gooch, *English Democratic Ideas of the Seventeenth Century* (1898; rpt. Cambridge: Cambridge University Press, 1927).
2. Lewis H. Berens, *The Digger Movement in the Days of the Commonwealth* (1906; rpt. London: Holland Press and Merlin Press, 1961).
3. Olivier Lutaud, *Winstanley: Socialisme et Christianisme sous Cromwell* (Paris: Didier, 1976); still unsurpassed, still untranslated, and still regularly overlooked by anglophone Winstanley scholars.
4. M.M. Kovalevskii, *Precursors of English Radicalism* (in Russian; St Petersburg, 1893); Eduard Bernstein, *Kommunistische und demokratisch-sozialistische Strömungen während der englischen Revolution des 17. Jahrhunderts* (1895; trans. as Cromwell and Communism: Socialism and Democracy in the Great English Revolution [London: Allen & Unwin, 1930]; rpt. New York: Schocken, 1963, and Nottingham: Spokesman, 1980).
5. Lutaud, *Winstanley*, p.467, translation mine.
6. For a historical etymology, see Steven Grant, "*Obshchina* and *Mir*", *Slavic Review* 35/4 (December 1976), pp.636–51. On the *mir* or *obshchina* and related writings in a marxist tradition, see Teodor Shanin's superb collection, *Late Marx and the Russian Road: Marx and "The Peripheries of Capitalism"* (New York: Monthly Review Press, 1983).
7. Gerrard Winstanley, *Breaking of the Day* (1648; rpt. in *Several Pieces Gathered into one Volume* [London 1649], p.18).
8. *Works*, p.375. I will quote most of Winstanley's works from this edition, modernizing spelling and capitalization.
9. Richard Schlatter, "Winstanley, Gerrard", in Richard Greaves and Robert Zaller (eds.), *Biographical Dictionary of British Radicals in the Seventeenth Century*, 3 vols. (Brighton: Harvester Press, 1982–84), pp.3.329–32, 332.

10. Paul Elmen, "The Theological Basis of Digger Communism", *Church History* 23 (1954), pp.207–18, 213.
11. David Mulder, *The Alchemy of Revolution: Gerrard Winstanley's Occultism and Seventeenth-Century English Communism* (New York: Peter Lang, 1990), p.16n.
12. John R. Knott, Jr., *The Sword of the Spirit: Puritan Responses to the Bible* (Chicago: University of Chicago Press, 1980), pp.86, 114.
13. Winthrop Hudson, "The Economic and Social Thought of Gerrard Winstanley: Was He a Seventeenth-Century Marxist?" *Journal of Modern History* 18/1 (1946), pp.1–21.
14. *Karl Marx, Frederick Engels: Collected Works* (Moscow and New York: International Publishers, 1975–), 46.356; translation mine; in future references, I abbreviate this edition as *MECW*.
15. See Shanin's "Marxism and the Vernacular Revolutionary Traditions", Shanin, *Late Marx*, pp.243–79. A *verna* was a slave born inside the Roman master's house.
16. John Gray, "Hollow Triumph: Why Marx Still Provides a Potent Critique of the Contradictions of Late Modern Capitalism", *Times Literary Supplement*, 8 May 1998, pp.3–4.
17. See Robert Brenner, "The Origins of Capitalist Development: A Critique of Neo-Smithian Marxism", *New Left Review* 104 (1977), pp.25–92.
18. *MECW* 4.309. Thanks for this reference to Ed White of Scipio Center, New York.
19. *MECW* 6.488.
20. *MECW* 11.187, 193n.
21. *MECW* 35.751n, quoting 6.495–6, 494.
22. Raymond Williams, *Politics and Letters: Interviews with New Left Review* (London: New Left Books, 1979), p.322.
23. See Ellen Meiksins Wood, *The Origins of Capitalism* (New York: Monthly Review Press, 1999) for a brief, clear introduction, and also chapter four of my *Ehud's Dagger.*
24. *MECW* 28.25. This passage precedes Marx's more stagist discussions in *Capital I* – we are dealing with continuing "moments" in Marx's thought, not an easy development between early and late Marx.
25. *MECW* 28.420, 404.
26. *MECW* 28.426, 421–2.
27. *MECW* 28.421–2.
28. *MECW* 28.409. Here Marx indulges a favourite, sardonic pun: because the ex-peasant is "free" of all property, he or she is constrained to enter into the "free" wage contract (*MECW* 28.430; 35.177–9, 705). Both Marx and Engels later applied the pun to the serfs "freed" by Alexander II in 1861 (*MECW* 27.38; 36.31).
29. See Marx's notes on Morgan, Phear, Maine, and Lubbock in Lawrence Krader, (ed.), *The Ethnological Notebooks of Karl Marx* (Assen: Van Gorcum, 1974).
30. See Marx's detailed notes on Kovalevskii, with associated writings, in Lawrence Krader (ed.), *The Asiatic Mode of Production* (Assen: Van Gorcum, 1975).
31. Shanin, *Late Marx*, pp.183, 187.
32. *MECW* 27.423.
33. *MECW* 43.423–4.
34. Shanin, *Late Marx*, pp.8–9. Marx recollects traces of the ancient commune "right in *my own* neighbourhood, on the *Hunsrück*, the old Germanic system survived until the *last few* years. I now remember my father talking about it to me from *a lawyer's point of view*" (*MECW* 42.557–8). For an English variant, see H.N. Brailsford's moving recollection of his visit to Laxton, with the last remaining open fields in England, and of his "talks in India with old men in the Pathan borderland, and in central Russian with peasants round Vladimir, who were familiar in their younger days with the village community of the one and the *mir* of the other" (*The Levellers and the English Revolution* [1961; rpt. Nottingham: Spokesman, 1976], p.422).
35. *MECW* 24.196–201, 199, 200. Haruki Wada dates the letter to late 1878 (Shanin, *Late Marx*, pp.56–60). Marx did not send the letter, but it circulated widely in Russia after his death.
36. See Jay Bergman, *Vera Zasulich: A Biography* (Stanford: Stanford University Press, 1983).
37. *MECW* 24.346–71, 360n.

38. *MECW* 24.359. Like Maine, to whom he dedicated *Modern Customs and Ancient Laws of Russia, Being the Ilchester Lectures for 1889–90* (1891; rpt. New York: Burt Franklin, 1970), the liberal Kovalevskii stressed the inevitability of the commune's dissolution (p.118).
39. *MECW* 24.365. See Aijaz Ahmad's powerful defense of this earlier Marx (*In Theory: Classes, Nations, Literatures* [London: Verso 1992], pp.221–43; see also p.338n.10).
40. *MECW* 24.363, 364.
41. *MECW* 24.355.
42. *MECW* 24.363, 353.
43. *MECW* 24.349.
44. *MECW* 24.353–54.
45. *MECW* 24.426.
46. *MECW* 37.10.
47. Georgi Plekhanov, *Selected Philosophical Works* (Moscow: Progress Publishers, 1974), 1.674–82. Vladimir Lenin, *Collected Works* (Moscow: Progress Publishers, 1977), 1.146.
48. Lenin, *Works* 1.396, 3.323–30. Lenin's own brother Alexander was a Narodnik executed in 1877 for plotting against the life of Alexander III (Christopher Hill, *Lenin and the Russian Revolution* [Harmondsworth: Penguin, 1971], p.35).
49. Shanin, *Late Marx*, pp.127–33.
50. Christopher Hill, *Lenin and the Russian Revolution*, pp.49–50, 68–71, 83.
51. Eric Hobsbawm (ed.), *Karl Marx: Pre-Capitalist Economic Formations* (New York: International Publishers, 1964), pp.49–50.
52. Raymond Williams, *Politics and Letters*, p.321.
53. Dorothy Atkinson, *The End of the Russian Land Commune, 1905–1930* (Stanford: Stanford University Press, 1983), p.380.
54. Raymond Williams, *Politics and Letters*, p.323.
55. Richard N. Hunt, *The Political Ideas of Marx and Engels. II. Classical Marxism, 1850–1895* (Pittsburgh: University of Pittsburgh Press; and London: Macmillan, 1984), p.313. See also Étienne Balibar, *The Philosophy of Marx* (London: Verso, 1995), pp.106–12.
56. Shanin, *Late Marx*, p.20.
57. Shanin, *Late Marx*, p.78.
58. Jean-Paul Sartre, *Critique of Dialectical Reason, Volume I: Theory of Practical Ensembles* (London: Verso, 1976), p.140; see also 142.
59. *MECW* 47.281.
60. Leon Trotsky, *The History of the Russian Revolution* (Ann Arbor: University of Michigan Press, 1957), 1.51. As an advocate of "primitive socialist accumulation", Trotsky later found himself accused of opening the door to an old/new exploitation of the peasantry. See Isaac Deutscher, *The Prophet Unarmed: Trotsky, 1921–1929* (New York: Vintage, 1959), p.103.
61. Shanin, *Late Marx*, p.255.
62. Isaac Deutscher, "Maoism – Its Origins and Outlook", in *Marxism, Wars and Revolutions: Essays from Four Decades* (London: Verso, 1984), pp.181–211, at p.198.
63. *The Country and the City* (New York: Oxford University Press, 1973), pp.36–7, 304.
64. *Works*, pp.353, 381, 388–89, 436, 466.
65. *Works*, p.506.
66. *Works*, p.304.
67. See E.P. Thompson, "The Moral Economy of the English Crowd in the Eighteenth Century", in *Customs in Common* (New York: New Press, 1991), pp.185–258.
68. See Lutaud's discussion of theses, antitheses, and myths in Winstanley's thought (*Winstanley*, pp.387–441).
69. Carlo Ginzburg, *The Cheese and the Worms: The Cosmos of a Sixteenth-Century Miller* (Harmondsworth: Penguin, 1982), p.16. Ginzburg's brilliant book resurrects Menocchio, a miller of Montereale whom the Inquisition burnt as a heretic in 1599. Menocchio's peasant materialist theology and his experience interweave profoundly with Winstanley's.
70. *MECW* 37.777–8. This passage occurs in a discussion of the transition between feudal and capitalist forms of land tenure and ground rent.
71. *Works*, p.493.
72. *Works*, p.281.

73. *Works*, pp.482, 479–80.
74. *Works*, pp.482–3.
75. *Works*, pp.456–7, 460–61.
76. Keith Thomas, "The Date of Gerrard Winstanley's *Fire in the Bush*", in Charles Webster (ed.), *The Intellectual Revolution of the Seventeenth Century* (London: Routledge, 1974), pp.138–42. On the series, see Sartre's *Critique*, pp.256–342, and also 149–50. For attacks on the Diggers, see *Works*, pp.284–85, 295–96, 368, and John Gurney's chapter in this volume.
77. *Works*, pp.484–6.
78. In an excellent reading of *Fire in the Bush*, T. Wilson Hayes compares the dialectical psychology of Marx and Winstanley in *Winstanley the Digger* (Cambridge, MA: Harvard University Press, 1979), pp.199–206.
79. *Works*, p.445. Andrew Bradstock criticizes "the myth that Winstanley held a *regressive* view of history" in *Faith in the Revolution: The Political Theologies of Müntzer and Winstanley* (London: Society for Promoting Christian Knowledge, 1997), p.123.
80. *Works*, pp.276, 363, 558.
81. *Works*, p.190.
82. Raymond Williams, *Politics and Letters*, pp.128–9.
83. On Winstanley, Hartlib, and improvement, see Joan Thirsk, "Agrarian Problems in the English Revolution", in R.C. Richardson (ed.), *Town and Countryside in the English Revolution* (Manchester University Press, 1992), pp.169–97, 183; Andrew McRae, *God Speed the Plow* (Cambridge: Cambridge University Press, 1996), pp.129–31; Mulder, *The Alchemy of Revolution*, pp.191–212; and Charles Webster, *The Great Instauration: Science, Medicine and Reform, 1626–1660* (London: Duckworth, 1975), pp.367–8. On the English culture of improvement, see Ellen Meiksins Wood, *The Pristine Culture of Capitalism: A Historical Essay on Old Regimes and Modern States* (London: Verso, 1991), pp.81–93; Nigel Smith, *Literature and the English Revolution* (New Haven: Yale University Press, 1994), p.334.
84. *Works*, p.565.
85. *Works*, pp.577, 579, 567.
86. *Works*, p.475.
87. *Works*, p.580. Gabriel Plattes, the Hartlibian theorist of capitalist agrarian improvement, starved to death in December 1644 (Charles Webster, "The Authorship and Significance of *Macaria*, in Webster (ed.), *The Intellectual Revolution*, pp.369–85, 375).
88. *Works*, pp.556–62, 570–71.
89. Rodney Hilton, "Introduction" to T.H. Aston and C.H.E. Philpin (eds.), *The Brenner Debate: Agrarian Class Structure and Economic Development in Pre-Industrial Europe* (Cambridge: Cambridge University Press, 1985), p.8.
90. Kevin Sharpe, *Criticism and Compliment* (Cambridge: Cambridge University Press, 1987), p.ix.
91. Lotte Mulligan and Judith Richards, "A 'Radical' Problem: The Poor and the English Reformers in the Mid-Seventeenth Century", *Journal of British Studies* 29 (April 1990), pp.118–46, 146. They are quoting Quentin Skinner.
92. Winstanley repeatedly denied any intent to liberate property through violence, but neither did he naïvely hope, as John Morrill suggests, that his prophecies would persuade the rich to surrender their superfluous property ("The Impact on Society", in Morrill (ed.), *Revolution and Restoration: England in the 1650s* [London 1992], p.97). Rather, his naïvety (or hopeful innocence) lay in thinking the English ruling class would refrain from crushing him as soon as he showed English agrarian workers how to reclaim the means of production.
93. See Perry Anderson, *English Questions* (London: Verso, 1992), p.285.
94. *MECW* 35.706.
95. Peter Lake, "Retrospective", J.F. Merritt (ed.), *The Political World of Thomas Wentworth, Earl of Strafford, 1621–1641* (Cambridge: Cambridge University Press, 1996), pp.252–83, 257.
96. Christopher Hill, *Liberty Against the Law: Some Seventeenth-Century Controversies* (London: Penguin, 1996), p.x.; E.P. Thompson *The Making of the English Working Class* (New York: Vintage, 1963), pp.12–13.

97. Anthony Fletcher, *The Outbreak of the English Civil War* (London: E. Arnold, 1981), pp.409, 418, 415.
98. Review of Christopher Hill's *The Experience of Defeat*, in *Times Higher Education Supplement*, 7 Sept. 1984.
99. Kevin Sharpe, "Battles of Words and Swords", review of Mark Kishlansky, *Monarchy Transformed*, in *Sunday Times* (London), 3 Nov. 1996; "Religion, Rhetoric, and Revolution in Seventeenth-Century England", *Huntington Library Quarterly* 57/3 (1994), pp.275, 284, 279.
100. George Juretic, "Digger No Millenarian: The Revolutionizing of Gerrard Winstanley", *Journal of the History of Ideas* 36 (1975), pp.263–80.
101. Christopher Hill, *Collected Essays of Christopher Hill* (Amherst: University of Massachusetts Press, 1986), 2. 185, 232; Foreword to Stephen Sedley (ed.), *The Pamphlets of John Warr* (London: Verso, 1992), p.ix. Much better is his comment, "Winstanley's relation to traditional theology is like Karl Marx's relation to Hegelianism: he found it standing on its head and set it the right way up" ("Introduction" to *LFOW*, p.53).
102. Andrew Bradstock, *Faith in the Revolution*, pp.117–18.
103. Conrad Russell, *The Causes of the English Civil War* (Oxford: Oxford University Press, 1990), pp.62, 63.
104. Jonathan Clark, *Revolution and Rebellion: State and Society in England in the Seventeenth and Eighteenth Centuries* (Cambridge: Cambridge University Press, 1986), pp.16, 106, 23, 108.
105. John Morrill, *The Nature of the English Revolution* (London: Longman, 1993), p.68.
106. Neal Wood, "African Peasant Terrorism and Augustine's Political Thought", in Frederick Krantz (ed.), *History from Below* (Montréal: Concordia University Press, 1985), pp.279–99; Rodney H. Hilton, *Bond Men Made Free* (London: Temple Smith, 1973).
107. On the Taiping Rebellion, see Eric R. Wolf, *Peasant Wars of the Twentieth Century* (New York: Harper, 1973), pp.118–23. *Rebellion in the Backlands* [*Os Sertões*] (Chicago: University of Chicago Press, 1944), Euclides Da Cuña's tragic epic about Conselheiro and the Brazilian republic, casts oblique light on the capitalist English republic's destruction of the Diggers.
108. Ernst Bloch, *The Principle of Hope*, 3 vols. (Cambridge, MA: MIT Press, 1986), pp.514–15.
109. Lotte Mulligan, John K. Graham and Judith Richards, "Winstanley: A Case for the Man as He Said He Was", *Journal of Ecclesiastical History* 28/1 (1977), pp.57–75, 58, 71, 65.
110. "The Religion of Gerrard Winstanley", *Collected Essays*, 2.185–251, 193–4.
111. *Works*, p.212.
112. *Works*, pp.570, 590.
113. J.G.A. Pocock, "Historical Introduction" to *The Political Works of James Harrington* (Cambridge: Cambridge University Press, 1977), p.96; *Works*, p.428.
114. *LFOW*, pp.156–7.
115. Lutaud, *Winstanley*, p.336.
116. Andrew Bradstock, *Faith in the Revolution*; see in particular his concluding meditation, "Building the Kingdom: Towards a Christian Contribution to Revolutionary Praxis" (pp.139–75); Lewis C. Daly, "'Saith the Spirit, to This Shattered Earth': Mid-Seventeenth-Century Puritan Radicalism and the History of Religious Forms of Class Struggle" (Diss. SUNY Buffalo, 1996); Christopher Rowland, *Radical Christianity: A Reading of Recovery* (Maryknoll, New York: Orbis Books, 1988); Christopher Hill, *The English Bible and Seventeenth-Century Revolution* (London: Penguin Press, 1993), pp.447–51. See also John Marsden, *Marxism and Christian Utopianism: Toward a Socialist Political Theology* (New York: Monthly Review Press, 1991).
117. See George E. Mendenhall, "The Hebrew Conquest of Palestine", *Biblical Archaeologist* 25/3 (1962), pp.66–87; Marvin L. Chaney, "Ancient Palestinian Peasant Movements and the Formation of Premonarchic Israel", in David Noel Friedman and David Frank Graff (eds.), *Palestine in Transition* (Sheffield, 1983), pp.39–94; and Gottwald's epochal *The Tribes of Yahweh: A Sociology of the Religion of Liberated Israel, 1250–1050 B.C.E.* (Maryknoll, NY: Orbis Books, 1979). I am grateful to Dr Lew Daly for introducing me to this material, and for many conversations on related subjects.
118. *Works*, p.182.

The Common People and the Bible: Winstanley, Blake and Liberation Theology

CHRISTOPHER ROWLAND

Gerrard Winstanley belongs to a long line of Christian radicals who, through their emphasis on the ability of all people to understand the ways of God, and stress on the priority of the Spirit over the intellect and inspiration over memory and learning, have contributed to the well-being of humanity.[1] In his "successor" William Blake we find the same concern, and in our own day these themes have been echoed in the writings of the liberation theologians and among the poor communities which have provided their inspiration.

Winstanley wrote that "the poorest man, that sees his maker, and lives in the light, though he could never read a letter in the book, dares throw the glove to al the humane learning in the world, and declare the deceit of it".[2] In a less polemical vein a contemporary advocate of grassroots bible study in Brazil writes that, with the poor, "the emphasis is placed not on the text itself but rather on the meaning the text has for the people reading it ... [on] ... understanding life by means of the Bible ... The discovery of meaning is not the product of scholarship alone, of human reasoning, but is also a gift of God through the Spirit."[3] These grassroots groups are a new way of being church, though that only demonstrates the extent to which many who profess faith in Jesus have forgotten words like those in Matthew 11.25: "I thank you, lord of heaven and earth, that you have kept these things from the wise and intelligent and revealed them to babes." According to liberation theology, understanding comes through action. Theology is the "second act", paralleling Winstanley's conviction that "words and writings were all nothing, and must die, for action is the life of all, and if thou dost not act, thou dost nothing".[4] In this essay Winstanley's relationship with a radical strain in Christianity will be traced, a strain which is deeply rooted in the character of the early Christian movement and Christianity's foundation documents.

In Gerrard Winstanley there arose a prophetic figure with distinctive views on the interpretation of prophetic texts linked to practical action. His writings display a sophisticated use of the Christian doctrine of the Fall, and the apocalyptic imagery of texts like Daniel and Revelation, to demonstrate the injustice and sinfulness of contemporary economic and political arrangements. His writing career spans the years 1648 to 1652, the period from the second civil war to the last years of the Commonwealth; no further theological and political writings outside that period have ever been discovered.[5] From April 1649 to March 1650 his life and writing were intimately bound up with the Digger commune established in Surrey, and, as the term "Digger" implies, this was a movement concerned to give practical effect to its convictions. Winstanley was prompted by a revelation that he and his companions should dig the common land, and this they began to do at St George's Hill near Weybridge (now, ironically, one of the most prosperous areas of housing in southern England) on Sunday 1 April 1649. Their action provoked hostility from local landowners and complaints to the Council of State, and, after relocating to Cobham, they were finally driven off the land in the spring of 1650. We know little of what happened to Winstanley, though there is some evidence that he became part of respectable society, leaving behind his Digger days as part of a moment of radical political opportunity (a *Kairos*, to use the biblical term which has been used in radical political theology) which had passed.

Winstanley himself had an acute consciousness of his own vocation, which he describes with the sense of immediacy familiar to us from the biblical apocalyptic tradition:

> As I was in a trance not long since, divers matters were present to my sight, which must not be here related. Likewise I heard these words, Worke together. Eat bread together; declare this all abroad. Likewise I heard these words. Whosoever it is that labours in the earth, for any person or persons, that lifts up themselves as Lords & Rulers over others, and that doth not look upon themselves equal to others in the Creation, The hand of the Lord shall be upon that labourer: I the Lord have spoke it and I will do it; Declare this all abroad.[6]

Winstanley believed that the prophetic spirit was again active in the momentous days in which he lived and that the prophetic images of the Bible were the currency with which latter day prophets could speak God's word. Indeed, the prophetic promises of the past were coming to fulfilment: "all the Prophecies, Visions, and Revelations of Scriptures, of Prophets, and Apostles, concerning the calling of the Jews, the Restauration of Israel; and making of that People, the Inheritors of the whole Earth; doth all seat themselves in this Work [i.e. the Digger experiment] of making the Earth a Common Treasury."[7] He considered that his insights were not merely the product of intellectual exercise but the proclamation of the "True Reason" dwelling within him. It was part of Winstanley's task to unmask the reality of an unjust contemporary society, and, in particular, the iniquities promoted by a monarchy supported by violence and the ideologues of an established religion. He did this by contrasting the present "normality" and the paradise which God intended and which had once existed before the Fall.

Fundamental to Winstanley's justification of the Diggers' communal experiment was the belief that the earth was a common treasury, that all men and women had a right to the land and its fruits; and this right was undermined whenever the land was owned as private property and bought and sold as a commodity.[8] Winstanley was concerned to expose the way in which the preoccupation with private property reflected a fundamental characteristic of humanity after the Fall of Adam and the dominance of the influence of the Beast. Winstanley's writings, like those of his predecessor, the early Reformation figure Thomas Müntzer,[9] betray a remarkable understanding of the intimate link which connects the struggle that goes on at the internal level between human acquisitiveness on the one hand and altruism and sharing on the other, and the parallel struggle in society at large between the maintenance of the private property system and common ownership of the creation.

According to Winstanley, at the Fall Adam consented to the serpent covetousness, fell from righteousness, was cursed, and was sent into the earth to eat his bread in sorrow. Private property is the curse, and those who possess it have gained it by oppression or murder, thereby following in the steps of Cain.[10] Its prevalence is typified by the rule of the Beast: a professional ministry; kingly power; the judiciary; and the buying and selling of the earth. These correspond to the four beasts in the book of Daniel, most clearly set out in one of Winstanley's later works, *The Fire in the Bush*:

> These foure powers are the foure Beasts, which Daniel saw rise up out of the Sea … And this Sea is the bulke and body of mankinde ... for out of Mankinde arises all that darknesse and Tyranny that oppresses it selfe ...
>
> The first Beast which Daniell saw rise up out of the deceived heart of mankinde, was like a Lion; and had Eagles wings: And this is kingly power, which takes the Sword, and makes way to rule over others thereby, dividing the Creation, one part from another; setting up the Conqueror to rule, making the conquered a slave; giving the Earth to some, denying the Earth to others ...
>
> The second Beast was like a Beare; And this is the power of the selfish Lawes, which is full of covetousnesse ... and he had three ribs in his mouth, which are these … the power of Prisons … the power of whipping, banishment, and confiscation of goods ... the power of hanging, pressing, burning, martering ... take these three ribs out of

> the mouth of the Law, or Innes of Court trade, and that Beast hath no power, but dies.
>
> The third Beast was like a Leopard … and this is the thieving Art of buying and selling the Earth with the fruits one to another ... this Beast had foure wings; Policy, Hypocrisie, Self-Love, and hardnesse of Heart; for this Beast is a true self-Lover, to get the Earth to himselfe, to lock it up in Chests and barnes, though others starve for want ...
>
> The fourth Beast is the Imaginary Clergy-Power, which indeed is Judas; and this is more terrible and dreadful then the rest ...
>
> When Christ the Anoynting spirit rises up, and inlightens mankind, then in his light, they shall see the deceit and falshood of this Beast, that hath deceived all the world; and shall fall off from him, and leave him naked and bare; and if he will teach and rule, let him shew his power over the Beasts; for the people will all looke up to God, to be taught and governed by him.[11]

This passage encapsulates many typical features of Winstanley's apocalyptic hermeneutics: the process of "updating" Daniel, already evident in Revelation and 4 Ezra,[12] is now applied to the particular manifestation of tyranny evident in the English monarchical state. The diabolical alliance of monarchy, military power, the legal system, a system of private property and religion – what Winstanley identifies collectively as "kingly power" – maintains a hegemony which crushes ordinary people. Salvation involves the overcoming of this power, and occurs when the scales fall off the eyes of deluded people and the spirit of Christ wells up within them bringing back the justice which existed before the Fall. Such a happening Winstanley believes he glimpses in the immediate aftermath of the execution of Charles I in 1649. That is the Kairos,[13] a moment of opportunity, which people could grasp and begin to institute the messianic age in their common life freed from the tyranny of the Beast. Unfortunately for Winstanley and his companions, the Beast raised its head when those who were expected to promote a different order turned out to be just as monarchical and upholders of "covetousness" as their predecessors. The Kairos passed, and with it the exemplification of the reign of God in the little Digger communes. Perhaps, as Winstanley's last extant work, *The Law of Freedom*, indicates, he recognized this and refused to allow himself to be led on by a millennial fantasy in a situation where there seemed little possibility of change. Other strategies were called for once the political opening was no longer there.

Winstanley's use of apocalyptic imagery anticipates what we find in the writing and painting of William Blake, where the Apocalypse becomes a means of reading the signs of the times.[14] He rejects any literal fulfilment of the apocalyptic material, his focus being on the present as a time of fulfilment rather than the distant future, the world of flesh and blood rather than an ethereal world of fantasy. Any naive identification of the Beast with some remote, eschatological figure inevitably removes the immediacy of the impact of a symbol whose import is then confined to remote eschatological times. By linking the Beast to contemporary institutions and persons (as is the case with the application of the Antichrist myth in 1 John) Winstanley makes the present a time for action: "But for the present state of the old World that is running up like parchment in the fire, and wearing away."[15] The new heaven and earth is something to be seen here and now. In *The New Law of Righteousnes* Winstanley dismisses the view that the New Jerusalem is only "to be seen hereafter" and asserts: "I know that the glory of the Lord shall be seen and known within the Creation, and the blessing shall spread in all Nations."[16] The kingdom of God is therefore very much a this worldly kingdom. Christ's second coming means the establishment of a state of community where the curse of Adam and the tyranny of the beast are overthrown. True freedom lies in the community in spirit and community in the earthly treasury, which is Christ spread abroad in the creation. A new creation will see a community of humankind which is typified by "the unity of spirit of Love, which is called Christ in you, or the Law writen in the heart, leading mankind into all truth, and to be of one heart and mind".[17] God's kingdom is not far above the heavens but is to be found in the lives and experiences of ordinary men and women. One looks for God within oneself and as a result has commune with the divine spirit and every other creature made in the divine image (a sentiment which reappears in the closing stanza of William Blake's "Divine Image" in his *Songs of Innocence*). The person that worships God "at a distance" is deceived by "the imagination of his own heart" and ignores the dwelling of God in humanity and the possibility for a new society without the curse of Adam, private property. Salvation comes not "by believing that a man lived and died long ago in Jerusalem, but by the power of the spirit within",[18] and God's kingdom comes when God arises in his saints. There then takes place "the rising up of Christ in sons and daughters", which is Christ's second coming, when flesh will never act unrighteously or trespass against others.[19]

William Blake thought of himself as standing in a tradition of prophets like John of Patmos, who described his own book as prophecy. Blake used the title prophecy for his illuminated books of the 1790s,[20] and in *Milton* Copies A & B Preface (the stanzas popularly known as "Jerusalem") he explicitly quotes Numbers 11.29: "Would to God that all the Lord's people were prophets." As with Winstanley, the sense of prophetic vocation and insight equips Blake to offer the meaning of contemporary events, like the biblical prophecies against the nations or the visions of the beast and Babylon in the book of Revelation. Indeed, Blake recognizes the prophets of the Bible as kindred spirits (in *The Marriage of Heaven and Hell* he writes of dining with Isaiah and Ezekiel). He can write in their style and use their images. He is no mere interpreter or exegete of the prophets and apocalyptic seers, but their successor, embodying their vocation and recasting their words for a new situation.[21] Blake's prophecies were not intended to predict exactly what would happen, for they were written after the events that are described, as he puts it succinctly in a marginal note he wrote in 1798:

> Prophets in the modern sense of the word have never existed. Jonah was no prophet, in the modern sense, for his prophecy of Nineveh failed. Every honest man is a prophet; he utters his opinion both of private and public matters. Thus: If you go on So, the result is So. He never says, such a thing shall happen let you do what you will. A Prophet is a Seer, not an Arbitrary Dictator.[22]

The prophecies rather lay bare the inner dynamic of history and revolution, the potential for positive change that exists and the corruption of those impulses. Blake's insight into social change is not that of the utopian, however. In *Europe* there is no naive expectation of the inevitable success of revolution, nor is there any of the optimism about revolution expressed in, for example, Coleridge's early "Religious Musings", written roughly at the same time as Blake's prophecies.[23] Indeed, quite the reverse. Throughout *Europe* there is recognition of the profound subversion of revolution and the multi-faceted forms of resistance to change, avoidance of reality, and temptation to delusion. Any revolutionary optimism that Blake may have harboured in the last decade of the eighteenth century is tempered by a need to plumb the complexities of the human personality and its tendency to succumb to the "dark delusions" of the world in which religion and theology have all too often played their part. Europe, a continent which was to be briefly lit with the flame of revolution, is seen as sleepy and immune to this spirit of change. Milton in "On the Morning of Christ's Nativity" saw the Incarnation as the moment when old errors were dispersed and the way of truth triumphed (a text probably alluded to in Blake's *Europe*); Blake, in less sanguine vein, sees the coming of Christ as a moment which increased rather than diminished the power of the pagan deities and the false religion and culture they encouraged.[24] Europe is entangled in a religion and an ethic which made it impervious to revolutionary change, a dreamy world cut off from reality. Revolution would only produce "the strife of blood" not the bliss of Paradise. The coming of Christ heralds not only the blissful salvation of the "Lamb" but the wrath of the "Tyger", to use Blake's contrasting images in *Songs of Innocence and Experience*. This parallels the awesome consequences of the exaltation of the Lamb in Revelation 5 which results in the cataclysmic apocalypse described in the following chapters of that book.

John's apocalyptic vision is a central component of Blake's visionary world and it also informs his understanding of his own political situation.[25] As he put it in 1798: "To defend the Bible in this year … would cost a man his life. The Beast and the Whore rule without control."[26] Blake explicitly traces a continuity between his own mythical world and the vision seen by John on Patmos, as he makes clear at the conclusion of the Eighth Night of *The Four Zoas*:

> Rahab triumphs over all; she took Jerusalem Captive a Willing Captive by delusive arts impell'd To worship Urizen's Dragon form, to offer her own Children Upon the bloody Altar. John saw these things Reveal'd in Heaven On Patmos Isle, & heard the souls cry out to be deliver'd. He saw the Harlot of the Kings of Earth, & saw her Cup Of fornication, food of Orc & Satan, pressd from the fruit of Mystery.[27]

Blake's use of the Apocalypse represents a visionary continuity with the text rather than a commentary or analysis of it. He stands in the prophetic tradition of which John of Patmos also is a part, donning the prophet's mantle and minting fresh prophetic words and images for his own day. As a prophet his hope is that his words of harsh indignation might enable humans to see that "every kindness to another is a little Death In the Divine Image, nor can Man exist but by Brotherhood".[28]

Blake's myth-making and creative use of Scripture is filtered through personal experience and social upheaval to liberate the Bible from the dominant patterns of interpretation of his day which had so enslaved ordinary people by their legalism. The Book of Job, for example, as illustrated by Blake, is the story of a conversion from "book religion", based on the diabolical religion of law and sacrifice, to the immediacy of vision and experience. A different perspective was needed to tell the story in language which might subvert a Bible used in support of a system which oppressed the poor and turned the religion of Jesus into a series of commandments which kept ordinary people in subjection. It was necessary by words and pictures to open people's eyes to other dimensions to life and an awareness of the epistemological shift which was required of dulled human intellects. A twentieth-century English successor of Blake and Winstanley speaks for them both in this succinct summary of the challenge confronting religious radicals and the difficult task before them:

> Blake found men and women using the Bible in the very way Christ had deplored, because they had ceased to learn to speak in the Spirit in their own tongues. They were as those who laboriously learned a dead language and made it the tomb of the Spirit. … Blake was shaping a new language to express a conception of human life, of

> incarnate love, of the triumph of Christ, of body and spirit made one flesh, for which there were no adequate images in the minds of men and women in his time. Such imagery has to be new-made over and over again. Only so can the old imagery be reborn, only so can the Scripture and the spiritual experiences of human beings of other generations become present truth and quickening words.[29]

One of the most remarkable aspects of Winstanley's and Blake's work is the easy and unselfconscious way in which biblical figures and places are interwoven with British events and places so that the biblical story becomes a kind of lens through which to view contemporary history. That kind of typological hermeneutics has a long history within the church and has a contemporary parallel in the grassroots biblical interpretation among the groups influenced by liberation theology in Latin America (often known as "Basic Christian Communities").[30] The way in which refugees from the north-east of Brazil can identify themselves with Abraham and Sarah in their wanderings offers a contemporary parallel to Winstanley's and Blake's exegesis. In their experience of oppression, poverty, hunger and death they believe God is speaking today and that God's presence is to be found among the millions unknown or unloved by humanity but blessed in the eyes of God. This is something confirmed by the witness of the Christian tradition, particularly the scriptures themselves.[31] For them the text becomes a catalyst in the exploration of pressing contemporary issues relevant to the community. There is an immediacy in the way in which the text is used. Resonances are found with the experience set out in the stories of biblical characters. The Bible offers a means by which the present difficulties can be shown to be surmountable in the life of faith and community commitment. The people go straight to the text with no concern to ask questions about its original historical context or meaning. The Bible then is less a treasury from which spiritual nuggets can be quarried than a lens which enables a degree of clear-sightedness to assist in the "pilgrim's progress". The difference from some evangelical, protestant, readings is the communitarian setting and political perspective which help avoid a narrowly individualist "religious" reading. The setting for the reading is not primarily the individual Christian's life but communities surrounded by a world of poverty, disease and death in which good news comes to offer hope and a path to life. So the experience of poverty and oppression is as important a text as the text of Scripture itself and remains in dialogue with it, just as it had, in somewhat different circumstances, for Winstanley and Blake. The God who identified with slaves in Egypt and promised that he would be found among the poor, sick and suffering reveals in everyday life of ordinary people that there is another "text" to be read as well as that contained between the covers of the Bible or the teachings of the church.

God's word is to be found in the continuing story to be heard and discerned by those with eyes to see in the contemporary world. That means that there must be a continuous dialogue between that present story told by the poor, of oppression and injustice, and the one that they read from the past. That twofold aspect of the interpretative practice is well brought out by Carlos Mesters:

> ... the emphasis is not placed on the text's meaning in itself but rather on the meaning the text has for the people reading it ... the common people are putting the Bible in its proper place, the place where God intended it to be. They are putting it in second place. Life takes first place! In so doing, the people are showing us the enormous importance of the Bible, and at the same time, its relative value – relative to life.[32]

Such a view of the use of the Bible could apply equally well to the approach found in Winstanley and Blake.[33]

This distinctive form of religion found in the small Christian communities of Latin America is one in which story, experience and biblical reflection are intertwined with the community's life. In all probability an experience of celebration, worship, and varied stories and recollections re-enacted in drama and festival, may lie behind the written words of scripture itself, which bears witness to the various, and often conflicting, accounts of a people oppressed, bewildered and longing for deliverance. While exegete, priest and religious may have their part to play in the life of the contemporary communities, the readings are largely uninfluenced by excessive clericalism and individualistic piety. Many theologians in Latin America spend a significant part of each week working with grass-roots communities in the shanty towns on the periphery of large cities or in rural communities, and as part of their pastoral work they listen to and help the process of reflection on the Bible which is going on in the grassroots communities. Their writing has not taken place solely in the context of academic institutions, therefore, which would have cut them off from personal and social pressures of the countries in which they live. Indeed, it is that experience of being alongside the poor and their involvement pastorally in their struggles which are the motivating forces driving their theology and what links them with the earlier work of Winstanley, Blake and others like them who have discovered God in a similar context. Revelation of God's ways is very much a present phenomenon, not one that is entirely past, in the deposit of faith, something to be preserved, defended and transmitted to the people by its guardians. The Bible is not, therefore, just about past history or struggles only, nor is it a manual of dogma; it is a means whereby the stories of today's people of God can be lent a new perspective. The way of reading the Bible common in the Basic Communities parallels many of the older methods of interpretation in which there is a stress on the priority of the spirit of the word rather than its letter. God speaks through life, but it is a word that is illuminated by the Bible: "the principal objective of reading the Bible is not to interpret the Bible but to interpret life with the help of the Bible", as Carlos Mesters puts it.[34] The major preoccupation is not the quest for the meaning of the text in itself but the direction which the Bible is suggesting to the people within the specific circumstances in which they find themselves. Such popular reading of the Bible is directed to contemporary practice and the transformation of a situation of injustice, often permitting the poor to discover meaning which can so easily elude the technically better equipped exegete.

As in many earlier radical movements in Christianity there is a stress on the immanence of God in the persons of the poor and as a catalyst for theology in history.[35] The emphasis is on experience as a prior "text" which must condition the way in which Scripture and tradition are read and the "signs of the times" interpreted. The positions of radicals in Christianity, varied as they are, do seem to exhibit certain tendencies and influences – the presence of God in the persons of the poor, the emphasis on action rather than belief, the hope for the reign of God on earth, and a reliance on an action-reflection model. What runs like a thread throughout is a recognition of the centrality of action and commitment as the sphere of understanding God; the conviction that God's presence is hidden in the poor; and a belief that the resources of Scripture are apocalyptic, in the strict sense of the word, a potent revelatory medium which may offer a searching political critique available for those who wish to resist the principalities and powers of their generation as they seek to allow Christ to rise in sons and daughters. Liberation theology echoes both the struggles and the insight of those like Winstanley and Blake who find in the Scriptures the resources for the critique of hegemony and oppression, but its adherents know that radicalism in theory is not enough and "if thou dost not act, thou dost nothing."

NOTES

1. See A. Bradstock, *Faith in the Revolution* (London: SPCK, 1997); G.E. Aylmer, "The Religion of Gerrard Winstanley", in J.F. McGregor and B. Reay (eds.), *Radical Religion in the English Revolution* (Oxford: Oxford University Press, 1984), pp.91–119; C. Hill *The Religion of Gerrard Winstanley* (Oxford: Past and Present Society, 1978); C. Rowland *Radical Christianity* (Oxford: Polity, 1988).
2. *The New Law of Righteousnes* in *Works*, p.214.
3. Carlos Mesters, *Defenseless Flower* (London: CIIR, 1991).

4. *A Watchword to the City of London and the Armie* in *Works*, p.315.
5. The standard collection of Winstanley's writings is at present *Works* (from which all the quotations here are taken). Unfortunately, this edition does not contain in full the early writings, which are more overtly theological, such as *The Breaking of the Day of God* and *The Saints Paradice*.
6. *The New Law of Righteousnes* in *Works*, p.190); cf. *The True Levellers Standard Advanced* in *Works*, p.261.
7. *The True Levellers Standard Advanced* in *Works*, p.260.
8. See Rowland, *Radical Christianity* pp.58–61.
9. Thomas Müntzer was radical theologian and leader of the peasants in Germany in 1525: see A. Bradstock, *Faith in the Revolution*.
10. See also I John 3.15; Josephus, *Jewish Antiquities* i.60; and Augustine, *De civitate Dei*, xv, where the Cain and Abel story is linked to property and social dislocation.
11. *The Fire in the Bush* in *Works*, pp.464–6, 470.
12. On the importance of 4 Ezra or II Esdras and radical Christianity, see A. Hamilton, *Apocryphal Apocalypse* (Oxford: Oxford University Press, 1999).
13. Compare the way in which the significant moment is used in the context of the struggle against the apartheid regime in South Africa in *The Kairos Document: The Challenge to the Churches* (London: CIIR, 1985)
14. There is something very similar in the late twentieth century US theologian and activist William Stringfellow's writings, for example: "Apocalypse about judgement and as such applicable to every age ... heaven is an estate of self-knowledge and hope offers a way of transcending time to see how in our history Eden and the Fall, Jerusalem and Babylon, Eschaton and the Apocalypse converge here and now" (*An Ethic for Christians and Other Aliens in A Strange Land* [Waco: Word, 1977], p.48).
15. *True Levellers Standard Advanced* in *Works*, p.252.
16. *Works*, p.153.
17. *New-Yeers Gift* in *Works*, p.386.
18. *The Saints Paradice* in *Works,* p.98.
19. *Works*, pp.162f.
20. D.W. Dörrbecker (ed.), William *Blake: The Illuminated Books; vol. 4: The Continental Prophecies* (London: William Blake Trust/The Tate Gallery, 1995).
21. Much the same idea occurs in Thomas Müntzer, who, at certain points in his career, *is* Elijah, John the Baptist, etc.
22. Annotations to Watson's "Apology for the Bible", in G. Keynes (ed.), *Blake: Complete Writings* (Oxford: Oxford University Press, 1957) (hereafter K), p.392.
23. See J. Mee, *Dangerous Enthusiasm: William Blake and the Culture of Radicalism in the 1790s* (Oxford: Oxford University Press, 1992), pp.35ff, and also Morton D. Paley, *Apocalypse and Millennium in English Romantic Poetry* (Oxford: Oxford University Press, 1999).
24. See L. Tannenbaum, *Biblical Tradition in Blake's Early Prophecies: The Great Code of Art* (Princeton: Princeton University Press, 1982); and M.J. Tolley "Europe: to those ychaind in sleep", in D. Erdman and J.E. Grant (eds.), *Blake's Visionary Forms Dramatic* (Princeton: Princeton University Press, 1970).
25. C. Burdon, *The Apocalypse in England: Revelation Unravelling 1700–1834* (London: Macmillan, 1997).
26. Marginal notes which Blake scribbled in his copy of Bishop Watson's "Apology" (K 383).
27. *Four Zoas* 8.597ff.
28. *Jerusalem*, 96.28.
29. Alan Ecclestone, *Yes to God* (London: DLT, 1975), p.62.
30. C. Rowland, *The Cambridge Companion to Liberation Theology* (Cambridge: Cambridge University Press, 1999).
31. See C. Rowland and M. Corner, *Liberating Exegesis: The Challenge of Liberation Theology to Biblical Studies* (London: SPCK, 1990), pp.35ff.
32. C. Mesters, "The Use of the Bible in Christian Communities of the Common People", in N.K. Gottwald (ed.), *The Bible and Liberation: Political and Social Hermeneutics*

(Maryknoll: Orbis Books, 1984), p.122, and see also his *Defenseless Flower*.

33. There is another interesting parallel, the relationship between text and illumination which forms an important part of the *Parabolas de Hoje* prepared for use in the Basic Christian Communities: see Rowland and Corner, *Liberating Exegesis*, pp.7ff.
34. Rowland and Corner, *Liberating Exegesis*, p.39.
35. See Rowland, *Radical Christianity*, and on the emphasis on immanentist theology in the writings and illustrations of William Blake, as a protest at the hegemonic theology of his day, see J. Mee, *Dangerous Enthusiasm*.

Abstracts

The Diggers in Their Own Time ***by Gerald Aylmer***

This paper seeks to set the Diggers of 1649–50 in a meaningful historical context. Their ideas, as expressed in the writings of Gerrard Winstanley, are shown to have been not merely radical but genuinely revolutionary, in the alternative which these offered to the society of their time and to its values and beliefs. The immediate economic situation in 1649 is shown to have been at least potentially revolutionary, but several reasons are advanced to show why the Digger movement did not develop into a full-scale popular revolution, and why in practice it could not have done so. These include repression by local property owners besides military action against them, but also political, legal and technical factors. Attention is paid to the work of several twentieth-century historians, in discussion of the historical context and in relation to Winstanley's ideas and the controversial question of how far these changed between 1649 and 1651–52. Finally, the inevitability of their failure does not make the Diggers less interesting, or less deserving of study and of admiration.

Gerrard Winstanley: What Do We Know of His Life? ***by James D. Alsop***

The obscurity of Gerrard Winstanley (1609–76) has long intrigued and puzzled scholars of seventeenth-century Britain. The absence of firm knowledge, particularly outside the critical years of 1649–51, has led to much speculation and occasionally ill-informed judgement. In particular, Winstanley's participation in the events of 1649–50 has been portrayed within a biographical context which is unsupported by surviving evidence. This investigation sets out to unearth what can be known with reasonable certitude from documentary sources about Gerrard Winstanley, the man. This is not all that is worth knowing, or speculating, about this enigmatic figure, but it is a critical starting point.

Gerrard Winstanley at Cobham ***by David Taylor***

The story of the Diggers' attempt to set up their commune on St George's Hill is well known, but perhaps less attention has been paid to the second episode in their history, which was enacted out wholly in the parish of Cobham. This essay explores the Diggers' – and in particular Winstanley's – connections with Cobham, both before and after the digging on the Little

Heath. In a postscript John Gurney challenges the idea, almost universally held so far by Winstanley scholars, that the Digger leader chose to come to Cobham in 1643, following the collapse of his business venture in London, on account of his father-in-law holding property there.

Gerrard Winstanley and the Literature of Revolution ***by Nigel Smith***

In his writings Winstanley plays down the importance of "writing" in favour of "digging": the former is a distraction, preventing men and women from meeting their true purpose, the return to Eden by union with the Godhead in the collective cultivation of the land. Yet the spoken, written and printed word was essential for the elaboration of Digger ideology, and Winstanley knew well the opportunities for written expression and printed circulation in his time, and exploited them with notable expertise. This essay explores Winstanley's skill and effectiveness as a writer – not only during the digging but before and after – and concludes that he did something quite remarkable, something achieved by no other contemporary, namely "digging" on the page as well as in the ground.

Winstanley, Women and the Family ***by Elaine Hobby***

When the Diggers challenged the law of property by sowing seeds and building houses on George Hill, the economic and social positions of the women and men were radically different. Male domination was enforced in law, and justified theologically. In the revolutionary years this came under direct pressure, as women formed and joined radical congregations of Quakers and Baptists, and argued that their divinely ordained role was one of action and intervention, not wifely obedience, or silence. This essay places Digger writings in the context of women's activism. It concludes that Digger pamphlets are haunted by the possibility that their arguments for equality might be extendable to women, but that the case is never fully developed.

"Furious divells?" The Diggers and their Opponents ***by John Gurney***

Throughout the period of their stay on St George's Hill and Cobham's Little Heath, the Diggers met with concerted and often violent opposition from sections of local society. Although large numbers of locals were involved in the campaign against them in the parish of Walton, this appears not to have been the case in Cobham. Opposition in this parish had a much narrower base, and it is evident that some local inhabitants came to support the digging venture. The Diggers' gentry opponents in Cobham did not simply seek to target them as a threat to their property interests. By portraying them also as atheists, drunkards and enemies of the state, these opponents succeeded in eliciting the support of the government in their campaign to end the digging. The claims made by Winstanley to Crown as well as common land is also likely to have alienated members of the army, many of whom had initially shown a tolerant attitude towards the Diggers. Digger settlements in Surrey and elsewhere were swiftly brought to an end in the spring of 1650.

"The Consolation of Israel": Representations of Jewishness in the Writings of Gerrard Winstanley and William Everard *by Claire Jowitt*

In the mid-seventeenth century Jewish history, practices and beliefs were highly charged subjects for English Protestants. Jewishness was often used to define what "Englishness" was not, but, at the same time, many Christian commentators noticed similarities between English and Jewish peoples. Despite the thirteenth-century banishment of Jews from England, there were increasing contacts and dialogue between Christians and Jews which lead to the debate about Jewish readmission in the 1650s. This article places Winstanley's frequent use of metaphors of Jewishness in his writings within this history of increased contact between Christians and Jews in the period. It explores the extent to which Winstanley was using an historical Israelite identity as a metaphor for the situation and aspirations of the Diggers. It also questions whether the Diggers' interest in Jewishness was purely historical, and examines the extent to which the movement engaged with contemporary Jewry.

Civil Liberty in Milton, the Levellers and Winstanley *by Warren Chernaik*

This essay argues that Milton, Winstanley, and such Leveller pamphleteers as Walwyn, Overton and Lilburne share in a common project: the creation of a public sphere of discourse which, by its very existence, challenged the hegemony of traditional ruling elites. Milton's stance in the opening sentences of *Areopagitica* is that of the private citizen offering "publick advice", exercising the right of "free born men" to "speak free" to those in positions of authority in the state. Civil liberty, here as in other pamphlets of Milton and by the Levellers Overton and Walwyn, is defined in terms of freedom of access, the willingness of those in power to listen to the grievances of those who seek redress. Winstanley's pamphlets on behalf of the Diggers, like the other works discussed here, employ the decorum of direct address, urging those who had gained power during the English

Revolution to recognize their common cause with the ordinary people, with whose aid and on whose behalf they had overthrown the monarchy. If Winstanley's *Law of Freedom* (1652) and Milton's *The Readie and Easie Way* (1660) differ in certain respects from earlier political pamphlets by these two authors, one possible reason for this is a consciousness of defeat, a recognition that the conventions of direct address, of counsel freely offered and received, have broken down, so that all that is left is prophetic lament, a farewell to liberty.

Communism, George Hill and the *Mir*: Was Marx a Nineteenth-Century Winstanleyan? *by James Holstun*

Anti-communist Winstanley scholars are quick to assure us that Winstanley was no seventeenth-century marxist, but they are a little too quick in assuming that everyone knows what it means to be a marxist. Marx, for one, fervently denied that he was one. I argue that Winstanley and Marx were neither marxists nor winstanleyans, but communists. First, I consider Marx's "regressive" interest in the peasant communism championed by Narodnik radicals. In his later years, he grew fascinated with the Russian peasant commune, or *mir*, which he thought might be the medium for an immediate transition to advanced communism, with no necessary intervening phase of proletarian destitution. Second, I consider Winstanley's "progressive" interest in communist improvement. As opposed to traditionalist opponents of agrarian capitalism, Winstanley constructed a materialist theory of history as class struggle, a dialectical psychology, a dialectical theory of the transition from oppressive enclosures to utopia, and a communist theory of agrarian improvement that cancelled and preserved the capitalist science of the Hartlibian Enlightenment. Just as Marx imagined a revolutionary communist Narodism as a third way beyond Slavophile paternalism and capitalist liberalism, so Winstanley imagined communist Digging as a third way beyond feudal paternalism and capitalist improvement. To those who fear that a comparison of Winstanley and Marx necessarily leads to reductive secularization, I argue that there are strong affinities among Winstanley's agrarian communism, Marx's vernacular communism, and contemporary liberation theology.

The Common People and the Bible: Winstanley, Blake and Liberation Theology *by Christopher Rowland*

Winstanley belongs to a long line of Christian radicals who have emphasized the ability of all people to understand the ways of God, and stressed the priority of the Spirit over the intellect and inspiration over memory and learning. This paper considers Winstanley alongside the eighteenth-century visionary William Blake and members of basic Christian communities in present day Latin America, noting how in approaching Scripture each is concerned to develop a new prophetic language to allow it to speak to and interpret their own situation, not to unlock its "meaning" with the tools of learning and scholarship. In particular each will want their new language to provide a critique of oppression, though that in itself will not be enough and must be accompanied by action.

Notes on Contributors

James D. Alsop is Professor of British History and Associate Dean of the Faculty of Humanities at McMaster University, Hamilton, Ontario, Canada. His publications on Winstanley have appeared in *Past and Present*, *The Historical Journal*, *The Journal of British Studies*, and other academic journals. He is the co-author with P.E.H. Hair, of *Seamen and Traders in Guinea, 1553–1565* and is presently completing *British Espionage, Propaganda and Political Intrigue during the War of the Spanish Succession*.

Gerald Aylmer has been Professor of History at York and Master of St Peter's College, Oxford. He has written on both Winstanley and the Levellers, and his books include *Rebellion or Revolution? England 1640-1660*, and *The Levellers in the English Revolution*.

Andrew Bradstock lectures in church history and political theology at King Alfred's College, Winchester, UK. He is author of *Faith in the Revolution: The Political Theologies of Müntzer and Winstanley* and *Radical Religion and Politics in the English Revolution*, and of books and articles on Victorian spirituality, liberation theology and the church and the Nicaraguan revolution.

Warren Chernaik is Emeritus Professor of English at the University of London, Visiting Professor at the University of Southampton, and Senior Research Fellow, Institute of English Studies, University of London. His publications include *The Poetry of Limitation: A Study of Edmund Waller*, *The Poet's Time: Politics and Religion in the Work of Andrew Marvell*, and *Sexual Freedom in Restoration Literature*. He is co-editor, with Martin Dzelzainis, of *Marvell and Liberty*, and, with others, of several other volumes of essays published in association with the Institute of English Studies.

John Gurney works for the Historical Manuscripts Commission in London. He has published on the Diggers and on George Wither, and is currently writing a book on Gerrard Winstanley and the Digger movement.

Elaine Hobby is Reader in Women's Studies in the English and Drama Department, Loughborough University, UK. Her writings on seventeenth-century women radicals include "'Come to Live a Preaching Life': Female Community in Seventeenth-Century Radical

Sects", in Rebecca D'Monte and Nicole Pohl (eds.), *Female Communities 1600–1800: Literary Visions and Cultural Realities*; "Prophecy, Enthusiasm and Radical Female Texts", in N.H. Keeble (ed.), *The Cambridge Companion to Writing of the English Revolution*; and "'Handmaids of the Lord and Mothers in Israel': Early Vindications of Quaker Women's Prophecy", *Prose Studies.*

James Holstun teaches in the English Department at the State University of New York, Buffalo. He is the editor of *Pamphlet Wars: Prose in the English Revolution*, and the author of *A Rational Millennium: Puritan Utopias of Seventeenth-Century England and America*, and *Ehud's Dagger: Class Struggle in the English Revolution.*

Claire Jowitt teaches Renaissance literature at the University of Wales, Aberystwyth. She has published articles on women's writing, travel literature and Jewish/Christian relations in the seventeenth century. She is currently writing a book on gender and colonialism for Manchester University Press.

Christopher Rowland is Dean Ireland's Professor of the Exegesis of Holy Scripture at the University of Oxford. His books on Christianity and politics include *Radical Christianity*, *Liberating Exegesis* (with Mark Corner), and (as editor) the recently published *Cambridge Companion to Liberation Theology.*

Nigel Smith has been Professor of English at Princeton University since September 1999, and was previously Reader in English at Oxford University, and a Fellow of Keble College. He is author of *Perfection Proclaimed: Language and Literature in English Radical Religion 1640–1660* and *Literature and Revolution in England 1640–1660*, and editor of *Ranter Pamphlets* and the Penguin edition of *George Fox's Journal.* He is currently preparing an edition of Andrew Marvell's poems for the Longman Annotated English Poets series.

David Taylor has lived all his life in Cobham and made a life-long study of the town's history. He has written several books on the history of the locality – most recently *Cobham Houses and their Occupants* – and is Honorary Local Secretary of the Surrey Archaeological Society and President of the Esher District Local History Society. He has a particular passion for the Diggers and has researched Winstanley's life in Cobham helped and inspired by Christopher Hill. His revised "Gerrard Winstanley in Elmbridge" has recently been published.

Index

Books of Related Interest

News, Newspapers and Society in Early Modern Britain

Joad Raymond, *University of Aberdeen* (Ed)

In early modern Britain news was transformed from a currency of conversation and social exchange to a potent and lucrative industry, capable of manufacturing public opinion and transforming perceptions of literature, medicine and history. This collection of essays explores the impact of printed periodicals on British culture and society between 1590 and 1800.

Using a variety of methods and disciplines (from literary criticism, through political history, the history of books, and the history of medicine) the contributors present a multi-faceted picture of the emerging periodical press, including discussions of the origins of printed newspapers; the role of manuscript transmission of news; the relationship between newsbooks and the theatre; the use of newspapers by political radicals during the civil wars of the mid-seventeenth century; the role of women in the early periodical press; the emergence of a public sphere of popular political opinion; the use of advertising as a form of communication; the distribution and readership of newspapers in the provinces; ideas of nationhood in the Scottish periodical press; and the role of medical and philosophical journals in promoting medical reform.

158 pages 1999
0 7146 4944 9 cloth
0 7146 8003 6 paper
A special issue of the journal Prose Studies

FRANK CASS PUBLISHERS
Newbury House, 900 Eastern Avenue, Ilford, Essex, IG2 7HH
Tel: +44 (0)20 8599 8866 Fax: +44 (0)20 8599 0984 E-mail: info@frankcass.com
NORTH AMERICA
5804 NE Hassalo Street, Portland, OR 97213 3644, USA
Tel: 800 944 6190 Fax: 503 280 8832 E-mail: cass@isbs.com
Website: www.frankcass.com